AWT Programming for Java

Miles O'Neal
Tom Stewart

M&T Books
A Division of MIS:Press, Inc.
A Subsidiary of Henry Holt and Company, Inc.
115 West 18th Street
New York, New York 10011
http://www.mispress.com

Printed in the United States of America

First Edition—1997

Library of Congress Cataloging-in-Publication Data

O'Neal, Miles.
AWT programming for Java / by Miles O'Neal, Tom Stewart.
p. cm.
ISBN 1-55851-494-5; jf11 to sl 96-46934
1. Java (Computer program language) I. Stewart, Tom.
II. Title.
QA76.73.J38082 1996
005.13'3--dc21 96-46934
CIP

MIS:Press and M&T Books are available at special discounts for bulk purchases for sales promotions, premiums, and fundraising. Special editions or book excerpts can also be created to specification.

For details contact: Special Sales Director
MIS:Press and M&T Books
Subsidiaries of Henry Holt and Company, Inc.
115 West 18th Street
New York, New York 10011

10 9 8 7 6 5 4 3 2 1

Associate Publisher: *Paul Farrell*

Executive Editor: *Cary Sullivan*
Editor: *Andy Neusner*
Copy Edit Manager: *Shari Chappell*
Production Editor: *Patricia Wallenburg*
Technical Editor: *Chuck McManis*
Copy Editor: *Sara Black*

Dedication

Miles O'Neal:

To my parents, Floyd and Billie O'Neal, who got me safely to adulthood in spite of myself, who instilled a love of learning that has only grown stronger with time, and taught me truth, love, and honor in a world often fleeing in the opposite direction.

Tom Stewart:

This book is dedicated to all the practical people in this land who know that their job is to get work done, not just to have their needs fulfilled. I pray that each person who reads this will remember that God ordained men to worship Him, work for Him, and live for Him.

May God bless you with the fruits of labor.

ACKNOWLEDGMENTS

The authors would like to thank: Pencom for the chance to do this book, Pencom Web Works for invaluable assistance, especially Dave Makower (for handling the details on the CD-ROM side), Edith Au and Patricia Ju (various suggestions and sanity checks), Mark Mangan (out publisher interface), Linda DiSanto, Jonathan Hines and Jonathan Wallace (for the opportunity). We especially thank Vignette Corporation for generously allowing us to use their Tab classes, saving us oodles of work (and providing excellent code, at that). Thanks also to Chuck McManis for handling the technical editing chores, and to all the folks at Henry Holt, especially our editor, Andy Neusner, and our publisher, Paul Farrell.

Miles O'Neal

First I must thank my family - Sharon, Esther and Josiah - for putting up with my playing Invisible Man these last few months; you are truly a gift from God.

I want to additionally thank the following Pencommies: Linda, Jonathan & Jonathan for generally keeping the rest of the world at bay, Dany Guindi, Tommy Morgan and Ed Taylor, without whom I'd never have ended up at Pencom in Austin, and all the recruiters and other staff who put up with us when we were too busy with this book to act like real employees, especially Jacqui Gallow, Kim Hastings and Mercedes Gamboa. And, of course, Joy Venegas and all the Timesheet Crew.

Thanks to the folks at Vignette for being so flexible and helpful, especially Neil Webber, for granting us permission to use the code and working out the details, and to Greg Hilton (Tab's dad) for elegant code and the extra pair of eyes.

Thanks to all the folks who brought us the Web, the Net, and all the fun, useful stuff that got us to the point that there is an AWT.

Thanks to Round Rock Chapel, rmct, OOG, tDOTb and all the RRU supporters, just for being there.

Most of all, thanks, God, for everything.

Tom Stewart

I want to express my thanks to my supervisor(s), my peers, and my co-author. I also want to thank my family for allowing me the time to work on this book. The love and encouragement my wife and kids give me each day provides the energy to take on projects like this.

I also want to express my thanks to all the friends who gave us so much support during the months we worked on this. May God's blessings fall on each of you.

Contents

CHAPTER 1

Introduction

- What is the Abstract Windowing Toolkit?
- Introduction for Managers
- Scope of this Book
- Related Java Packages
- Compiling AWT Code
- Our Example Code

What is the Abstract Windowing Toolkit?

The Abstract Windowing Toolkit (AWT) is the first set of nontrivial, publicly available, basic objects with which to build Java programs, with the focus on graphical user interfaces, or GUIs. The AWT was built by Sun's JavaSoft unit and is provided free for anyone to use for any reason whatsoever, in binary form.

There is some controversy as to whether the AWT in its present condition will survive, but it does have three things going for it:

- It is the first Java toolkit available,
- It has gained rapid acceptance, and
- JavaSoft is committed to it.

The AWT is similar in concept to most other packages of widgets, objects, controls, and whatnots, such as those provided in the OSF's Motif, NEXTSTEP's Appkit, and Windows' SDK. Like these packages, AWT provides most of the basic pieces needed to build GUIs; however, it's missing a few, and it has some definite quirks. These pieces include everything from basic layout controls, buttons, menus, and text boxes.

The AWT works with a native windowing toolkit (such as Motif) to provide the actual GUI look and feel, through a mechanism known as *peers*. This allows Java code to be portable across platforms regardless of GUI, trading similarity of look and feel for familiarity of the native GUI. This concept is similar to that used in the XVT toolkit used by many C programmers.

Figures 1.1 and 1.2 show the same program on different platforms; the same user code is being run in each case. The first is from an X-Windows system; the second is run from Windows 95.

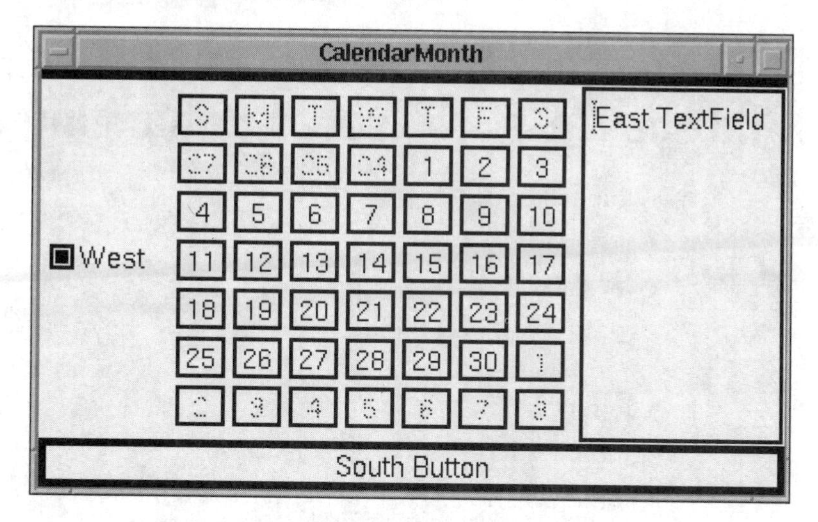

Figure 1.1 Java program in a UNIX window.

You should notice the variation in text display. The sizing of text displayed in a window is not handled well by the current AWT. You'll find that each platform occasionally crops text improperly.

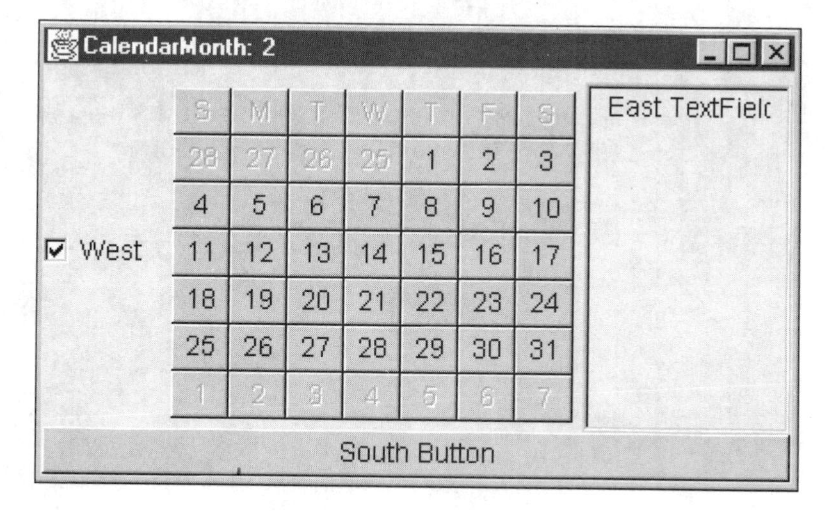

Figure 1.2 The same Java program in a Windows 95 window.

Introduction for Managers or Why Java and the AWT are Career-Enhancing

- Intranet good
- Java good
- AWT good
- COBOL bad

- Intranets empower employees.
- Intranets have a positive impact on bottom lines.
- Intranets impress people you need to impress.
- You will be considered a dinosaur if you don't have an Intranet.

- Java is object oriented.

- Java'a Abstract Windowing Toolkit seamlessly integrates with all standard GUI platforms.
- Java integrates desktop computing, client server, and departmental and corporate MIS functionality.
- Enough Java books are produced in a single day to feed and power the average third-world country.

Java is supported by:

- Microsoft
- Netscape
- IBM
- Apple
- Sun, SGI, and all those weird UNIX vendors

- Intranet experience is worth at least a 15% premium on your next job offer.
- Java experience is worth at least a 15% premium on your next job offer.
- Java puns gain you valuable peer points in networking conversations.
- The opposite sex finds Intranetters irresistable.

Scope of this Book

This book will help you understand the Java AWT and learn to build useful, real-world programs with it. Consequently, this book is not about Java, per se. For an introduction to Java, see *Java Programming Basics* (Edith Au, Dave Makower, and Pencom Web Works, MIS:Press).

This book is targeted primarily at beginning to intermediate users but includes information we have seen nowhere else, much of which we had to determine by experimentation or perusing source code. The situation has been rather like that of the early releases of X11, when there was little documentation, and the primary sources of information were news groups, email with the developers, and lots of late-night hacking sessions. This book will answer most of your questions about the AWT and how to use it, provide some useful objects not included with AWT, add missing functionality to some of the AWT objects, provide work-arounds or alternatives for buggy objects, and, hopefully, everything else you wanted in an AWT book. It will not, at this time, wash your car or whiten your teeth, but if even half of the current Java hype is correct, a later edition may eventually help with those tasks as well.

Related Java Packages

As of this writing, several *packages* (collections of objects) are available from JavaSoft:

- **java.applet**
- **java.awt**
- **java.awt.image**
- **java.awt.peer**
- **java.io**
- **java.lang**
- **java.net**
- **java.util**

java.awt, **java.awt.image**, and **java.awt.peer** are AWT-related. This book is primarily concerned with the actual **java.awt** package, as the **java.awt.image** is still fairly limited, and the **java.awt.peer** package is useful primarily to those porting to new platforms, or at least different native toolkits. Parts of the other packages may be mentioned or used at times in example code, but the emphasis here is on the AWT and building GUIs.

Versions

This book focuses on release 1.0.2 of the Java Development Kit (JDK). Preliminary information on the 1.1 release is available at http://java.sun.com/products/JDK/1.1./.

Compiling AWT Code

AWT code can be compiled in the same way as any other Java code.

The Java Development Kit

The Java Development Kit (JDK) is covered more fully in *Java Programming Basics*, but we will recap the use of the **javac**.

The Java compiler is invoked with the command **javac** (or **javac_g**, which generates debugging symbols and includes them in the compiled bytecodes). The syntax for an invocation of the Java compiler is

```
% javac [options] sourceFile.java [moreSourceFiles.java …]
```

javac takes one or more source files (whose filenames end in the **.java** extension) and creates Java bytecodes, which it stores in one or more class files. Each class in the source file is put into its own output file, whose name consists of the name of the class, followed by the **.class** extension.

The **.class** files are stored in the same directory as the **.java** source files, unless an alternative destination directory is specified with the **-d** option. This option allows the user to specify a different root directory for the class hierarchy of output **.class** files.

For more information about the JDK tools, see Appendix A of *Java Programming Basics*.

Netscape Navigator

For basic compilation chores, Netscape Navigator versions 2.01 and above works fine. On some platforms (such as Linux a.out platforms), this may be your only choice.

In this case, Netscape works purely in a command-line mode. The basic format is

```
%netscape -java sun.tools.javac.Main class_file_name
[other_files]
```

The **sun.tools.javac.Main** class is available with the JDK, which is available on the accompanying CD or via the Internet from http://java.sun.com/products/JDK/1.0.2/.

Some versions of Navigator 3.0 may not work properly for this task; you may need Navigator 2.1.

Currently, Navigator supports the following Java compilation options (available via `netscape -java -help`):

```
Usage: -java [-options] class
```

where options include:

-help	Print out this message
-version	Print out the build version
-v, -verbose	Turn on verbose mode
-debug	Enable JAVA debugging
-noasyncgc	Don't allow asynchronous Graphics Contexts (GCs)
-verbosegc	Print a message when GCs occur
-cs, -checksource	Check if source is newer when loading classes
-ss<NUMBER>	Set the C stack size of a process
-oss<NUMBER>	Set the JAVA stack size of a process
-ms<NUMBER>	Set the initial Java heap size
-mx<NUMBER>	Set the maximum Java heap size
-D<NAME>=<VALUE>	Set a system property
-classpath	<directories separated by colons> List of directories in which to look for classes
-prof	Output profiling data to ./java.prof
-verify	Verify all classes when read in
-verifyremote	Verify classes read in over the network [default]
-noverify	Do not verify any class

We suggest that you create a script to handle the compilation. On UNIX systems, we use the following script (named **javac**).

```
#!/bin/sh
CLASSPATH=.:/usr/local/netscape/java/classes/classes.zip:\
/usr/local/netscape/java/classes/moz2_01.zip
export CLASSPATH

while [ q$1 != q ] ; do
        Files="$Files $1.java"
        shift
done
/usr/local/bin/netscape-2.01 -java -cs sun.tools.javac.Main $Files
```

Set the CLASSPATH variable as needed; we are getting **sun.tools.javac.Main** from **/usr/local/netscape/java/classes/classes.zip**.

Use the script as follows:

```
% javac file1 [file2 . . .]
```

Our Example Code

The examples in this book, as well as the classes we develop to fill gaps in the AWT, are available on the included CD and over the Internet, in both source and compiled formats.

The CD

The CD contains the examples used in the text and classes developed to fill small gaps in the current AWT.

Online

The code is also available via the World Wide Web at

`http://www.pencom.com/awt/examples.hqx` (Mac)

`http://www.pencom.com/awt/examples.tgz` (UNIX tar/gzip)

`http://www.pencom.com/awt/examples.zip` (Windows)

or via anonymous ftp from

`ftp://ftp.rru.com/pub/pww/awt/`

If you are not familiar with anonymous ftp, you simply use the name "anonymous" as the login, and your email address as your password. The email address must be valid, must be of the form *login@domain* or *login@hostname.domain*, and must be verifiable via DNS.

Copyrights

All the included PWW code and some other code is freely available under the PWW copyright notice on the CD-ROM.

The other code on the CD-ROM may be shareware, GNU copylefted, or otherwise restricted (copyrights and redistribution rules accompany the code).

Running the Examples

Unless otherwise specified, the examples are set up as applets. This means that anyone with a Java-enabled browser or Sun's Applet Viewer can easily run the examples. These applets may generally be invoked in a web browser by accessing the HTML file with the same prefix as the applet. For instance, the **hw1.class** applet may be invoked by viewing the **hw1.html** file.

CHAPTER 2

Using the AWT

- Where to Get It
- How to Use It
- The Original Hello World
- Bells and Whistles

Where to Get It

We believe most readers of this book will already have a Java development environment available. However, we want to quickly outline what products are easily obtainable, so you can jump right into development.

There are two ways to get the Java AWT cheaply. The first is to download Netscape Navigator version 2.x or 3.x. Both versions of this web browser and their related products contain support for Java and the AWT (with constraints). The second way is to download the JDK from JavaSoft. This is the original development package that all other current products have grown from.

If you prefer to have a supported Java development environment, you can purchase one of several commercial products. Borland, Symantec, and others are shipping products that are at least the equivalent of the JDK, with some added Visual GUI builder capabilities. Their products (and others) are evolving rapidly as better compilers, more complete GUI builder ports, and other components of mature development environments arrive.

To obtain the Java Developer's Kit, you can access the JDK web pages at

```
http://java.sun.com/products/JDK/.
```

To get a copy of Netscape Navigator, look on the Web at

```
http://www.netscape.com/
```

or anonymous ftp at

```
ftp://ftp.netscape.com/pub/navigator/
```

Addresses for commercial product vendors are included in Appendix B.

How to Use It

Using the AWT is no different from using any other Java package. The source file must import the parts of the package you want. You can do this in either of two ways:

- Explicitly import just the classes you need.

```
import java.awt.FlowLayout;
import java.awt.Button;
```

- Import everything in one easy statement.

```
import java.awt.*;
```

Then you simply write your code and compile it as explained in Chapter 1.

NOTE

Okay, we lied. We're sorry. To get everything, you also have to import **java.awt.image.***. Normally, real programmers don't do images.

A Word About Applets in HTML Files

You can easily access an applet from a web page (HTML file) by using the <APPLET> tag. The applets in this chapter were tested using simple pages like those shown in Listing 2.1, with a Java-enabled browser. We used Netscape Navigator 3.0 beta to test and view the applets, and Navigator 2.01 to build them.

Listing 2.1 Basic Hello World applet test page

```
<BODY BGCOLOR=#ffffff TEXT=#000000>
<CENTER>
<APPLET code="hw1.class" WIDTH=120 HEIGHT=80></APPLET>
</CENTER>
</BODY>
```

Because this page was used intended for use inside `<FRAME>` tags, no `<HTML>` or `<HEAD>` tags appear.

The Original Hello World

With Java, you can create a simple applet as shown in Listing 2.2 with about the same amount of source as any other language (excluding COBOL, of course!).

Listing 2.2 Basic Hello World.

```
import java.applet.*;
import java.awt.*;
// Uses an AWT Graphics object
public class hw1 extends Applet {
   public void paint(Graphics g) {
      g.setColor(Color.red);
      g.drawString("Yo!  Adrian!", 10, 10);
   }
}
```

This applet uses nothing from the AWT besides the **Graphics** class. It is actually one line longer than necessary; invoking the `setColor()` method is unnecessary. It draws directly onto the applet's window. The result is a simple line of text as shown in Figure 2.1.

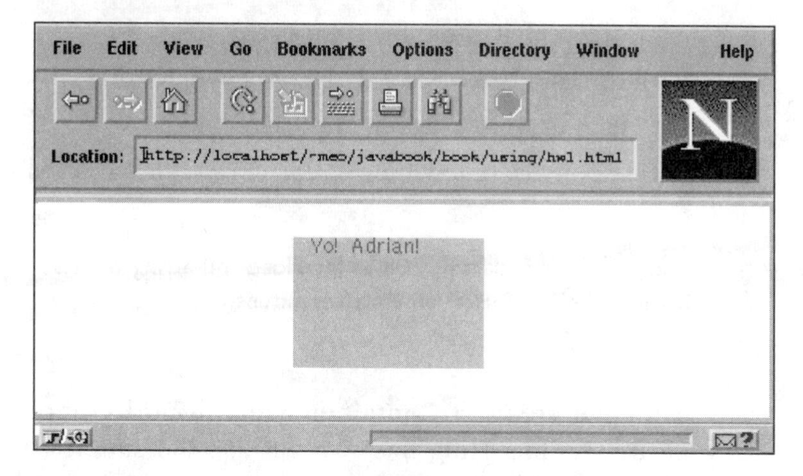

Figure 2.1 Basic Hello World applet.

The gray background is a default in the browser. If you are writing applets for web pages, you probably want to set the background color of the web page in the HTML file (as we did), and set the background color of the applet to the same thing (as we did not do in this example, but will from now on). This is easy to do with most of the AWT objects, but doing it with raw graphics requires painting the whole area!

Bells and Whistles

We can duplicate Listing 2.2 with a Label object. Before we add objects to our applet, we need to create a container to hold them. We will choose a LayoutManager to go with the container. A LayoutManager lets you specify layout semantics.

A Java app normally uses a subclass of Frame, which allegedly includes a container. To date, this has problems (at least on systems we have tested), and you should therefore add your own container.

AWT objects fall into three basic categories:

- Graphics classes (Point, Polygon, Event, etc.)
- Containers (FlowLayout, CardLayout, etc.)
- Components (everything else, such as Button, Scrollbar, etc.)

NOTE

The **java.lang.*** classes, such as Int, Float, and String will also be covered, because the AWT uses these classes extensively.

After we create a Container, we can add components as necessary. In Listing 2.3, we will use the simplest Container (FlowLayout) and include one component (a Label).

Listing 2.3 Basic Hello World with label.

```
import java.applet.*;
import java.awt.*;
// Uses an AWT Label object
public class hw2 extends Applet {
   public void init()   {
      FlowLayout layout = new FlowLayout();
      this.setBackground(Color.white);
      this.setForeground(Color.red);
      this.setLayout(layout);
      this.add("howdy", new Label("Howdy!"));
   }
}
```

We also set the background color in this applet for a cleaner appearance, and the foreground color for impact as shown in Figure 2.2. We could also have set the font, drawn all sorts of cool things around it, and otherwise enhanced the appearance (or wasted time, depending on your viewpoint), but we will save that for later.

NOTE

This is the last time you'll see us using code font unless it's necessary. Java assumes that method calls without an object specifier apply to `this`. We wanted to show you that it's okay to make a style choice, and it certainly makes global search and replace operations more interesting.

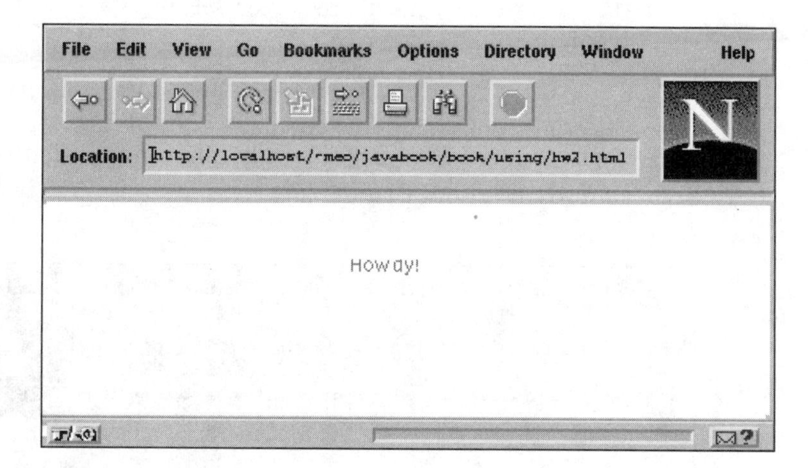

Figure 2.2 Basic Hello World using label object.

This is the basic approach to take in developing any Java app. For most sophisticated GUIs, you will of course use a more sophisticated LayoutManager, often layering one inside another. This will be discussed in Chapter 5.

Almost Real Functionality

It's as simple to use a Button as a Label as shown in Listing 2.4 (as long as we don't expect the Button to actually do anything!).

Listing 2.4 Basic Hello World with Button.

```
import java.applet.*;
import java.awt.*;
// Uses an AWT Button object
public class hw3 extends Applet {
```

```
    public void init()    {
        FlowLayout layout = new FlowLayout();
        this.setBackground(Color.white);
        this.setForeground(Color.red);
        this.setLayout(layout);
        this.add("howdy", new Button("Good Evening"));
    }
}
```

As you can see in Figure 2.3, the only difference is that we now see a Button instead of plain text.

Figure 2.3 Basic Hello World using Button object.

At Last! An Applet That Responds

To make the Button actually do something, we have to handle the event generated when the Button is activated. We will do this with a handleEvent( ) method. Since we have only the one control, we will assume all events come from it. we will only test for an ACTION_EVENT, which the Button generates whenever it is activated by a mouse button or keystroke.

In Listing 2.5, we will change the Button label whenever the Button is activated.

Listing 2.5 Hello World that does something.

```
import java.applet.*;
import java.awt.*;
// Uses an AWT Button object and an event handler
public class hw4 extends Applet {
   Button b;
   boolean orig = true;
   public void init()    {
      FlowLayout layout = new FlowLayout();
      this.setBackground(Color.white);
      this.setForeground(Color.red);
      this.setLayout(layout);
      b = new Button("Howdy, you all!");
      this.add("howdy", b);
   }
   public boolean handleEvent(Event e) {
      switch (e.id) {
         case Event.ACTION_EVENT:
            if (orig) {
               b.setLabel("Buenas Noches!");
               orig = false;
            } else {
               b.setLabel("Good Evening!");
               orig = true;
            }
            return true;
      }
      return false;
   }
}
```

The initial Button state is shown in Figure 2.4a. The first activation changes the Label as shown in Figure 2.4b. The next activation changes the Label as shown in Figure 2.4c.

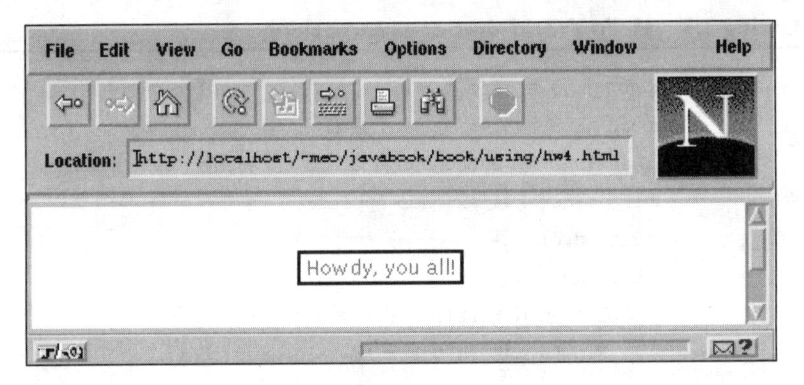

Figure 2.4a Initial Hello World state.

Figure 2.4b Hello World Button after first activation.

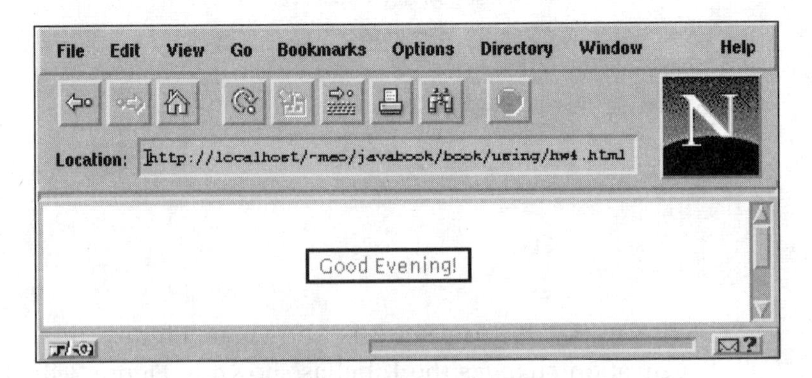

Figure 2.4c Hello World Button after second activation.

Subsequent activations toggle the Button Label between the states shown in Figures 2.4b and 2.4c.

Summary

Now you have the gist of a Java AWT program—Container/LayoutManager, Components, and event handlers. All other Java programs are simply more complex versions of Hello World (in the same sense that an operating system written in C is simply a more complex version of Hello World)!

Throughout the rest of the book, we'll show you how to manage some of that complexity.

CHAPTER 3

AWT Class Overview

Before we get into detailed examples of the various classes and how to use them, let's take a look at all the pieces. We'll cover basic data classes—Points, Dimensions, Rectangles and Polygons—in detail here but just provide an overview of the GUI components and other higher-level classes, as these are described in more detail in later chapters.

- Basic Objects
- Point, Dimensions, Rectangles, and Polygons
- Fonts and Colors
- Events
- Selection Controls
- Labels and Text
- Scrollbars
- Canvas and Graphics
- Containers and LayoutManagers

- Panels, Frames, Dialogs, Windows, and Applets
- Miscellaneous

Basic Objects

Because of Java's object orientation, Sun did not simply provide a library similar to libc, but provided object wrappers around even the most basic data types. In most cases, the name is the same, except that the first letter is capitalized. A couple of these have no classless equivalent. These are actually from the **java.lang** package, but because they appear throughout the AWT, we cover them here because they provide the functionality you will need. Table 3.1 lists the basic data objects.

These wrappers are also useful when you need to pass something by reference.

Table 3.1 Basic Data Objects

Object	Equivalent Data Type
	Numeric Types
Double	double
Float	float
Integer	int
Long	long
Number	none (superclass of all numeric types)
	Other Types
Boolean	boolean
Character	char
String	none (similar to C's `static char *`)
StringBuffer	none (similar to C's `char *`)

One of the most commonly used methods throughout the AWT is `Object.toString()`. Each AWT class overrides this method to provide useful class-specific output. You can use it with output of your own either by overriding the inherited method in your class

```
Object x;
class MyClass extends Panel {
   public String toString() {
         return ("MyClass personal output " +
            x.toString());
}
```

or by using the inherited text output like so:

```
...
if ( ... ) {   // some error
  System.out.println("EEK! x.toString() is " +
       x.toString());
}
```

Numeric Types

The basic numeric classes—Double, Float, Int, and Long—provide a common set of methods for converting between the classes and their equivalent Java data types, methods for converting between the classes and strings, and some basic tests. Some methods for converting between the classes are also provided. Table 3.2 lists the most useful, common routines.

Table 3.2 Common Numeric Methods

Method	Returns	Notes
`typeValue()`	type*	none
`toString()`	String	none
`isInfinite()`	Boolean	You can also test against NEGATIVE_INFINITY and POSITIVE_INFINITY
`isNaN()`	Boolean	True if not a number
`equals()`	Boolean	True if instance value is equal to method parameter

*The string type should be changed to the actual data type, such as Int.

A common usage for these methods is to convert a standard data type into a String. Rather than invoke an I/O conversion routine, you simply write code like that in Listing 3.1.

Listing 3.1 Converting an int to a string.

```
int msgNum = 0;
    ...
messages.appendText((new Integer(msgNum++)).toString());
```

Or, with less typing overhead, and roughly the same efficiency:

```
int msgNum = 0;
...
messages.appendText("" + msgNum);        // implicit string
conversion
```

You could as easily make msgNum an Integer, but depending on what else you are doing with it, this could introduce unnecessary complexity, and if you don't need an Integer most of the time, it would introduce unnecessary overhead.

Each numeric class includes methods to produce each of the basic, numeric data types, including the type from which the class is derived. Listing 3.2 shows how to use these.

Listing 3.2 Class to basic type conversion.

```
float flimit;
int ilimit;
Integer limit = new Integer(i);
    :
    :
flimit = limit.floatValue()
ilimit = limit.intValue()
```

You can also use typecasting to convert these basic types. Unlike C and some object-oriented languages, a lot of the basic date type objects are really part of the language. It's a lot simpler to type

```
float flimit = (float)limit;
```

even if the compiler does have to generate the same machine code.

Constructors are provided for each numeric class to create a new instance initialized from the basic data type, or from a string. The latter throws a format exception if the string contains anything other than a representation of the appropriate data type.

There are also class methods called `valueOf(String)`, that are used to convert strings into numbers. These methods are commonly used for simple conversions where you don't want to impact performance and garbage collection.

Each class also comes with two constants, MAX_VALUE and MIN_VALUE, designating the maximum and minimum values available in the underlying data types.

Additional Numeric Methods

Float and Double also provide class methods `typeToIntBits(type)` and `intToTypeBits(int)`, to convert between their respective data types and an int representation of the bit value of the data. This allows you to twiddle the bits in a float or double number.

Integer and Long provide an additional `toString(String val, int radix)` method to produce string representations in any base between MIN_RADIX and MAX_RADIX (currently defined as 2 and 36, respectively). The string representation is simple numbers, with no prefix (such as "0x" for hexadecimal in C). Table 3.3 shows some examples of the number 64 (base 10) converted to string in this manner and printed via the `System.out.println()` method.

Table 3.3 Sample toString() Conversion Output

Base	Output
2	1000000
4	1000
8	100
10	64
12	54
16	40
36	1s

Note the value in base 36; each base beyond 10 uses an additional character beginning with "a" to represent numbers beyond 9.

The Integer and Long classes provide class methods to convert Strings directly to Integers and Longs, respectively, `parseInt(String num)`, `parseLong(String num)`, `parseInt(String num, int radix)`, and `parseLong(String num, int radix)`, all of which throw NumberFormatException on conversion errors.

The Integer and Long classes also provide class methods to get Integer and Long property values (these have nothing to do with Monopoly) from objects, as shown in Table 3.4.

Table 3.4 Getting Property Values

Method	Notes
`getInteger(String name)`	None
`getInteger(String name, int val)`	If no matching name, looks for matching val
`getInteger(String name, Integer val)`	If no matching name, looks for matching val
`getLong(String name)`	None
`getLong(String name, long val)`	If no matching name, looks for matching val
`getLong(String name, Long val)`	If no matching name, looks for matching val

The Number Class

The Number class is the superclass of the types in Table 3.4. It has only a constructor and methods to convert to each of the above numeric types. It is primarily useful for those writing new numeric classes.

Other Basic Types

Boolean

Boolean is a simple object wrapper around the boolean data type. It has only a few basic methods. Two constructors are provided; one will initialize from a boolean and the other from a String. It provides class methods to get a property value (`getValue(String name)`) and to convert a String to a boolean (`getValue(String)`).

The expected instance methods (`booleanValue()` and `toString()`) are provided as well.

Character

Character provides a wrapper around the basic char class and provides methods for a few character classification and manipulation routines, including case checking and conversion. Beyond those, AWT 1.0 provided only checks for digits and white space and for conversion of digits based on a radix. AWT 1.1 provides more functionality, including classification for purposes of valid Java variable name characters.

All of these are class methods that operate on char data.

A `charValue()` method is provided to return the current char value of a character, along with the inevitable `toString()`.

It is still a far cry from C's standard library functions for character comparison.

String

A *String* is an immutable string of characters. While its list of methods is fairly long, they are all pretty intuitive, and you will probably find the functionality you expect and need.

Constructors are provided for most likelihoods, accepting data of type `String`, `StringBuffer`, `char[]`, and `byte[]`.

A number of class methods are provided. Two versions of `copyValue()` copy a `char[]` array. A set of `getValue()` methods turn each of the basic data types (such as int) into a String.

A variety of instance methods handle the rest of the standard chores, as noted in Table 3.5.

Table 3.5 String Instance Methods

Type	Method	Notes
char	`charAt(int index);`	None
int	`compareTo(String anotherString);`	None
String	`concat(String str);`	Same as "+" operator
boolean	`endsWith(String suffix);`	None
boolean	`equals(Object anObject);`	None
boolean	`equalsIgnoreCase(String anotherString);`	None
void	`getBytes(int srcBegin, int srcEnd, byte[] dst, int dstBegin);`	None
void	`getChars(int srcBegin, int srcEnd, char[] dst, int dstBegin);`	None
int	`indexOf(int ch);`	None
int	`indexOf(int ch, int startIndex);`	None
int	`indexOf(String str);`	None
int	`indexOf(String str, int fromIndex);`	None
String	`intern();`	Guarantees all identical Strings are the same String
int	`lastIndexOf(int ch);`	None
int	`lastIndexOf(int ch, int fromIndex);`	None
int	`lastIndexOf(String str);`	None
int	`lastIndexOf(String str, int ; fromIndex)`	None
int	`length();`	None
boolean	`regionMatches(boolean ignoreCase, int strOffset, String other, int otherOffset, int len);`	Substring matching
boolean	`regionMatches(int strOffset, String other, int otherOffset, int len);`	Substring matching

continued...

Type	Method	Notes
String	`replace(char oldChar, char newChar);`	Replaces all occurrences in this String
boolean	`startsWith(String prefix);`	None
boolean	`startsWith(String prefix, int offset);`	None
String	`substring(int beginIndex);`	Creates new String with substring
String	`substring(int beginIndex, int endIndex);`	Creates new String with substring
char[]	`toCharArray();`	None
String	`toLowerCase();`	None
String	`toUpperCase();`	None
String	`trim();`	Remove leading and trailing white space

StringBuffer

The StringBuffer class is conceptually similar to the String class except that the text is modifiable. There is very little overlap in methods. To get String functionality, you must convert with the `toString()` method and operate on that object. The new String shares the actual string contents array with the StringBuffer object until the StringBuffer contents are modified, at which time the StringBuffer makes a new copy for itself. Table 3.6 lists the StringBuffer methods.

Table 3.6 StringBuffer Instance Methods

Type	Method	Notes
StringBuffer	`append(boolean b)`	None
StringBuffer	`append(char c)`	None
StringBuffer	`append(char[] str)`	None

continued...

Type	Method	Notes
StringBuffer	`append(char[] str, int offset, int len)`	None
StringBuffer	`append(double d)`	None
StringBuffer	`append(float f)`	None
StringBuffer	`append(int i)`	None
StringBuffer	`append(long l)`	None
StringBuffer	`append(Object obj)`	Implicitly uses `obj.toString()` to produce the text to be appended.
StringBuffer	`append(String str)`	None
Int	`capacity()`	Returns buffer size
Char	`charAt(int index)`	None
void	`ensureCapacity(int minimumCapacity)`	Grows buffer if necessary
Void	`getChars(int srcBegin, int srcEnd, char[] dst, int dstBegin)`	None
StringBuffer	`insert(int offset, boolean b)`	None
StringBuffer	`insert(int offset, char c)`	None
StringBuffer	`insert(int offset, char[] str)`	None
StringBuffer	`insert(int offset, double d)`	None
StringBuffer	`insert(int offset, float f)`	None
StringBuffer	`insert(int offset, int i)`	None
StringBuffer	`insert(int offset, long l)`	None
StringBuffer	`insert(int offset, Object obj)`	None
StringBuffer	`insert(int offset, String str)`	None
int	`length()`	Returns current character count
StringBuffer	`reverse()`	not in AWT 1.0
void	`setCharAt(int index, char ch)`	None
void	`setLength(int newLength)`	null—fills any extra space

Points, Dimensions, Rectangles, and Polygons

Despite their names, Points, Dimensions, Rectangles, and Polygons are not really graphics-related classes but rather GUI-related classes.

Points

Point represents a standard set of (*X*, *Y*) coordinates. This class is used by several others. You can access the *X* and *Y* coordinates individually as the instance variables *x* and *y*. You may set the coordinates through the `move(int x, int y)` method, or offset them by the `translate(int dx, int dy)` method. The code fragment shown in Listing 3.3 results in the point (10, 10), with the output of the `toString()` method shown in Listing 3.4.

Listing 3.3 Using point methods.

```
Point p1 = new Point(4, 6);
p1.translate(6, 4);
System.out.println(p1.toString());
```

Listing 3.4 Point string representation.

```
java.awt.Point[x=10,y=10]
```

This output is useful for debugging rather than production work. A useful `toString()` for production work would be as shown in Listing 3.5:

Listing 3.5 Better point string method.

```
import java.applet.*;
import java.awt.*;
```

```
// production-useful Point.toString()

public class myPoint extends Point {
   public myPoint(int x, int y) {
      super(x, y);
   }

   public String toString()   {
       return("(" + x + "," + y + ")");
   }
}
```

The above `toString()` method is a perfect example of how Java's support for the basic objects as part of the language makes typing a lot easier. Here's the explicit object + method oriented equivalent:

```
return new String("(" + Integer.toString(this.x) +
   "," + Integer.toString(this.y) + ")");
```

This results in a String formatted in the standard point notation, as in Listing 3.6.

Listing 3.6 Better point string representation.

```
(10,10)
```

Dimensions

Dimension is a simple class with public variables `width` and `height`, and a `toString()` method. It isn't often used in the AWT, and its use is inconsistent. Nevertheless, it's there if you need it.

Rectangles

Rectangle is defined by an origin (upper left corner, which may be a point or an (*X*, *Y*) pair) and a size (either a Dimension or a `width` and `height`. Methods include `add()`, which adds a point to the Rectangle (resizing to be the smallest box that includes the origin and the new point), `grow()`, which increases the size of the Rectangle, `translate()`, which offsets the Rectangle by a displacement; and a set of methods to assist with clipping, bounding boxes, and general "set theory" concepts—intersection, union, and the like.

Polygons

Polygon is defined by a set of points defined in a pair of arrays (one each for *X* and *Y* coordinates). The Polygon is closed by a line from the last point to the first point. Methods are provided to append a point to the list (growing the Polygon), get the bounding box for the Polygon, and check if a point is inside the Polygon. Note that all points are (*X*, *Y*) pairs; the Point class is not used here.

Fonts and Colors

These two classes are not actually related in the AWT, but we are grouping them together as GUI graphics concepts.

Fonts and FontMetrics

Font handling is rather simple and straightforward and, hence, limited. For those coming from the X11, Motif, and OpenWindows world, it is extremely limited. On the other hand, it is much easier to comprehend.

A font is defined by its name, style, and size. Only four styles of fonts are provided: BOLD, ITALIC, PLAIN, and BOLD+ITALIC. In the binary distribution of the JDK, Sun hides the explanation of where the names are defined, or how to add new fonts, or even if you can. However, you can look in the source code that accompanies the JDK.

The limited interface provides methods to query a number of font aspects such as size, family (platform specific naming), and whether a font is a certain style.

Listing 3.7 includes examples of basic, common Font manipulation in Java.

Listing 3.7 Basic Font class usage.

```
mainFont = new Font("Dialog", Font.PLAIN, 14);
moduleFont = new Font("Dialog", Font.BOLD, 18);

this.setFont(mainFont);
module1.setFont(moduleFont);
module2.setFont(moduleFont);
```

A FontMetric class is also provided. It includes methods to return various font metrics such as `height` and `descent`.

Colors

The Color class provides more useful functionality than the Font class. Thirteen colors are predefined and named, but you can create colors as you need them.

Both RGB (Red/Green/Blue) and HSB (Hue, Saturation, and Brightness) color models are supported, although most of the support is for RGB. You can get the individual red, green, and blue channel values but must set the color as a whole.

Listing 3.8 is a Java code excerpt showing typical Color usage.

Listing 3.8 Basic Color class usage.

```
// Set the default colors for a standard
// white paper appearance.  Make messages
// stand out.

this.setBackground(Color.white);
```

```
this.setForeground(Color.black);
messages.setBackground(Color.lightGray);
messages.setForeground(Color.red);

// Now define the custom colors for the
// trademarked plaid.

plaid.color1 = new Color(210, 180, 140);
 :
```

RGB colors are created from int data, while HSB values are created from float data.

Events

The Event class primarily consists of static, public instance variables that describe event types and related information, public instance variables with specific event information, event modifiers, a few methods to test for event modifiers (such as the **Control** key being down during a key event), and a method to translate event coordinates by an offset. Events are in one of several categories:

- action,
- focus,
- key,
- list,
- file selection,
- mouse,
- scrollbar, and
- window.

Most likely, you will be primarily concerned with action events, which are all referenced as ACTION_EVENT.

Selection Controls

Selection Controls are the various familiar GUI controls for making things happen. Since the AWT uses the underlying windowing system's toolkit, the appearance and semantics should be familiar to the user.

Buttons, Checkboxes, Lists, Choices, and Menus

Buttons, checkboxes, lists, choices, and menus are extremely straightforward. The API model should be reasonably close to something you've used before. We'll start with the simplest class.

Buttons

The Button class is very straightforward. It has a label that you can set and retrieve. The main thing to know about buttons is that when one is activated, it generates an ACTION_EVENT (in all versions of the AWT).

NOTE

As of AWT 1.0.2, a Button will receive all mouse, keyboard, and motion events that occur while the cursor is over it. This is the standard trade-off of functionality versus elegance and speed.

Checkboxes

You can think of a Checkbox as a toggle, or latching, Button with the label beside it instead of on it. In addition to the Button's methods, a Checkbox includes methods to set and get its state (off or on) and to set its CheckboxGroup.

CheckboxGroups (Radio Button Behavior)

A CheckboxGroup object enforces radio button behavior among a designated set of Checkbox objects. This means that only one Checkbox in each group may be on at a given time;

selecting a new Checkbox in a group sets all others in that group to off. This class provides methods to set and get the current Checkbox that is on within a group.

A Checkbox joins a group via its `setCheckboxGroup()` method; a CheckboxGroup has no way of adding or removing a Checkbox.

Lists

Again, the List class is fairly close in concept to most list APIs. The List class methods allow you to:

- add and delete items,
- replace an item,
- select and deselect items,
- get selected items or the indexes of selected items,
- determine whether an item is selected,
- allow and check for multiple selections, and
- set the minimum, maximum and preferred size.

Menus and Choices

The AWT provides for both pop-up, or option, menus (Choice objects) and pull-down, or drop, menus (Menu objects).

Choices

A Choice class displays a labeled button. Selecting the button pops up the choice menu. Selecting a menu items causes three things to happen.

- An ACTION_EVENT is generated with the label of the selected item as its argument.
- The menu is popped down.
- The button label is changed to reflect the choice.

NOTE

As of AWT 1.0.2, a Choice will receive all mouse, keyboard and motion events that occur while the cursor is over it. This is the standard trade-off of functionality versus elegance and speed.

Methods are included to add an item, return the selected item, return the item count, and make a selection. There is no method for removing an item; the list of choices can either grow or remain static.

Menus

Pull-down menus in the AWT are always associated with a MenuBar. A Menu may contain MenuItems, CheckboxMenuItems, or other Menus.

A MenuBar is initially created empty. The `add()` method adds a menu to the MenuBar. Other methods are provided to remove a menu, determine how many menus are on a menubar, get a particular menu, and set and get the Help menu. The Help menu (if set) is always positioned in a reserved place (set by the peer toolkit).

Frames have a special method for attaching a MenuBar.

A Menu is a pull-down component of a MenuBar. A Menu may optionally be a tear-off menu, which remains on the screen instead of disappearing.

NOTE

The user interface for tearing off a menu is peer-dependent and thus varies across operating systems.

Menus may also contain separators. A Menu is created empty. Items are added with the `add()` method. Methods are also provided to remove an item, add a separator, return the item count, get an item, and set whether the menu is a tear-off.

MenuItems

A MenuItem is a simple menu component with a Label. It is essentially a Button in a menu pane, with additional methods to enable or disable the item and to test whether the item is currently enabled.

NOTE

Disabled items are typically grayed out, but this is a peer-dependent action, which varies by operating system and toolkit.

Selecting a MenuItem generates an ACTION_EVENT.

NOTE

As of AWT 1.0.2, a MenuItem will receive all mouse, keyboard, and motion events that occur while the cursor is over it. This is the standard trade-off of functionality versus elegance and speed.

CheckboxMenuItems

CheckboxMenuItem is a subclass of MenuItem. It adds the same sort of toggle capability provided by the Checkbox object except that no radio button behavior is offered. New methods set the state to on or off.

Selecting a CheckboxMenuItem generates an ACTION_EVENT.

NOTE

As of AWT 1.0.2, a CheckboxMenuItem will receive all mouse, keyboard, and motion events that occur while the cursor is over it. This is the standard trade-off of functionality versus elegance and speed.

Labels and Text

The AWT provides standard label and text objects. A Label can display a single line of text. A TextField can display a single line of text, but it is also editable.

NOTE

If you just want to display a single line of text, you should generally use a Label instead of a noneditable TextField.

The TextArea can display any number of lines of text and is optionally editable.

Both the TextField and the TextArea classes are subclassed from TextComponent.

Label

A Label displays a single line of text which may be left, center, or right aligned. Methods are provided to set and get the label text, and set the alignment (which may also be set via the constructor).

TextComponent

The TextComponent class has no GUI component but defines methods common to all text components. These methods allow you to get and set the text, get and set the current selection, and set and check whether a text object is currently editable.

Textfield

A TextField displays a single line of text, which is (by default) editable by the user. Methods are available to set and retrieve the preferred and minimum size, get the number of columns, and control the echo character. If the echo character is set, user-typed text is not displayed; instead, the echo character is displayed in place of each character typed. This makes it easy to (for instance) hide passwords as they are entered.

TextArea

TextArea is similar to the TextField class, except that it allows multiple lines of text and has additional methods to append, insert, and replace text and to set the number of rows. There is no explicit method to delete text.

No explicit scrollbar interface is included, but reasonable peer behavior is used. Generally speaking, you should expect to see scrollbars around a TextArea.

Scrollbars

Scrollbar is a fairly standard scrollbar implementation, although of course the final appearance depends on the peer. The thumb (or bubble or slider) length can be an absolute size or a percentage of the current size.

Methods are provided to get and set the orientation, get and set the minimum and maximum values, get and set the line increment values, get and set the page increment values, and get and set the value.

User interaction with a scrollbar can generate any of various scrollbar-specific events.

Canvas and Graphics

While the Canvas and Graphics classes can be used independently, their functionality is interrelated enough that we will address them together. The Graphics class is often used with other classes, but the Canvas class is fairly useless without Graphics.

Canvas

Canvas is a basic component with no built-in drawing or event-handling code. It handles key and mouse events. You can subclass it or simply draw directly on it.

Obvious uses include drawing and painting programs, CAD programs, plotting displays, and the like, but it has much broader uses. For instance, we will implement a custom GUI for the CardLayout based on Canvas.

Graphics

Graphics is the class you use to actually draw something—whether on or off screen. It is similar to graphics contexts in some windowing systems and toolkits and defines primitive drawing operations such as drawing a line, a rectangle, or a filled rectangle. It does not include some of the more complex primitives, which are implemented in packages such as X11, such as drawing a set of lines. You can add these if you need them, but in Java they are purely programmatic conveniences; there will be no speed gain.

All drawing is handled in the current Color, paintMode, and Font unless otherwise specified. Color and Font were covered earlier in this chapter; paintMode will be covered in the Chapter 11, Drawing.

Containers and LayoutManagers

What Are They?

Containers contain things, of course. In reality, you never deal directly with a Container, but rather invoke a child, such as a Frame, Panel, or Dialog, unless you are writing your own Container subclass. A Container contains components, which may be either Components or other containers.

A LayoutManager is actually an interface for controlling Container layout of components. These interface methods are actually invoked via the Container for which the LayoutManager is defined, as shown in Listing 3.9.

Listing 3.9 Basic Container/LayoutManager usage.

```
FlowLayout layout = new FlowLayout();
 :
this.setLayout(layout);
this.add("howdy", new Label("Howdy!"));
```

Do I Need a LayoutManager?

You can bypass a LayoutManager and position things with absolute coordinates. This, of course, removes all guarantees of platform independence, except in the simplest of interfaces, or if you live with less than optimal positioning (extra space for growth, etc.) and can ensure that things like font differences will not cause problems.

So in general, yes, you should use a LayoutManager.

Provided LayoutManagers

BorderLayout

BorderLayout is a simple LayoutManager commonly used for simple interfaces. It defines five regions in which to place components, arranged around the four sides of the (rectangular) window, labeled NORTH (top), EAST (right), SOUTH (bottom), WEST (left), and a central component labeled CENTER.

BorderLayout is the default LayoutManager for all windows, such as Frame and Dialogs.

FlowLayout

FlowLayout is the default manager for Panels. Each new component is added to the current row until a new one will not fit, at which time a new row is started. No scrolling or autoresizing is provided; you will need to take care of this yourself.

The only control you have over this container beyond size control is whether rows are left, center, or right aligned.

GridLayout

GridLayout implements an extremely simple grid layout with equal-sized rectangular cells at each grid point. Each cell can contain one component of any type. You can set the number of columns and rows when you create the grid. You may set either the columns or rows to 0, meaning an unlimited number of cells is allowed in that dimension.

Components are added across a row until the maximum (if any) has been reached, after which subsequent components will be added to the next row (if any).

Other than the order in which you add components, you have no control over the layout. The GridLayout class does not allow removing an object. Figure 3.1 is an example of a grid with two columns.

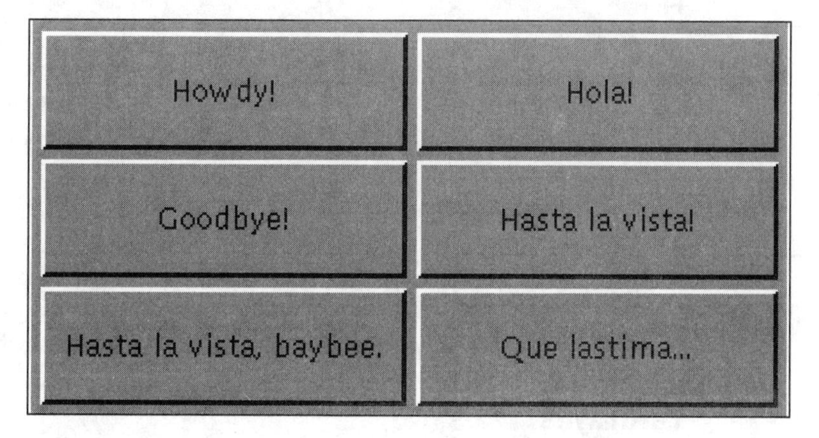

Figure 3.1 GridLayout example.

Note that the components automatically resize to fill the cells.

For more control over layout within a grid, use GridBagLayout.

GridBagLayout

GridBagLayout is a complex container which offers some very nice, and occasionally bizarre, control over component layout, based loosely on a grid model.

Each component added to a GridBagLayout has a set of constraints associated with it; to override a component's default constraints, you must associate a GridBagConstraints object with that component's cell with the `setConstraints()` method.

GridBagConstraints

The GridBagConstraints class is used exclusively with GridBagLayout. It defines how a component appears within a GridBagLayout cell.

Several public fields are available, of which the most important are listed in Table 3.7.

Table 3.7 GridBagConstraints Fields

Field	Use
`anchor`	Justification
`fill`	whether/how to resize for extra space in a cell
`gridwidth, gridheight`	number of cells to use for a single component
`gridx, gridy`	cell after which this cell appears
`weightx, weighty`	how to distribute extra cells

Additional fields control padding.

The only new method clones a GridBagConstraints object.

CardLayout

The CardLayout manager which contains multiple components on separate cards or pages. Each component can, of course, be a Container.

This is a fairly crude LayoutManager, with no GUI to control the cards. In actual use, another container is created to contain both the container using the CardLayout manager and its controls. Methods are provided to move between the cards, and to add and remove cards. You can use any GUI model you like to control the cards; most of the simple Java apps available on the web use a simple, menu-based interface.

A fairly standard way of handling this is to use a BorderLayout object to contain the controls at the top and the CardLayout manager, at the bottom. If you want anything more sophisticated than a menu at the top (which is pretty pathetic), you will need to add a container there (with perhaps a FlowLayout manager) to hold the controls or simply write a custom interface. We will show examples of both. Figure 3.2 shows an example of a card layout; only one card is showing. The other cards would appear in sequence when you clicked on the buttons at the top.

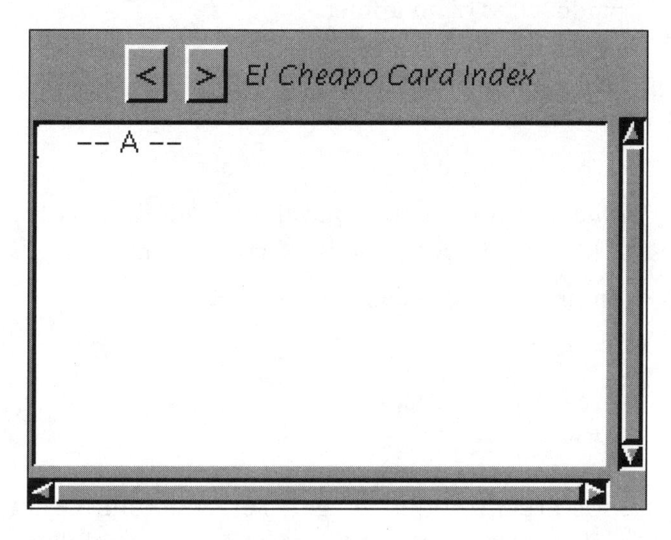

Figure 3.2 CardLayout example.

Panels, Frames, Dialogs, and Applets

Panels, Frames, Dialogs, and applets are all top-level containers. The vast majority of Java apps and applets ultimately work with one of these. Note that applications can be built without any visual interface (a server process, for example), but we assume that you're working on a client. Why else would you be reading this book?

Panels

A *Panel* is a Container with no window of its own. Normally, you'll have several panels in every application you deal with. Panels have several uses:

- top-level container for a Frame or Dialog,
- general container within another Panel, and
- parent class of an applet.

Panel has no additional methods.

Frames

A *Frame* is a top-level application window. It is (optionally) resizable and has several optional components:

- programmer-specified title,
- menu bar,
- icon, and
- cursor.

Methods are provided to get, set and remove any of the optional components and to set and test resizability. A limited set of cursors is provided.

Dialogs

The Dialog class is for pop-up dialog windows. Dialogs may be modal, have a programmer-specified title, and are resizable. Modality is set when the dialog window is created. Methods are provided to test modality and to set and test resizability and title.

FileDialog is a subclass of Dialog and implements a standard file selection dialog. The mode (LOAD or SAVE) is set at creation. Methods are provided to get the mode, and to get and set the directory, file, and filename filter.

Applets

Applet is the top-level container for a Java program running inside another program, such as a web browser. We will defer further discussion of this class until Chapter 15.

Applet is not actually a part of the AWT package, but rather of its own **java.applet** package. This package includes other classes, but they are of little concern at this point unless you are implementing an applet viewer.

Miscellaneous

The miscellaneous classes either didn't fit in other categories or are not worth much attention for most of you. A few of you might use Image; a few might care about Insets. Very few will care about either MediaTracker or Window.

Images

Image is an abstract class for representing an image. There is no constructor; an image is created by invoking either `Applet.getImage()` or `Component.createImage()`. The Image methods are complex enough that we will not discuss them here.

Insets

Insets is a class containing variables describing the four margins (in pixels) of any component in a Container. It includes a `clone()` method and a `toString()` method.

MediaTracker

Despite its name, MediaTracker is used primarily for tracking the status of image loading. You can also set priorities for the various images being loaded and synchronize further processing based on completion of all outstanding loads. While useful for integrating Java viewers into multiconnection web browsers and a handful of image processing applications, it is of little use to most people. We will do little more than document the public interface.

Window

This is simply a top-level window with nothing on it. The vast majority of applications have no need to access this class directly. Frame and Dialog are much more useful.

What's Missing?

There is no easy way to create a Dialog from an applet, since a Dialog must be associated with a Frame when it is created. We will develop a simple Dialog-like object later on.

The LayoutManagers are limited in many areas. A better interface is needed for CardLayout. GridbagLayout has some annoying limitations. A TableLayout class would be helpful. We will develop some of these classes as we go along.

CHAPTER 4

The Top Layers

- Panels
- Applets
- Frames
- Dialog Windows
- File Dialog Windows

In this chapter, we'll develop a simple Java application that manipulates dates to demonstrate the various uses of Panels, Frames, and Dialog windows. We'll also convert the program to an Applet, just to show the differences between applets and applications.

As we introduce new concepts, we'll change the program one step at a time to demonstrate each feature. This evolution closely models formal object-oriented development methodologies, which stress a continuing design/model/test approach.

Panels

For applet and application designers, Panels are extremely useful devices. As the most basic of useful container objects, panels are used in combination with layout managers to group and constrain the arrangement of other components (Buttons, TextFields, images, etc.).)

As a subclass of Container, Panel inherits more than the ability to collect components for grouping. The delivery of events is also an important part of the Container class.

Underneath Container, the Component class provides useful methods to allow and disallow mouse, keyboard, and event handling; to modify color, font, and display attributes; and to control input focus handling.

Table 4.1 outlines some of the useful methods that Panel inherits. We will demonstrate the use of each of these in this chapter.

Table 4.1 Panel Interface

Method	Returns	Notes
	Useful Panel Interface	
`panel()`		The default layout is FlowLayout
	Useful Inherited Container Interface	
`add(Component comp)`	Component	Adds the component to the end of the container's array of "contained" objects
`add(Component comp, int pos)`	Component	Adds the component to the container's array of "contained" objects at a particular slot
`add(String name, Component comp)`	Component	Adds the component to the end of the container's array of "contained" objects and also to the layout manager with the specified name

continued...

Method	Returns	Notes
countComponents()	Int	
getComponent(int n)	Component	Useful when interrogating non-object-oriented Panels
getComponents(n)	Component[]	Also useful when interrogating non-object-oriented Panels
getLayout()	LayoutManager	Get the current layout manager
insets()	Insets	Find out what the Panel inset or border is
locate(int x,int y)	Component	While this is normally called from the event-handling mechanisms, it can be useful to find out where an object is currently located
remove(Component comp)	Void	Could be used with locate to cause "random" deletions from a Panel
setLayout(LayoutManager mgr)	Void	Use once, or with getLayout to change the layout of a Panel without changing the contained objects
	Useful Inherited Component Interface	
disable()	Void	The Panel stays visible, but will not receive input events (mouse, keyboard, etc.)
enable()	Void	The Panel will once again receive input events
getBackground()	Color	
getFont()	Font	Returns the current font for the Panel
getFontMetrics(Font font)	FontMetrics	Returns the font metrics for the peer object
getParent()	Container	Returns the Container that this component is in
gotFocus(Event evt, Object what)	Boolean	Use this to change colors, fonts, or other attributes when the Panel becomes active

continued...

Method	Returns	Notes
`handleEvent(Event evt)`	Boolean	This is where you respond to input (mouse, keyboard, etc.)
`hide()`	Void	The visible Panel disappears; as opposed to `disable()`
`isenabled()`	Boolean	When you're checking on another Panel; usually you know this without asking
`lostFocus(Event evt, Object what)`	Boolean	Use this to change colors, fonts, or other attributes when the Panel becomes inactive
`setBackGround(Color c)`	Void	Useful for providing visual differentiation for subpanels
`setForeGround(Color c)`	Void	Change the color for text, etc.
`show()`	Void	Cause the Panel to (re)appear
`validate()`	Void	Cause the Panel and contents to be laid out if necessary

Very simple applications often use Panel objects directly rather than creating a subclass that extends Panel. Active components added to the Panel are retained as instance variables of another object so they can be updated. Because most of the function of arranging components belongs to the layout manager, Panels provide just the right amount of capability for simple use.

For example, the following simple Java application (Listing 4.1) shows the use of a Panel to group a set of components (a Label and TextField) to allow a layout manager to place them as a group. Since the only active component is the text field, the program doesn't really need to do anything with the panel other than set the background color. The TextField is allocated as a static instance variable of the Panel's creator and may be manipulated without any further reference to the Panel containing it.

Figure 4.1 A Simple Panel.

Listing 4.1 Call.java, a simple Panel.

```
import java.awt.*;
import java.util.*;

public class Call1 {

    public static void main(String args[]) {
    TextField t;
    Frame x = new Frame("Call1");
    Panel p = new Panel();
    Date d = new Date();

        p.setLayout(new FlowLayout());
        p.add(new Label("Calendar Date:"));
        t = new TextField((d.getMonth()+1)+"/"+d.getYear());
        p.add(t);
        p.setBackground(Color.gray);

        x.setLayout(new BorderLayout());
        x.add("North",p);

        x.pack();
        x.show();
    }
}
```

In Listing 4.1, TextField is initialized with the current month and year. The user can type in the field, but the application doesn't recognize the modification. Adding the capability to recognize changes and update the contents programatically requires some additional code. Because we're going to add quite a bit throughout the remainder of the chapter, we'll take this opportunity to convert our example program to true object-oriented code.

First, we'll subclass Panel to produce a Cal2 class. Then we'll move the components of the Panel into the Cal2 constructor. This will give us a proper class to which we can easily add functionality. The operation of our new Cal2 example (Listing 4.1) is identical to Cal1.

Listing 4.2 Cal2.java, a subclassed Panel.

```
import java.awt.*;
import java.util.*;

public class Cal2 extends Panel {

    public Cal2() {
    Date d = new Date();
    TextField t;
        t = new TextField((d.getMonth()+1)+"/"+d.getYear());
        setLayout(new FlowLayout());
        setBackground(Color.gray);
        add(new Label("Calendar Date:"));
        add(t);
    }

    public static void main(String args[]) {
    Frame x = new Frame("Cal2");
    Cal2 p = new Cal2();

        x.setLayout(new BorderLayout());
        x.add("North",p);

        x.pack();
        x.show();
    }
}
```

Even though Cal2 is now a proper subclass, it still doesn't do much. The first thing we want to add is functionality to recognize when a user types a new date into the text field. This involves adding an event handler for our Cal2 object.

First, we'll add the event handler method `public boolean handleEvent(Event e)` to our class. This method is called by the AWT when an event is detected in our component (for more information on events, see Chapter 8). In this case, we'll detect only the user pressing the **Enter** key. When the **Enter** key is pressed, we'll grab the first string of digits (up to a "/") from the text field and convert them to the integer month. We'll grab the digits after the "/" and convert them to the integer year (0–99).

We'll also add a new Label to our Panel. The Label will start out with some innocuous message and be updated by the `handleEvent()` method with the new month and year typed into the text field.

The new example, along with a screen grab of the Panel after typing in a new date (Figure 4.2) is in Listing 4.3.

Listing 4.3 Cal3.java, a Panel with input/output.

```
import java.awt.*;
import java.util.*;

public class Cal3 extends Panel {
    public static TextField t;
    public static Label l = new Label("no change yet to input
TextField!");

    public Cal3() {
        Date d;
        d = new Date();
        t = new TextField((d.getMonth()+1)+"/"+d.getYear());
        setLayout(new FlowLayout());
        setBackground(Color.gray);
        add(new Label("Calendar Date:"));
```

```
        add(t);
        add(l);
        validate();
    }

    public boolean handleEvent(Event e) {
        if (e.id == Event.ACTION_EVENT) {
        TextField x = (TextField)e.target;
        String s;
        int month;
        int year;
            s = t.getText();     // t is a public variable of Cal3
            month = new
Integer(s.substring(0,s.indexOf("/"))).intValue();
            year = new
Integer(s.substring(s.indexOf("/")+1)).intValue();
            l.setText("now " + month + "/" + year);
            return true;
        }
        return super.handleEvent(e);
    }

    public static void main(String args[]) {
    Frame x = new Frame("Cal3");
    Cal3 p = new Cal3();

        x.setLayout(new BorderLayout());
        x.add("North",p);

        x.pack();
        x.show();
    }
}
```

Figure 4.2 Panel with input/output.

At this point, there's no error handling, so invalid input will generate a Java Virtual Machine (JVM) dump that looks like this:

```
C:\java\SRC\awtbook # java Cal3
Exception in thread "AWT-Callback-Win32"
java.lang.StringIndexOutOfBoundsException: String index out of
range: -1
        at java.lang.String.substring(String.java:625)
        at Cal3.handleEvent(Cal3.java:28)
        at java.awt.Component.postEvent(Component.java:844)
        at java.awt.Component.postEvent(Component.java:861)
        at
sun.awt.win32.MTextFieldPeer.action(MTextFieldPeer.java:78)
        at sun.awt.win32.MToolkit.run(MToolkit.java:66)
        at java.lang.Thread.run(Thread.java:294)
```

Exceptions are covered in detail in Chapter 8, so we'll add only a small amount of code to handle the conversion errors here. Until we learn more, just change the initialization of month and year in `handleEvent()` to

```
try {
     month = new Integer(s.substring(0,s.indexOf("/"))).intValue();
     year = new Integer(s.substring(s.indexOf("/")+1)).intValue();
     l.setText("now " + month + "/" + year);
} catch (Exception ev) {
     // some conversion error
      l.setText("Not a valid date in MM/YY format");
     return true;
}
return true;
```

Applets

Applets are extensions to Panel that provide enough program context to act as a small, semi-useful program. They commonly appear as animations or other things in WWW pages. Because they inherit from Panel and are run by a WWW browser, they exist in the context of a pre-existing window that is created by the browser rather than by the developer's Java application.

As a subclass of Panel, all the normal Panel functionality is available to every applet. Layout managers may be assigned, Component objects added, and input events managed by the Applet object.

Applet Invocation

Changing the Java code to let our program behave as an application and applet was simple. However, if you try to open the Java class with appletviewer or with a Java-enabled browser, you'll find the results discouraging:

```
C:\java\SRC\awtbook # appletviewer Cal4.class
Warning: No Applets were started, make sure the input contains an
<applet> tag.
use: appletviewer [-debug] url|file ...
```

What the appletviewer is trying to tell us (in its own stupid way) is that what it is really expecting to see it HTML. To invoke an applet, you use the `<Applet>` tag in your HTML page, as shown in Listing 4.4.

Listing 4.4 cal4.html to invoke the Cal4 applet.

```
<title>AWT Cal4 Test<title>
<hr>
<applet code=Cal4.class width=500 height=100> <applet>
<hr>
<a href="Cal4.java">The Cal4.java source.<a>
```

The <Applet> tag has a small set of required parameters: code, width, and height. The code parameter specifies where to find the compiled Java applet. Note that the value is a URL, and can be either a local filename (as in our example) or a normal HTTP-server-based URL. The width and height parameters indicate to the browser what size window object to preallocate for the applet. Remember that applets inherit from Panels, and Panels must be contained in windows. Each browser has some flexibility in the actual window characteristics, because HTML is a markup language rather than a strict formatting language. Video display settings, preferred font settings, and other system- and user-specific settings affect how the applet is actually displayed.

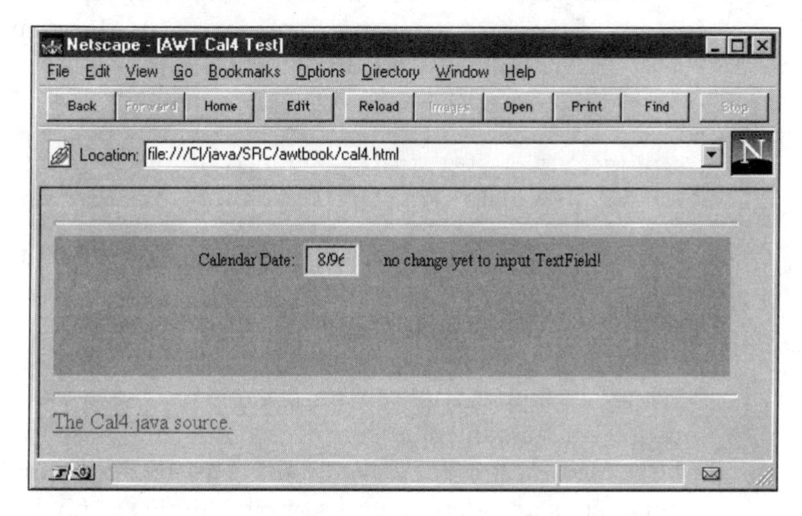

Figure 4.3 Cal4 viewed with Netscape Navigator 2.2 Gold.

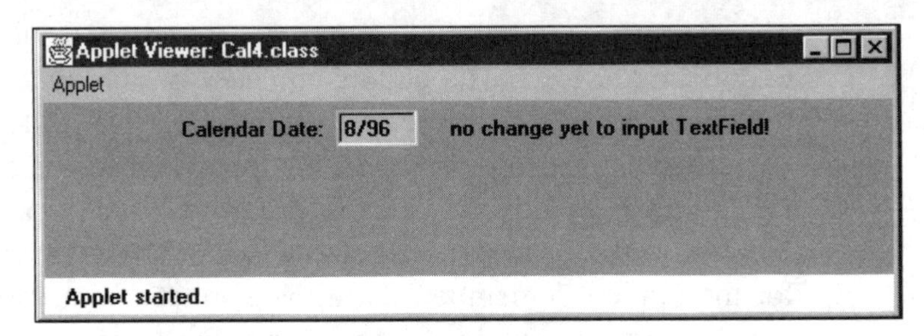

Figure 4.4 Cal4 viewed with appletviewer.

Various browsers behave in different ways when required parameters are omitted. For example, when Netscape is used to view the HTML file, the Java window is merely sized to the width of the browser window. However, the appletviewer is very strict about the width and height parameters:

```
C:\java\SRC\awtbook # appletviewer Cal4.html
Warning: <applet> tag requires width attribute.
Warning: No Applets were started, make sure the input contains an
<applet> tag.
use: appletviewer [-debug] url|file ...
```

Basic Applet Conventions

While a minimal applet is implemented as we've described, a couple of fundamental "bug features" are exposed if we stop here. Most of these revolve around passing applet initialization parameters and starting and stopping applets. Another problem is that the applet runs continuously; in other words, it's a huge drain on the CPU. Nice applets usually must implement threads and the `Runnable` interface to behave appropriately in a WWW page shared with other applets. We'll leave the thread discussion for a later chapter, and now we'll focus on the supporting methods that the applet class provides.

Table 4.2 outlines some of the useful methods that applets implement. We will demonstrate the use of each of these in this chapter.

Table 4.2 Applet Interface

Method	Returns	Notes
`destroy()`	Void	Implement this to clean up threads started in the `init()` method
`getAppletInfo()`	String	Applets use this to report ownership, copyrights, etc.
`getCodeBase()`	URL	Used if an applet needs additional resources (images, etc.) from the location of the applet
`getDocumentBase()`	URL	Used if an applet needs additional resources (images, etc.) from the location of the HTML WWW page
`getParameter(String name)`	String	Call this method with the name of an HTML-named parameter
`getParameterInfo()`	String[][]	Where you should return an array of strings that provide help in using the applet
`init()`	Void	Where initialization of the applet normally occurs (including threads)
`isActive()`	Boolean	Threads can check to see if their applet is currently running
`resize(Dimension d)` `resize(int width, int height)`	Void	Use this to try to resize the containing window
`showStatus(String msg)`	Void	This is fairly useless in a HTML page with multiple applets
`start()`	Void	Browsers tell applets to turn themselves "on"
`stop()`	Void	Browsers tell applets to turn themselves "off"

Minimum Changes to Create an Applet

The minimum changes required to convert our previous example to operate as both an applet and an application are trivial. First, add a line to import the applet hierarchy. Then change our class to inherit from Applet. Applet is a subclass of Panel so we keep every single bit of behavior we had previously. This means that our application still works as it did before. However, we add all the cool WWW-based behavior that Java is currently being used for. Here are the two changes we made:

```
import java.awt.*;
import java.util.*;
import java.applet.*;

public class Cal4 extends Applet // was "Panel"  {
    public static TextField t;
```

Proper Initialization in Java Applets

As part of properly following the conventional applet API used by browsers, we need to implement the `init()` method, which performs some of the function that we formerly implemented in the object constructor. Because we are maintaining the dual applet/application nature of our program, we will keep the object constructor method. We'll also add `start()` and `stop()` methods that print a little debug information to the Java system object. (If you use Netscape, look in the Java Console window for the debug output.) Here are the two additional instance variables we add:

```
public class Cal5 extends Applet {
    public static TextField t;
    public static Label l = new Label("no change yet to input
TextField!");
    boolean userPause = false;
    boolean inApplet = false;
```

The `inApplet` variable is used to tell our code whether we are running as an applet or an application. This is required, because we must know when we can use methods implemented in the Applet class.

The `userPause` variable is used to tell our applet whether we are to "be active" or not. In our applet, we just use it for debug output and to prevent input in the text field object. Animations or complex multithreaded applications would start and stop running threads or perhaps send messages to other programs.

Here are the three methods that will help us meet the applet browser conventions; add them just after the object constructor:

```
public void init() {
    inApplet = true;
    userPause = false;
}
public void start() {
    Date s = new Date();
    if (inApplet)
        showStatus("Cal5 started at " + s.toString());
    System.out.println("Cal5 started at " + s.toString());
    userPause = false;
}

public void stop() {
    Date s = new Date();
    if (inApplet)
        showStatus("Cal5 stopped at " + s.toString());
    System.out.println("Cal5 stopped at " + s.toString());
    userPause = true;
}
```

After you make these changes, run the program as both applet and application. You'll note that there is no status line when it's running as an application and that "stopping" the application doesn't really stop anything. Only when leaving the HTML page will the browser invoke the start and stop methods. This lets the applet run while the page is displayed, but stop (and save resources) while you are browsing some other page.

To make the start and stop methods useful in the general case, you'll either want to add either a **START/STOP** button to the applet or just use mouse clicks to start and stop. We'll choose the second method, because it's more easily done in WWW pages.

To simplify our discussion, following is the event handler as modified to support mouse clicks.

```
    public boolean handleEvent(Event e) {
        if (e.id == Event.ACTION_EVENT) {
            TextField x = (TextField)e.target;
            String s;
            int month;
            int year;
            if (userPause)          // don't allow activity when
paused
                return true;
            s = t.getText();    // t is a public variable of Cal5
            try {
                month = new
Integer(s.substring(0,s.indexOf("/"))).intValue();
                year = new
Integer(s.substring(s.indexOf("/")+1)).intValue();
                l.setText("now " + month + "/" + year);
            } catch (Exception ev) {
                // some conversion error
                l.setText("Not a valid date in MM/YY format");
                return true;
            }
            return true;
        } else if (e.id == Event.MOUSE_DOWN) {
            if (userPause) {
                start();
            } else {
                stop();
            }
```

```
            return true;
        }
        return super.handleEvent(e);
    }
```

When you run this version of the applet, you'll quickly discover that the status messages displayed by the applet are erased by the browser as other events occur. If you have any important information to show, you'll want to choose some other method than `showStatus();` perhaps you can use a separate label or even a new frame.

One final refinement to the start/stop functionality is to add code to disable the text field when the applet is stopped. Adding `enable()` and `disable()` calls to the text field within the start and stop methods, respectively, will cause the text field to work sensibly.

```
    public void start() {
        Date s = new Date();
        if (inApplet)
            showStatus("Cal5 started at " + s.toString());
        System.out.println("Cal5 started at " + s.toString());
        userPause = false;
        t.enable();
    }

    public void stop() {
        Date s = new Date();
        if (inApplet)
            showStatus("Cal5 stopped at " + s.toString());
        System.out.println("Cal5 stopped at " + s.toString());
        userPause = true;
        t.disable();
    }
```

The only other change is to add a line in the event handler's `MOUSE_DOWN` code to ignore `MOUSE_DOWN` clicks only on the `textfield` component. This way, the user has to specifically start the application before typing a new date. The `locate()` method returns the component under the mouse click; if that component is the `textfield t`, we ignore the click by returning `true`:

```
} else if (e.id == Event.MOUSE_DOWN) {
    if (t == locate(e.x,e.y))
        return true;
    if (userPause) {
        start();
```

Passing Parameters to Java Applets

Real applets (and applications) don't just start with static values each time they're run. For example, our Cal4 class always starts with today's date (August of 1996 in Figures 4.3 and 4.4). This may be OK for certain uses, but WWW page designers usually require more flexibility in an applet.

The HTML required to pass an argument directly to a Java applet (rather than to the browser as in `width` and `height`) is fairly simple. The `<PARAM>` tag always uses `name` and `value` parameters to construct the argument passed to the Java applet. For each `<PARAM>` tag, the browser constructs one argument to the Java applet.

To demonstrate this capability, we'll add a `startdate` argument to our applet/application. The additional code to support applet parameters is limited to calls to `getParameter()`. Our single `startdate` parameter is easy to parse. To add the applet side initialization, change the `init()` method to

```
public void init() {
    String startDate = getParameter("startdate");
    if (startDate != null) {
```

```
            t.setText(startDate);
        }
        inApplet = true;
        userPause = false;
        t.enable();
    }
```

The HTML we need to invoke the applet with the `startdate` parameter is given in Listing 4.5.

Listing 4.5 cal5.html to invoke the Cal5 applet.

```
<title>AWT Cal5 Test with startdate parameter<title>
<hr>
<applet code=Cal5.class width=500 height=100>
<param name=startdate value=4/89>
<applet>
<hr>
<a href="Cal5.java">The Cal5.java source.<a>
```

Adding Information and Help to an Applet

If an Applet is provided to a user with appropriate written documentation and a personal guarantee of "I swear it works right," a user can decide whether to use it or not. If you're planning to deliver an applet without such guarantees, the following two methods should be included in your code:

```
public String getAppletInfo() {
    String s;
    s = "This Simple Applet produced by Pencom Web Works\n" +
        "    copyright (c) 1996, Pencom Systems, Inc.\n" +
        "Code Base is " + getCodeBase() + "\n" +
        "Document Base is " + getDocumentBase() + "\n";
    return s;
}
```

```
public String[][] getParameterInfo() {
    String pinfo [][] = {
        {"startdate","mm/yy","An initial month and year"}
        };
    return pinfo;
}
```

The `getAppletInfo()` method should provide basic information about the applet, including where to get it, who's responsible for it, and what legal restrictions may apply to the applet. The `getParameterInfo()` method provides each parameter name, the input range and/or type, and a simple description of what the parameter is for.

What's Missing from Our Applet Discussion

We've covered much of what is required of applets in this section. About the only thing we've ignored is thread management, because we've provided a separate chapter on threads. You'll find discussions of the runnable interface and more information on `init()`, `start()`, `stop()`, and `destroy()` there as well.

Frames

While WWW applets use a single Panel for most of their on-screen interaction, the Frame is the basic container object for applications. Applications and applets that provide multiple on-screen windows or open and close windows regularly, normally would instantiate a single frame for each window. Because Frame is a direct subclass of Window and is significantly more useful for most applications, we'll focus our discussion on frames rather than windows.

The primary reason for using Frames rather than Windows is the capability to support AWT menus, titles, and window borders. Because most applications regularly require these features, Frames are used much more often than Windows.

In this section, we'll show examples of using free-standing Windows to provide more flexibility in the user interface for applications and applets. Note that there are some security implications when creating Windows from within browsers.

Useful Windowing Interfaces

The Frame and Window classes provide the following useful methods listed in Table 4.3 along with the inherited Container and Component methods mentioned in the discussion on Panels.

Table 4.3 Frame Interface

Method	Returns	Notes
`Frame()` `Frame(String title)`		A new frame with optional title
`dispose()`	Void	Event handlers often call this method to make the window go away and free up system resources; you can still call `show()` to make the window reappear
`getCursorType()`	Int	Cursor types are enumerated in the Frame class
`getIconImage()`	Image	Returns null if there's no image associated with the inconized window
`getMenuBar()`	MenuBar	Use this method to get a handle to the menu
`getTitle()`	String	
`isResizable()`	Boolean	
`remove(MenuComponent m)`	Void	Remove the menu component from this frame

continued...

Method	Returns	Notes
`setCursor(int cursorType)`	Void	
`setIconImage(Image image)`	Void	
`setMenuBar(MenuBar mb)`	Void	Add MenuBar to this frame
`setResizable(boolean resizable)`		Void
`setTitle(String title)`	Void	
Useful Inherited Window Interface		
`getWarningString(String title)`	String	Useful for debugging security problems or for confusing users
`pack()`	Void	Cause the contained components to be laid out at their preferred size
`show()`	Void	Make the window visible; don't forget `Component.hide()`
`toBack()`	Void	Send the window to the back of the window stack
`toFront()`	Void	Send the window to the front of the window stack

Cursor Configuration

While most systems allow the mouse cursor to be set to any bit map, the AWT limits the choices to the following:

- CROSSHAIR_CURSOR
- DEFAULT_CURSOR
- E_RESIZE_CURSOR
- HAND_CURSOR
- MOVE_CURSOR
- N_RESIZE_CURSOR
- NE_RESIZE_CURSOR
- NW_RESIZE_CURSOR
- S_RESIZE_CURSOR

- SE_RESIZE_CURSOR
- SW_RESIZE_CURSOR
- TEXT_CURSOR
- W_RESIZE_CURSOR
- WAIT_CURSOR

While the AWT specifies the cursor in a device-independent way, each peer windowing system has the freedom to implement the specific bit map displayed by each call to `setCursor()`. Even with this behavior, it's a good idea to implement as much normal cursor behavior as possible within your code. Most of the component objects do implement appropriate behavior, but any code that draws directly into a canvas should probably attempt to maintain reasonable cursor shapes as hints to the user.

If you add the following code to the event handler for your Frame, you can easily cause the cursor to change appropriately every time the mouse crosses the Frame. Note, however, that this can have an impact on performance, because it changes every time the mouse passes over the Frame, even if another program is the current application.

```
int oldCursor;

...

} else if (e.id == Event.MOUSE_ENTER) {
    oldCursor = getCursorType();
    setCursor(Frame.CROSSHAIR_CURSOR);
    return true;
} else if (e.id == Event.MOUSE_EXIT) {
    setCursor(oldCursor);
    return true;
}
```

Assorted Window Management

To implement "normal" behavior of windows, the Window class provides a small group of methods dealing with positioning of the window relative to other windows. `show()`, `hide`, `toFront()`, and `toBack()` provide support for the traditional stack management of windows. However, there is no direct support for ordering of windows (i.e., you can't say "put this window in front of that window").

In addition to the ordering of windows, you can use inherited component behavior to manage placement of the windows relative to the screen boundaries. The `move()` method positions a component relative to its parent's boundaries. Because windows are positioned relative to the WindowManager display space, you can use the `move()` method to position windows at particular locations.

If the following code is added to an **Arrange Windows** menu entry in your program, each custom window you create will be staggered down the screen. Note that 15-pixel offsets may be too much or too little for any particular display system.

```
    static int left = 0;    // (x) position of class always starts
here
    static int top = 0;     // (y) position of class always starts
here
    myFrame w[];            // references to every myFrame you
created

    ...

    for (i=0;i<w.count();i++) {
        w[i].move(left,top);    // put window at current start
position
        left += 15;             // next window 15 pixels right
        top += 15;              // next window 15 pixels down
    }
```

Frames also support title bars; to change the title, just use the `getTitle()` and `setTitle()` methods. The frame constructor can also accept a `String` as the initial title.

```
Frame f = new Frame("the original title");

f.setTitle(f.getTitle() +
" and a longer title");
```

We have seem some applications that use the contents of the title bar to store the filename or other window content-specific information. Using `getTitle()`, they extract the filename from the window title and use that to open a file or connect to a host. We are not sure this is good style, but it seems to work.

Hiding (minimizing, iconizing, etc.) frames is simple; the user just clicks on the peer windowing system's **minimize** button. The AWT was designed to meet basic programming requirements. The AWT doesn't provide a way to programatically iconize AWT windows. The closest you can come is to completely `hide()` windows and then `show()` them later.

However, in the AWT tradition of exceptions, there is a way to set the icon image for iconized windows. For those who like iconized windows with meaningful icons that are on a system that can iconize windows, here's a simple method to change or restore the icon image in a frame. The method saves the previous icon and returns it to the caller. If the passed image is null, the previous icon is restored. Remember that not all windowing systems will display the icon.

```
static Image windowImage = getIconImage();

public Image setIcon(Image passedImage) {
    if (passedImage != null) {        // set or restore?
        windowImage = getIconImage(); // save previous Icon
        setIconImage(passedImage);
    } else {
```

```
            setIconImage(windowImage);      // restore previous Icon
        }
        return windowImage;
    }
```

Some windows, especially those without layout managers or with certain custom layout managers, shouldn't be resized. Frame provides two methods—`isResizable()` and `setResizable()`—to check and set this capability on a Frame. Like most methods discussed in this section, these are Frame methods, not Window methods.

```
if (isResizable() == true)     // flip resizable attribute
    setResizable(false);
else
    setResizable(true);
```

Dialog Windows

Dialog windows are subclassed Frames with the additional capability of operating in a modal fashion. This means that once they gain focus, they don't give it up until they're ready. Usually, Dialog windows manage error conditions, open/close, connect/disconnect, or other exceptional conditions that must be completed before an application can continue (see Table 4.4).

NOTE

On Microsoft platforms, with JDK release 1.0.1 and 1.0.2 (and their derivatives), Dialog windows are relatively buggy. Modal operation doesn't work correctly, and displaying newly created Dialogs is also fairly buggy. Our example code attempts to work around the display problems but doesn't solve the modality problem. The 1.1 release of the JDK is supposed to fix these problems.

Table 4.4 Dialog Interface

Method	Returns	Notes
`Dialog(Frame parent, boolean modal)` `Dialog(Frame parent,String title, boolean modal)`		Modal doesn't yet work
`getTitle()`	String	Get the title from this dialog/frame
`isModal()`	Boolean	Check if it's modal or not
`isResizable()`	Boolean	Check if the frame is resizable
`setResizable(boolean resizable)`	Void	Make it resizable
`setTitle(String title)`	Void	Set the dialog/frame title

Traditional Error Handling Dialog Windows

One of the most common uses of dialog windows in other windowing systems is that of acknowledging an error condition or status message. Figure 4.5 is an error dialog window that requires a user to **Accept**, **Cancel**, or **Exit** and returns a matching `true` (**Accept**) or `false` (**Cancel**) Boolean. The exit case performs an immediate `System.exit()` and terminates the program.

Figure 4.5 A simple error dialog window.

While this is not a full-featured error dialog window, it does at least provide reasonable functionality. We've used it in some of our Java applications to good effect, and we invite you to use it as a basis for your own dialog windows. However, once modal operation is finally implemented properly, you'll want to redesign this class.

Listing 4.6 Basic dialog window.

```
interface DialogInterface {        // allows subclass of Window or
Frame
    public void dialogResponse(boolean state);
}
class YesnoDialog extends Dialog {
    static Label l = new Label();
    static Button accept = new Button("Accept");
    static Button cancel = new Button("Cancel");
    static Button exit = new Button("Exit");
    static DialogInterface parent;

    YesnoDialog(DialogInterface f) {
        this(f,"Press Accept, Cancel, or Exit");
    }
    YesnoDialog(DialogInterface f,String s) {
        super((Frame) f, "Error Dialog", false);
        setLayout(new FlowLayout());
        parent = f;
        add(l);
        add(accept);
        add(cancel);
        add(exit);
        l.setText(s);
        pack();
    }

    public void setText(String s) {
        l.setText(s);
        pack();
        validate();
        show();
    }
    public boolean action(Event event, Object arg) {
        // message parent object with results
        if (event.target == accept)
```

```
            parent.dialogResponse(true);
        else if (event.target == cancel)
            parent.dialogResponse(false);
        else {
            System.exit(0);         // ACK!   oh well, he said go
away
        }
        hide();
        return true;
    }
}
```

Note that a Java interface called `DialogInterface` is used to communicate the results back to the parent object. The object that desires to see the **Accept** or **Cancel** condition should include code like this to create the dialog window. Note that the first time, we create the dialog window; other times, we can merely call `setText()` to update the message and redisplay the dialog window.

```
class xx extends Frame implements DialogInterface {
    YesnoDialog myDialog;
    ...
    // create the dialog here
    if (myDialog == null) {
        myDialog = new YesnoDialog(this);     // pass a handle back
to us
        myDialog.show();                      // paint the dialog
    } else {
        myDialog.setText("Bigger Message to Show in Dialog
TextField ");
    }
```

The `YesnoDialog` class uses a method called `dialogResponse()` to communicate the user response back to the parent object. If the Boolean passed to `dialogResponse` is `true`, the **Accept** button was clicked. If the `false` condition is passed, the

Cancel button was clicked. Of course, if the user clicks on the **Exit** button, the `YesnoDialog` class terminates the entire Java application with `System.exit(0)`:

```
public void dialogResponse(boolean state) {
    if (state == true)
            // Accept pressed in YesnoDialog
    else
            // Cancel pressed in YesnoDialog
}
```

File Dialog Windows

The other primary use of dialog windows in applications is to select a file or device. The Java AWT provides a class called FileDialog to simplify development efforts that involve opening files.

When creating the dialog window, pass the constructor either **FileDialog.LOAD** or **FileDialog.SAVE** to indicate the direction in which the dialog is to operate. Note that the dialog window doesn't actually open any file selected, it merely travels the file tree to allow easy selection of a file in the native format.

For security reasons, WWW browsers do not support FileDialog. Attempts to create FileDialog within a browser implementation of the AWT cause a JAVA Virtual Machine dump similar to:

```
java.awt.AWTError: FileDialog is unimplemented.
        at
sun.awt.win32.MToolkit.createFileDialog(MToolkit.java:132)
        at java.awt.FileDialog.addNotify(FileDialog.java:78)
        at java.awt.Window.show(Window.java:93)
        at Message.action(Cal8.java:154)
        at java.awt.Component.handleEvent(Component.java:900)
```

```
        at Message.handleEvent(Cal8.java:143)
        at java.awt.Component.postEvent(Component.java:838)
        at java.awt.MenuComponent.postEvent(MenuComponent.java:94)
        at java.awt.MenuComponent.postEvent(MenuComponent.java:94)
        at java.awt.MenuComponent.postEvent(MenuComponent.java:94)
        at
sun.awt.win32.MMenuItemPeer.action(MMenuItemPeer.java:50)
        at sun.awt.win32.MToolkit.run(MToolkit.java:57)
        at java.lang.Thread.run(Thread.java:289)
```

The FileDialog class provides the interface shown in Table 4.5. Remember that, on some platforms, the native file dialog windows may have additional functionality that the AWT does not provide access to.

Table 4.5 Useful FileDialog Interface

Method	Returns	Notes
`FileDialog(Frame parent,String title)` `FileDialog(Frame parent, String title,int mode)`		Create file dialogs with an optional `LOAD` or `SAVE`
`getDirectory()`	String	Returns the current directory selected in the FileDialog
`getFile()`	String	Returns the current filename selected
`getFilenameFilter()`	FilenameFilter	
`getMode()`	Int	Is this a `FileDialog.LOAD` or `FileDialog.SAVE` FileDialog
`setDirectory(String dir)`	Void	Set the directory to be selected in the dialog
`setFile(String file)`	Void	Set the filename to be selected (and made the default if the dialog has not been "shown" yet)
`setFilenameFilter (FilenameFilter filter)`	Void	Establish the filename filter object which is to handle filtering for this dialog

The only complication to using the file dialog is the FileFilter. This Java interface is part of `java.io` and provides only one method, `accept(File dir, String filename)`. The intent of the file filter is to constrain the display of files in the file dialog window to those that are of the potentially correct type. For instance, a text file filter `accept()` method would return `true` when passed filenames that end in **.txt**. Note that the object containing the `accept` method does not necessarily have to be a file-oriented object, it just must implement the FileFilter interface.

Problems with Dialog Windows

Currently, the biggest problem with dialog windows as implemented in the JDK is the failure of modal operation. Because modality is what dialog windows are designed for, this problem makes standard dialog windows next to useless. In fact, when combined with the display problems in the Win-32 JDK, it's probably easier just to use Frame to implement everything.

FileDialog allows only one selection at a time. A significant improvement would be to allow multiple selections. However, because the underlying windowing systems have different behavior for multiple selections in a listbox, this useful extension may never be implemented in the basic AWT.

CHAPTER 5

Basic Layouts

- LayoutManager
- BorderLayout
- FlowLayout
- GridLayout
- GridBagLayout
- GridBagConstraints
- CardLayout
- What's Missing?

LayoutManager

A layout manager is a class for controlling the layout of components in a container. The LayoutManager is the interface for all layout managers. The layout managers provided with the AWT vary from simplistic (which end up being useful for only the simplest user interfaces) to fairly complex (but still not quite able to do everything we want).

LayoutManager Methods

The LayoutManager interface consists primarily of five methods, defined in Table 5.1. This is a relatively stable interface. A useful layout manager will also provide a constructor, and probably a `toString` method.

Table 5.1 LayoutManager interface.

Method	Returns	Notes
`addLayoutComponent (String name, Component comp)`	void	Usually called by `add()`
`removeLayoutComponent (Component comp)`	void	Usually called by container's `remove` or `removeAll` method
`layoutContainer (Container parent);`	void	Usually called by container's `layout` method
`minimumLayoutSize (Container parent)`	Dimension	Usually called by container's `layout` method
`preferredLayoutSize (Container parent)`	Dimension	Usually called by container's `preferredSize` method

None of these methods are usually invoked directly by an application or applet. As shown in Table 5.1, most of them are automatically invoked by the container itself, and the remaining method (`addLayoutComponent`) is usually invoked by the `add()` method (the usual method by which an application adds a component to a container).

Unless you are interested in the nitty gritty of layout managers (which probably means you plan to write one), you can skip ahead to the descriptions of the LayoutManager classes provided with the AWT.

addLayoutComponent

```
public abstract void
addLayoutComponent(String name, Component comp)
```

This `addLayoutComponent` method adds the designated component to the layout, using `name` (also known as a *tag*), which is a string relevant to this layout manager.

Most of the actual work is done elsewhere; this method primarily handles anything special with regards to the tag. Layout managers without tag requirements generally have an empty `addLayoutComponent` method.

removeLayoutComponent

```
public abstract void
removeLayoutComponent(Component comp)
```

The `removeLayoutComponent` method removes the designated component's tag from a layout. It is typically called from either the `remove` or the `removeAll` method of a container. Containers that do not use tags typically have an empty `removeLayoutComponent` method.

layoutContainer

```
public abstract void
layoutContainer(Container parent)
```

The `layoutContainer` method performs most of the real work of a layout manager, actually handling the layout management for the designated container (the parent of this instance of the layout manager).

`layoutContainer` may reshape the components within its parent container as necessary to satisfy current layout constraints.

This method is normally called by a container's `layout` method.

minimumLayoutSize

```
public abstract Dimension
minimumLayoutSize(Container parent)
```

The `minimumLayoutSize` method determines and returns the minimum dimensions of the parent container necessary to hold its current components, given the current layout constraints.

This method is normally called by a container's `layout` method.

preferredLayoutSize

```
public abstract Dimension
preferredLayoutSize(Container parent)
```

The `preferredLayoutSize` method determines and returns the preferred dimensions of the parent container necessary to hold its current components, given the current layout constraints. This method can be as clever as you wish to make it.

This method is normally called by a container's `layout` method.

Examples

After we look at the layout managers provided by the AWT we will develop some other layout managers and go through their interface methods to show how these methods work together.

BorderLayout

The BorderLayout manager is useful only for simple GUIs. It handles up to five components, one along each of the top and bottom borders of a rectangle, one along each of the left and right borders of a rectangle, and one in the center.

This manager uses tags to designate the borders, named after the four major compass points, and `Center` for the center component, as shown in Figure 5.1.

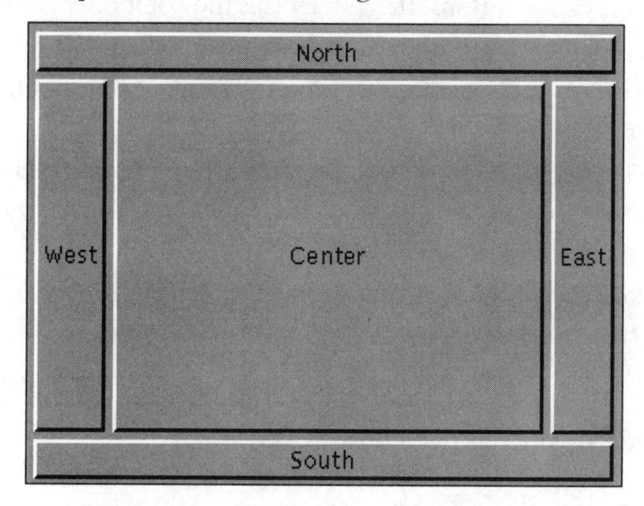

Figure 5.1 Basic BorderLayout.

The code for this example is shown in Listing 5.1.

Listing 5.1 Basic BorderLayout applet.

```
import java.applet.*;
import java.awt.*;

public class Border extends Applet {
    public void init() {
```

```
        this.setLayout(new BorderLayout());
        this.add("North", new Button("North"));
        this.add("West", new Button("West"));
        this.add("South", new Button("South"));
        this.add("East", new Button("East"));
        this.add("Center", new Button("Center"));
    }
}
```

As you can see, BorderLayout resizes the components as follows:

1. The `North` and `South` components are stretched horizontally to the width of the container. These components are not vertically resized.
2. The `East` and `West` components are then stretched vertically to the remaining height of the container. These components are not horizontally resized.
3. The `Center` component is then resized to fill any remaining space in the center of the container between the border components.

BorderLayout has two constructors:

```
public BorderLayout();
public BorderLayout(int hgap, int vgap);
```

The latter version allows you to set horizontal and vertical gaps between the components; the default is 4.

If you're wondering why everyone uses almost identical examples for this layout manager, it's because in this case the obvious example is the right one. Buttons show the results of the resize with the least programming; the labels show the tags.

For a more useful example, let's revisit the CardLayout example in Chapter 4 (Figure 5.2). A BorderLayout is used for the outermost container, but you can't tell from looking at the applet.

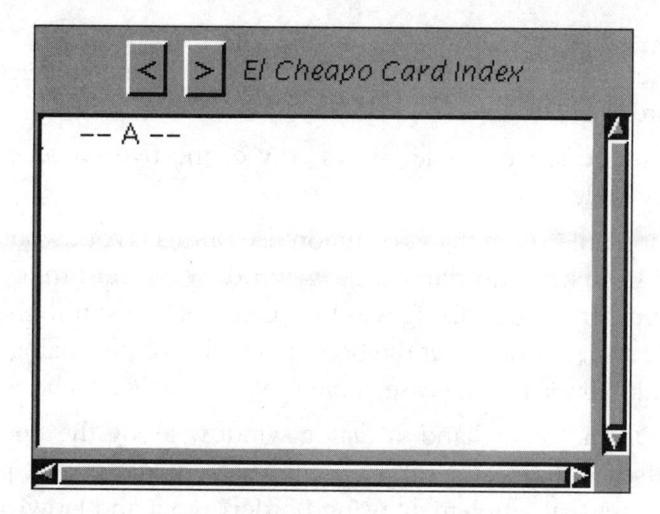

Figure 5.2 Real Use for BorderLayout.

The BorderLayout-related code (Listing 5.2) is extremely straightforward. Note that all components managed in this example are other containers.

Listing 5.2 BorderLayout code in card index.

```
Panel buttons, cards;

BorderLayout borderLayout = new BorderLayout();
FlowLayout flowLayout = new FlowLayout();
CardLayout cardLayout = new CardLayout();

public void init() {
    :
    this.setLayout(borderLayout);
    buttons = new Panel();
    buttons.setLayout(flowLayout);
    this.add("North", buttons);
    cards = new Panel();
    cards.setLayout(cardLayout);
    this.add("Center", cards);
    :
}
```

Very little is handled directly by this BorderLayout object; all other objects are children of the two containers managed by the BorderLayout object.

As the last example shows, any of the five layout positions may be left empty.

It would seem that a common use of this layout would be for an industry-standard dialog window appearance, with a menubar on top, dialog window area of some sort in the center, and a set of buttons at the bottom, much like the Dialog class. In reality this is not the case; a menubar can only attach to a frame.

On the other hand, a dialog window along the lines of the Netscape Navigator (albeit somewhat cruder) option panels is fairly easy to implement using BorderLayout and FlowLayout.

Details, Details

There aren't many gory details to worry about other than how the minimum and preferred size are determined; if you don't care about these, feel free to skip ahead to FlowLayout.

minimumSize

BorderLayout determines minimum size based on the managed components' minimum sizes, the container's insets, and the horizontal and vertical gaps.

```
min_height = min_height(North) + min_height(South) +
             maximum_of(min_height(West),
                        min_height(Center),
                        min_height(East)) +
             (2 * vgap);

min_width =  maxiumum_of((min_width(West) + min_width(East) +
                           min_width(Center) + (2 * vgap)),
                        min_width(North),
                        min_width(South));
```

preferredSize

BorderLayout determines preferred size based on the managed components' preferred sizes, the container's insets, and the horizontal and vertical gaps.

```
pref_height = pref_height(North) + pref_height(South) +
              maximum_of(pref_height(West),
                         pref_height(Center),
                         pref_height(East)) +
              (2 * vgap) + Insets.top + Insets.bottom;

pref_width =  maxiumum_of((pref_width(West) + pref_width(East) +
                          pref_width(Center) + (2 * vgap)),
                         pref_width(North),
                         pref_width(South)) +
              Insets.left + Insets.right;
```

FlowLayout

The FlowLayout manager treats components much like a simple word processor or editor treats words and lines in a paragraph. It just keeps adding new components to the right, and when a new component won't fit, a new line is started. Like a simple word processor, FlowLayout can also handle left, center, or right adjustment.

FlowLayout implements only the standard LayoutManager methods and two additional constructors:

```
public FlowLayout(int align);
public FlowLayout(int align, int hgap, int vgap);
```

`align` can be any of **LEFT**, **CENTER**, or **LEFT**. The default adjustment is **CENTER**. `ggap` and `vgap` are the standard horizontal and vertical gap parameters and default to 8.

This layout manager is typically used to handle a set of buttons on a single line, but it can contain any type of component. The card index shown in Figure 5.2 uses a `FlowLayout` to manage the buttons and logo at the top of the applet. The relevant code is shown in Listing 5.3.

Listing 5.3 Using FlowLayout.

```
Label logo;
Panel buttons;
Button button[] = new Button[2];

BorderLayout borderLayout = new BorderLayout();
FlowLayout flowLayout = new FlowLayout();

this.setLayout(borderLayout);
buttons = new Panel();
buttons.setLayout(flowLayout);
this.add("North", buttons);
:
button[0] = new Button("<");
buttons.add("Prev", button[0]);
button[1] = new Button(">");
buttons.add("Next", button[1]);
buttons.add("Logo", new Label("El Cheapo Card Index"));
```

Details, Details

There aren't many gory details to worry about other than how the minimum and preferred size are determined; if you don't care about these, feel free to skip ahead to GridLayout.

minimumSize

FlowLayout determines minimum size based on the managed components' minimum sizes, the container's insets, and the horizontal and vertical gaps and assumes all components will be placed on one row.

```
min_height = min_height_of_tallest_component +
             (2 * vgap) +
             Insets.top + Insets.bottom;

min_width =  sum_of_component_min_widths +
             ((num_components + 1) * hgap) +
             Insets.left + Insets.right;
```

preferredSize

FlowLayout determines preferred size based on the managed components' preferred sizes, the container's insets, and the horizontal and vertical gaps and assumes all components will be placed on one row.

```
pref_height = pref_height_of_tallest_component +
              (2 * vgap) +
              Insets.top + Insets.bottom;

pref_width = sum_of_component_pref_widths +
             ((num_components + 1) * hgap) +
             Insets.left + Insets.right;
```

GridLayout

This implements an extremely simple grid layout with equally sized rectangular cells at each grid point. A cell contains a single component, and each component will be resized to fill the cell. Components are added to the next available cell in a row or, if the row is full, to the first cell in the next row, until all defined cells have been filled. You have no other control over where a given component goes.

You define the number of columns and rows when you create the grid. Either the number of rows or the number of columns (but not both) may be unlimited; setting the appropriate dimension to 0 defines this behavior.

The GridLayout class does not allow you to remove an object.

There are two constructors:

```
public GridLayout(int rows, int cols);
public GridLayout(int rows, int cols, int hgap, int vgap);
```

Listing 5.4 contains examples of typical grid construction.

Listing 5.4 Typical grid layouts.

```
GridLayout g1, g2, g3, g4, g5;
g1 = new GridLayout(3, 2);     // 3 rows of 2 columns
g2 = new GridLayout(1, 0);     // 1 row, unlimited columns
g3 = new GridLayout(2, 0);     // Why is this pointless?
g3 = new GridLayout(0, 1);     // 1 column, unlimited rows
g3 = new GridLayout(0, 2);     // 2 columns, unlimited rows
```

The first layout `g1` should be obvious. Figure 5.3 shows an example.

Figure 5.3 GridLayout example.

Listing 5.5 shows the code that produced this grid.

Listing 5.5 Typical grid layouts.

```
public class Grid extends Applet {
   public void init()
```

```
    {
        this.setLayout(new GridLayout(3, 2));

        this.add(new Button("Howdy!"));
        this.add(new Button("Hola!"));
        this.add(new Button("Goodbye!"));
        this.add(new Button("Hasta la vista!"));
        this.add(new Button("Hasta la vista, baybee."));
        this.add("a", new Button("Que lastima..."));
    }
}
```

Note that GridLayout does not really use a tag. The final add method call does not do anything differently than the previous add calls; the tag is discarded.

The next two grids in Listing 5.4 (g2 and g3) define grids with an unlimited number of columns. Since the only control you have over position is the order in which you add components (and your knowledge of the grid dimensions), it should be obvious that the second row of g3 is pointless; new objects will always be added to the first row.

The final two grids in Listing 5.4 (g4 and g5) stack grow vertically. The first grid g4 always adds a new row for a new component. The final grid g5 creates a new row for every other component. The effect is that of a two-column table that can grow vertically as necessary.

Grids are not as useful as one might hope, for several reasons:

- They always attempt to grow horizontally first; there is no way to have a multicolumn grid fill up in column order. If you must have this, you need a single-row grid (or something similar) whose children are single-column grids. This requires slightly more work to get all the components in the right positions.

- Grids always resize their children to the cell size. This means that GridLayout is probably not an appropriate choice for grouping other containers of related dialog windows. Nor can you set up a grid where all cells in a row must be the same height but different rows may be different heights.
- You cannot skip cells; it is impossible to have an empty cell with components in subsequent cells. To implement this requires placeholder components, which must be of the correct type since you cannot replace them later.
- There is no way to span cells.

Some (but not all!) of these limitations are solved by the GridBagLayout class.

Details, Details

There aren't many gory details to worry about other than how the minimum and preferred size are determined; if you don't care about these, feel free to skip ahead to GridBagLayout.

layoutContainer

GridLayout determines cell size by dividing the appropriate dimension of the container (less any horizontal gap or vertical gap space and less any insets) by the number of columns or rows.

minimumSize

GridLayout determines minimum size based on the managed components' minimum sizes, the container's insets, and the horizontal and vertical gaps.

```
min_height = (min_height_of_tallest_component *
              num_components) +
             ((num_components + 1) * vgap) +
             Insets.top + Insets.bottom;

min_width =  (min_width_of_widest_component *
```

```
                num_components) +
               ((num_components + 1) * hgap) +
               Insets.left + Insets.right;
```

preferredSize

GridLayout determines preferred size based on the managed components' preferred sizes, the container's insets, and the horizontal and vertical gaps.

```
pref_height = (pref_height_of_tallest_component *
                num_components) +
               ((num_components + 1) * vgap) +
               Insets.top + Insets.bottom;

pref_width =  (pref_width_of_widest_component *
                num_components) +
               ((num_components + 1) * hgap) +
               Insets.left + Insets.right;
```

GridBagLayout

This is the most sophisticated and complex of the standard AWT layout managers; it's also the most complex to use. It usually behaves like you want it to or expect it to, but not always. Most of the control available with this manager is actually implemented through its companion class GridBagConstraints. We will cover the basics of GridBagLayout here but defer the in-depth discussion until GridBagConstraints.

GridBagLayout has only a basic constructor:

```
public GridBagLayout();
```

Unlike GridLayout, this class does not require all components to be the same size. It allows a component to span cells. You may place a component anywhere within the grid. Cells may be empty. Thus it seems to resolve all the complaints of the GridLayout class. In reality, there are still holes, and GridBagConstraints can be annoying to use.

A set of default constraints is provided, yielding behavior similar to GridLayout, except that the components are not resized to fit the cells. Do not try to place multiple components in the same cell.

Only a basic constructor is provided:

```
public GridBagLayout()
```

Two constants are also provided in the public interface, as designated in Table 5.2.

Table 5.2 GridBag constants.

Name	Use	Default
MAXGRIDSIZE	Maximum number of cells (same for horizontal and vertical)	128
MINSIZE	Minimum number of cells (same for horizontal and vertical)	1

GridBagLayout does not use the `addLayoutComponent` method. It does have additional methods for working with constraints, as defined in Table 5.3.

Table 5.3 GridBagLayout constraint methods.

Method	Returns	Notes
`getConstraints (Component comp)`	GridBagConstraints	Returns copy of constraints for designated object
`lookupConstraints (Component comp)`	GridBagConstraints	Returns actual constraints for designated object (not a copy)
`setConstraints (Component comp, GridBagConstraints constraints)`	void	Sets constraints for designated object

As shown in Listing 5.6, minimal usage of the GridBagLayout is simple.

Listing 5.6 Minimal GridBagLayout example.

```
this.setLayout(new GridBagLayout());
this.add("ignored", button1);
```

But this makes no use of the rich functionality available. For that, you need to set some constraints, which are described soon.

Details, Details

There aren't many gory details to worry about here. If you don't care about these, feel free to skip ahead to GridBagConstraints.

layoutContainer

GridLayout has to construct a new grid layout whenever a new component is added. It basically works its way through the grid, one cell at a time across each row, until all rows are done.

removeLayoutComponent

GridLayout has to construct a new grid layout whenever a component is removed. It basically works its way through the grid from the point of the removed component, one cell at a time across each row, until all rows are done.

minimumSize

GridLayout determines minimum size based on the managed components' minimum sizes, the container's insets, and the horizontal and vertical gaps.

```
min_row_height = min_height_of_tallest_component_of_row;
min_height = (sum_of_min_row_heights +
```

```
                ((num_components + 1) * vgap) +
                Insets.top + Insets.bottom;

min_col_width = min_width_of_widest_component_of_cols;
min_width =     (sum_of_min_col_widths +
                ((num_components + 1) * hgap) +
                Insets.left + Insets.right;
```

preferredSize

GridLayout determines preferred size based on the managed components' preferred sizes, the container's insets, and the horizontal and vertical gaps.

```
pref_row_height = pref_height_of_tallest_component_of_row;
pref_height = (sum_of_pref_row_heights +
                ((num_components + 1) * vgap) +
                Insets.top + Insets.bottom;

pref_col_width = pref_width_of_widest_component_of_cols;
pref_width =    (sum_of_pref_col_widths +
                ((num_components + 1) * hgap) +
                Insets.left + Insets.right;
```

GridBagConstraints

This class defines the constraints for the GridLayout class. The public interface consists of a set of fields, some with predefined constants. These are noted in Table 5.4.

Table 5.4 GridBagConstraints interface.

Field	Type	Notes	Defaults
`anchor`	Int	When component is smaller than cell, this determines how to position the component, with possible values of: CENTER, NORTH, NORTHEAST, EAST, SOUTHEAST, SOUTH, SOUTHWEST, WEST, and NORTHWEST.	CENTER
`fill`	Int	When component is smaller than cell, this determines if and how to resize the component, with possible values of: NONE, HORIZONTAL, VERTICAL, and BOTH	NONE
`gridheight`	int	Number of cells in a column	
`gridwidth`	Int	Number of cells in a row	
`gridx`	Int	Cell position within row, or RELATIVE (to right of last component added)	RELATIVE
`gridy`	Int	Cell position within column, or RELATIVE (below last component added)	RELATIVE
`insets`	Insets	Padding between component and cell edges	(0, 0, 0, 0)
`ipadx`	Int	Component's internal horizontal padding	0
`ipady`	Int	Component's internal vertical padding	0
`weightx` `weighty`	Double	Described later	0.0

As an example of using GridBagConstraints, let's create an interface to hold a message box with standard GUI buttons at the bottom: **Apply**, **Cancel** and **Help**, as in Listing 5.7.

Listing 5.7 "Simple" GridBagConstraints example.

```
GridBagLayout gridbag = new GridBagLayout();
GridBagConstraints gbc = new GridBagConstraints();
TextArea text = new TextArea(4,20);
Button apply = new Button("Apply");
Button cancel = new Button("Cancel");
Button help = new Button("Help");

public void init() {
    this.setLayout(gridbag);
    gbc.gridx=0;
    gbc.gridy=0;
    gbc.gridwidth=3;
    this.add(text);
    gridbag.setConstraints(text, gbc);

    gbc.gridy=1;
    gbc.gridwidth=1;
    gbc.anchor=GridBagConstraints.WEST;
    this.add(apply);
    gridbag.setConstraints(apply, gbc);

    gbc.gridx=1;
    gbc.anchor=GridBagConstraints.CENTER;
    this.add(cancel);
    gridbag.setConstraints(cancel, gbc);

    gbc.gridx=2;
    gbc.anchor=GridBagConstraints.EAST;
    this.add(help);
    gridbag.setConstraints(help, gbc);
}
```

This, of course, is a simple example. Unfortunately, as you can plainly see in Figure 5.4, it's also not quite what we wanted.

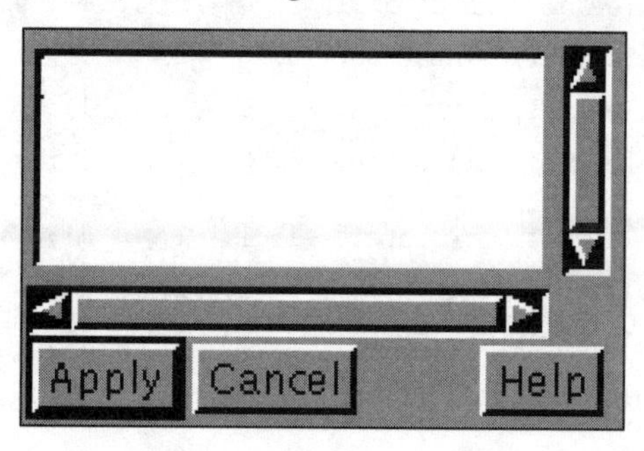

Figure 5.4 GridBagLayout example 1.

The problem is that the GridBagLayout makes each cell only as large as it has to. Any extra space in a row or column is added to the last cell in that row or column, whereas the GridLayout class allocated extra space evenly between all cells in a row or column. Later, when we discuss weights, we will explain how to get the desired GUI.

So what is a GridBagLayout good for? It really comes into its own when you have a more complex set of components. For instance, the waveform scope shown in Figure 5.5 uses several GridBagLayout objects.

Each of the numbered modules (beginning with a number on the left and ending with a display on the right) is a panel using a GridBagLayout as its layout manager. In each module, the number and display span two rows. Note how each row and column is the height or width of the largest cell within that row or column. Listing 5.8 shows the code for modules 1 and 2.

Listing 5.8 GridBagLayout example 3 code.

```
modulePanel = new Panel();
modulePanel.setLayout(gridbag);

//          parent,     component,  x, y, cols, rows
```

```
constrain(modulePanel, moduleNum,  0, 0,  1,    2);

constrain(modulePanel, shapeLabel, 1, 0,  1,    1);
constrain(modulePanel, sinButton,  2, 0,  1,    1);
constrain(modulePanel, squButton,  3, 0,  1,    1);
constrain(modulePanel, triButton,  4, 0,  1,    1);

constrain(modulePanel, freqLabel,  1, 1,  1,    1);
constrain(modulePanel, freq      , 2, 1,  1,    1);
constrain(modulePanel, invButton,  3, 1,  1,    1);
constrain(modulePanel, offButton,  4, 1,  1,    1);

constrain(modulePanel, display,    5, 0,  1,    2);
```

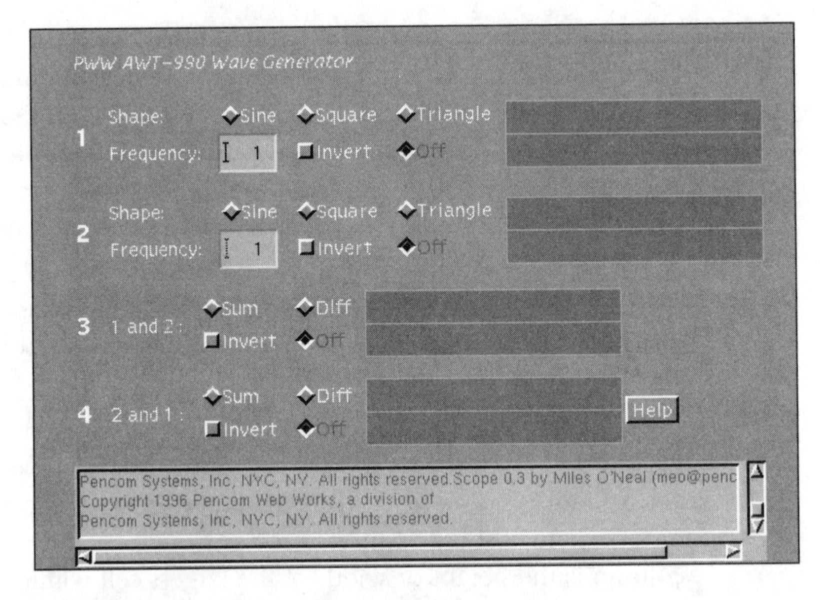

Figure 5.5 GridBagLayout example 2.

This probably isn't what you expected to see; since so much redundant code goes into constraints, we have created a `constrain` method to handle most of it. The main thing to note here are the x and y coordinates and the columns and rows (`gridx`, `gridy`, `gridwidth`, and `gridheight`, respectively), and see how they map into what you see in Figure 5.5.

Notice that the first and last components span multiple rows and that both of these have a `gridx` (x coordinate) of 0. All other components are laid out as you would expect.

A Constrain Method

The simple `constrain` method for the preceding example is detailed in Listing 5.9. Constraints not used in this method use their default settings.

Listing 5.9 Basic constrain method.

```
public void constrain(Container cont, Component comp,
    int x, int y, int cols, int rows)
{
    GridBagConstraints gbc = new GridBagConstraints();
    gbc.gridx = x;
    gbc.gridy = y;
    gbc.gridwidth = cols;
    gbc.gridheight = rows;
    ((GridBagLayout)cont.getLayout()).setConstraints(comp,
        gbc);
    cont.add(comp);
}
```

Other Constraints

Other constraints likely to be used in a `constrain` method are `anchor` and `fill`. The remaining fields are used less often, but we will describe their use anyway.

Anchor and Fill

Most of the time you will use at most one of these fields. For complex layouts, however, you may wish to use them together. This is meaningful only if you use one in a columnar sense and the other in a row sense.

For instance, you might set `fill` to `HORIZONTAL` and `anchor` to `NORTH`.

Padding

Insets are padding added to a component's size, whereas `ipadx` and `ipady` define extra padding between a component and its containing cell.

Weights

`weightx` and `weighty` are used to define how extra space within a container is distributed. By default, these constraints have a value of 0.0, and cells are never resized to use extra space. When any cells within a row or column have nonzero values for these constraints, those cells have any extra space divided between them proportionately by their weights. For example, consider the code in Listing 5.10.

Listing 5.10 Extra space redistribution.

```
public void init() {
    this.setLayout(gridbag);
    constrain(this, new Button("1"), 0, 0.0);
    constrain(this, new Button("2"), 1, 2.0);
    constrain(this, new Button("3"), 2, 0.0);
    constrain(this, new Button("4"), 3, 1.0);
}

public void constrain(Container cont, Component comp,
    int x, double weight)
{
    GridBagConstraints gbc = new GridBagConstraints();
    gbc.gridx = x;
    gbc.fill = GridBagConstraints.HORIZONTAL;
    gbc.weightx = weight;
    ((GridBagLayout)cont.getLayout()).setConstraints(comp,
```

```
        gbc);
    cont.add(comp);
}
```

This should produce four buttons in a single row. Buttons 1 and 3 should be just large enough to display their labels, while buttons 2 and 4 should use the extra space with a ratio of 2:1. As Figure 5.6 shows, this is exactly the behavior we observe (the applet was displayed with a size of 320 x 240).

Figure 5.6 Extra space redistribution.

With this example, we at last know enough to finally solve the problem of the standard GUI dialog buttons, as shown in Listing 5.11.

Listing 5.11 Standard GUI dialog code.

```
public void init() {
    this.setLayout(gridbag);
    constrain(text,   0, 0, 3, 0.0, 1.0,
        GridBagConstraints.CENTER);
    constrain(apply,  0, 1, 1, 1.0, 0.0,
        GridBagConstraints.WEST);
    constrain(cancel, 1, 1, 1, 1.0, 0.0,
        GridBagConstraints.CENTER);
    constrain(help,   2, 1, 1, 1.0, 0.0,
        GridBagConstraints.EAST);
}

public void constrain(Component comp, int x, int y,
    int cols, double weightx, double weighty, int fill)
{
    GridBagConstraints gbc = new GridBagConstraints();
    gbc.gridx = x;
```

```
        gbc.gridwidth = cols;
        gbc.fill = GridBagConstraints.HORIZONTAL;
        gbc.weightx = weightx;
        gbc.weighty = weighty;
        gbc.fill = fill;
        ((GridBagLayout)this.getLayout()).setConstraints(comp,
            gbc);
        this.add(comp);
    }
```

We used a custom `constrain` method to cut down on code size as compared to Listing 5.6. The results are shown in Figure 5.7.

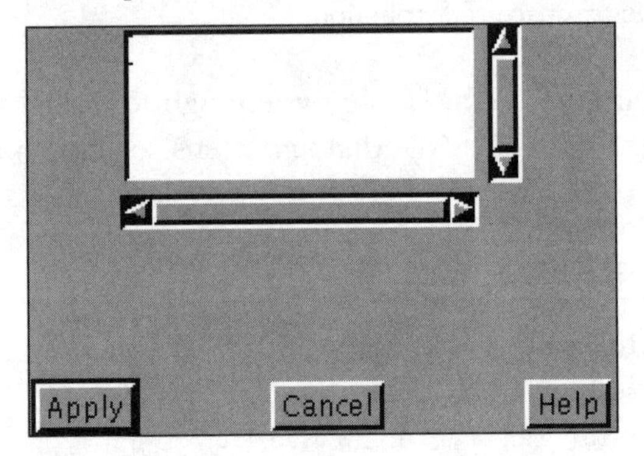

Figure 5.7 Standard GUI dialog at last.

CardLayout

As we discussed in Chapter 3, the CardLayout manager displays one of a number of panels (cards), but has no UI for selecting which card is currently displayed. The metaphor is apparently intended to be like that of index cards in a file (hence our dirt cheap card file approach in Chapter 3), but we could certainly use any metaphor that makes sense when displaying 1 of *N* items.

CardLayout has two constructors:

```
public CardLayout();
public CardLayout(int hgap, int vgap);
```

The latter version allows you to set horizontal and vertical gaps between the card and its container.

Details, Details

CardLayout has two types of methods—the standard, layout-related methods and methods to select which card is displayed. We will cover the latter first, as you will probably use them the most.

```
public void first(Container target);
public void last(Container target);
public void next(Container target);
public void previous(Container target);
public void show(Container target, Sring name);
```

These methods do just what their names suggest; the first four cause the designated target CardLayout to display its first last, next, or previous card. `next()` and `previous()` wrap around; if they are on the last or first card (respectively), they display the first or last card (respectively). `show()` causes target to display the card whose name matches the designated name. The `target` argument seems redundant, but it is required.

addLayoutComponent

`addLayoutComponent` is the one layout-related method you will always use.

```
public void
    addLayoutComponent(String name, Component comp);
```

Each card added has a name attached; individual cards may be referenced only by name.

layoutContainer

```
public void layoutContainer(Container target);
```

`layoutContainer()` lays out the target container.

CardLayout uses this method to resize all components to the size of the container, less space for any insets and horizontal or vertical gaps. Most applications do not call this method directly.

minimumSize

CardLayout determines minimum size based on the managed components' minimum sizes, the container's insets, and the horizontal and vertical gaps.

```
min_height = min_height_of_tallest_card +
    (2 * vgap) + top_inset + bottom_inset;
min_width =  min_width_of_widest_card +
    (2 * hgap) + left_inset + right_inset;
```

preferredSize

CardLayout determines preferred size based on the managed components' preferred sizes, the container's insets, and the horizontal and vertical gaps.

```
pref_height = largest_preffered_height_of_cards +
    (2 * vgap) + top_inset + bottom_inset;
pref_width =  largest_preffered_width_of_cards +
    (2 * hgap) + left_inset + right_inset;
```

Removing Components

You remove cards in the usual way by calling the `remove()` or `removeAll()` method. There is no way to remove a component by name; to do this you need to look up the object based on its name and remove that object.

Using CardLayout

Even though the CardLayout class is fairly simple, practical use does require some extra work, as we have noted before. Listing 5.12 shows the pertinent code from our El Cheapo Card Index to set up a CardLayout, add cards, and add CardLayout card control methods to a GUI layer.

Listing 5.12 Typical card layout usage.

```
import java.applet.*;
import java.awt.*;

public class Cards extends Applet {
   Label logo;
   Panel buttons, cards;
   Button button[] = new Button[2];
   TextArea card[] = new TextArea[3];

   static private Font mainFont, logoFont, cardFont;

   // The layout manager for each of the containers.
   BorderLayout borderLayout = new BorderLayout();
   FlowLayout flowLayout = new FlowLayout();
   CardLayout cardLayout = new CardLayout();

   public void init() {
      :
      logo = new Label();
      logo.setText("El Cheapo Card Index");

      // put the CardLayout and control container
      // (FlowLayout) in a BorderLayout.

      this.setLayout(borderLayout);
      buttons = new Panel();
      buttons.setLayout(flowLayout);
      this.add("North", buttons);
      cards = new Panel();
```

```
      cards.setLayout(cardLayout);
      this.add("Center", cards);

      // add the controls and logo

      button[0] = new Button("<");
      buttons.add("Prev", button[0]);
      button[1] = new Button(">");
      buttons.add("Next", button[1]);
      buttons.add("Logo", logo);

      // create the cards themselves and add them
      // to the CardLayout object

      card[0] = new TextArea();
      card[0].appendText("      -- A --");
      cards.add("A", card[0]);
      card[1] = new TextArea();
      card[1].appendText("      -- B --");
      cards.add("B", card[1]);
      card[2] = new TextArea();
      card[2].appendText("      -- C --");
      cards.add("C", card[2]);
        :
      ((CardLayout)cards.getLayout()).show(cards, "A");
   }

   // EVENT HANDLING

   // If it's the left arrow button, go to the
   // previous card; if it's the right arrow
   // button, go to the next card.

   public boolean action(Event e, Object arg) {
      if (e.target instanceof Button) {
         Button b = (Button) e.target;
         if (e.target == button[0]) {
            ((CardLayout)cards.getLayout()).previous(cards);
            return true;
```

```
            } else if (e.target == button[1]) {
                ((CardLayout)cards.getLayout()).next(cards);
                return true;
            }
        }
    return false;
    }
}
```

What's Missing?

One of the main things missing is a GUI for the CardLayout class. We provide one as part of the sample code on the companion CD-ROM.

CHAPTER 6

Labels and Text

- Labels
- Text Class
- TextField Class
- TextInteger Class
- TextArea Class

Building on what we've learned about Frames, Dialog windows, and layout managers, we'll use this chapter to talk about what the AWT provides in the way of text handling. The AWT provides both editable and noneditable text objects.

Labels

Label objects provide the noneditable text objects in AWT. They are generally limited to single-line messages (Labels, short notes, etc.). Figure 6.1 shows an example Panel with a Label.

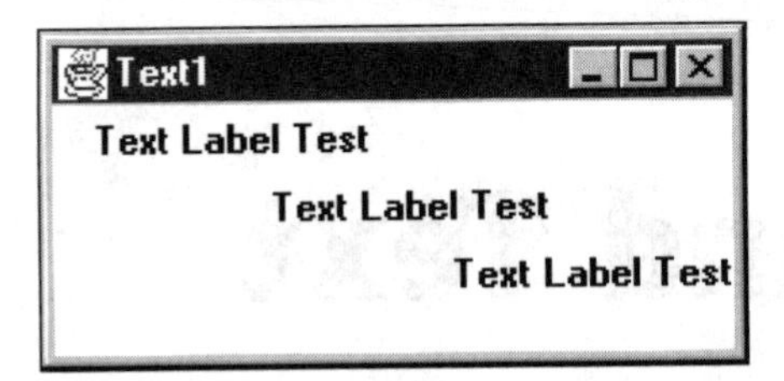

Figure 6.1 Simple Label.

The Label has no surrounding border that might indicate that it's an editable text object. It also has virtually no use in user interaction. For example, you wouldn't normally attempt to detect mouse clicks or other events over the Label.

The Java API documentation produced by Sun/JavaSoft specifically states that version 1.0.x of the AWT does not send events to Label or TextComponents. It also states that version 1.0.x will send events to Label and TextComponents. We don't recommend trying to use Labels for user interaction.

For such a simple class, Label actually has a full-featured set of methods, as shown in Table 6.1. It also inherits from Component, so there are many subversive things you can do with and to a Label.

Table 6.1 Label Interface

Method	Returns	Notes
`Label()` `Label(String label)` `Label(String label, int alignment)`		An empty label is somewhat unusual, but possible alignment is either Label.CENTER, Label.LEFT, or Label.RIGHT

continued...

Method	Returns	Notes
`getAlignment()`	Int	Returns LEFT, CENTER, or RIGHT
`getText()`	String	What's on the Label right now?
`setAlignment(int alignment)`	Void	Change the alignment of the existing text
`setText(String label)`	Void	Paint a new text string in the same Label; this implies a layout manager relayout

The following excerpt shows how to produce simple labels. Note that the constructor can either implicitly specify "left align" or explicitly specify the alignment with a second argument.

```
public Text1() {
    Label l;
    setLayout(new FlowLayout());
    l = new Label("Text Label Test");
    add(new Label("Text Label Test",Label.CENTER));
    add(new Label("Text Label Test",Label.RIGHT));
    add(l);
    pack();
}
```

While we've retained a handle to the first Label object in 'one', many times you simply instantiate the object and add it at the same time (as the last two Labels are handled).

NOTE

To track down this Label later, you can run the list of components in the container object with `Container.countComponents()`, `Container.getComponent(int)`, and `Label.getText()`. If you really have a dynamic text Label, it's usually better to either retain a handle as in our first example or use one of the other text objects.

This is easily the most common place for typing errors. One of the authors almost always gets typing dyslexia and leaves off the last parenthesis. Luckily, the compiler catches this particular typing error.

The only other methods in Label deal with changing the text. The standard `getText()` and `setText()` methods are used. You can also use any of the inherited component methods, but be forewarned that some platforms do not implement the underlying changes yet. For instance, changing colors with `setForeground()` works on UNIX but not on Win32 systems. Perhaps this will eventually be corrected, but probably not any time soon.

Text Class

Dealing with user text input and output is fairly simple in Java. The AWT provides Labels for simple static Labels and two working objects that inherit from the TextComponent class. The TextField class supports single-line input and output operations, while the TextArea class provides a rectangular area (in rows and columns) for user interaction. Both objects implement the standard cursor movement, clipboard, and in-place editing operations that are common to most windowing systems now. The text objects can also use fonts and colors to provide emphasis, but you have to look in Chapter 9 for more details.

Figure 6.2 shows what the standard text objects look like.

Figure 6.2 AWT text objects.

Text Classes User Interface

Table 6.2 Text Objects Interface

Method	Returns	Notes
	TextComponent Useful Interface	
`getSelectedText()`	String	The string returned is only the selected text
`getSelectionEnd()`	Int	The index to the last character selected
`getSelectionStart()`	Int	The index to the first character selected
`getText()`	String	The entire contents of the text object
`isEditable()`	Boolean	If true, the user can type in the text object
`select(int selStart, int selEnd)`	Void	Use this to "pre-mark" text (as in a search)
`selectAll()`	Void	Mark the whole text object contents (as in a file dialog window)
`setEditable(boolean t)`	Void	If true, the user can type in the object
`setText(String t)`	Void	Replace the entire contents of the text object
	TextField Useful Interface	
`TextField()` `TextField(int cols)` `TextField(String text)` `TextField(String text, int cols)`		Columns are approximate, some windowing systems don't seem "perfect"
`echoCharIsSet()`	Boolean	False if we're echoing the keystrokes properly, true if we're echoing a single character (like password echo)
`getColumns()`	Int	How wide is the text field?
`getEchoChar()`	Char	What is the password echo character?
`minimumSize()`	Dimension	Tell us (in pixels) what the minimum space required is
`minimumSize(int cols)`	Dimension	Tell us (in pixels) what the minimum space required is
`preferredSize()`	Dimension	

continued...

Method	Returns	Notes
`preferredSize(int cols)`	Dimension	
`setEchoCharacter(char c)`	Void	Set the character to echo on keystrokes (password echo)
	TextArea Useful Interface	

`TextArea()`
`TextArea(int rows, int cols)`
`TextArea(String text)`
`TextArea(String text, int rows, int cols)`
		Rows and columns are approximate, some windowing systems don't seem "perfect"

`appendText(String str)`	Void	Tack the string on the end of the area
`getColumns()`	Int	How wide is the text area
`getRows()`	Int	How tall is the text area
`insertText(String str, int pos)`	Void	Insert the string in the existing text at the index passed in; note that this doesn't use rows and columns
`minimumSize()`	Dimension	
`minimumSize(int rows, int cols)`	Dimension	
`preferredSize()`	Dimension	
`preferredSize(int rows, int cols)`	Dimension	
`replaceText(String str, int start, int end)`	Void	Same as `TextField.setText()`

Text Objects and Peers

Recall from the basics of AWT portability that each on-screen component has a peer object that manages the interaction with the native windowing system. Text components use their peer object to calculate the size of the component in real-world coordinates (usually pixels). If the component doesn't have a peer, the superclass's size methods are used to calculate the Dimension object used by the layout manager.

While using the AWT text classes is fairly intuitive, understanding the way the AWT uses `minimumSize` and `preferredSize` is not necessarily so. We also touched on minimum and preferred size in Chapter 5, but defer the remainder of the discussion to Chapter 9.

One other interesting feature of the TextField class (actually Component, but who can keep track of this stuff) is to use the TextField class as a deviant Label. By turning the field on and off with `enable()` and `disable()`, you can make the field be either interactive or static (like a Label). This works well when you have TextFields that are dependent on the state of another component on your container, but you don't want to repaint or re-lay out the whole container.

TextField Class

This section will cover common TextField operations in detail. Since TextFields are used very often in applets and applications, the extra effort we spend now will make development quite a bit easier. First, let's discuss the constructor methods for the TextField class.

Note that you can create an empty TextField with the default constructor. To add text to it, you would use `setText(String s)`.

```
TextField t = new TextField();
```

The second constructor, with a single-integer width argument initializes TextField with a display width roughly equivalent to the number of columns specified by the integer.

```
TextField t = new TextField(10);
```

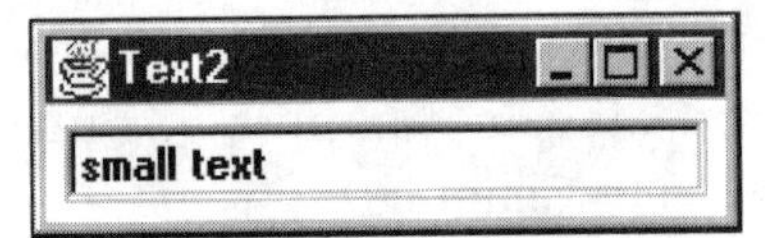

The third constructor, with one string argument combines the instantiation operation with some initial text. The width of the displayed TextField is set to the number of characters in the string argument.

```
TextField t = new TextField("now with some text");
```

The fourth constructor, with a string argument and a width argument. Note that the width of the string passed in (or contained in the TextField) can be as large or as small as desired. The width argument simply sets the displayed width (and then at the whim of the layout manager).

```
TextField t = new TextField("small text",20);
```

TextField Editing

After the TextField object is initialized, there is significant work to be done. TextField can perform all user editing on its own. Typing, correcting, scrolling, and selecting text in the displayed TextField can all be done without any code on our part.

Here's the same TextField after we've typed in it.

Note that we removed characters (with the **Backspace** key or the edit operations: **Cut**, **Copy**, **Paste**), added the text `TYPED HERE`, and currently have selected `xxxx` with the mouse. All these operations came without any code on our part—no event handler, no callback, no nothing. So, this is handled pretty well by the AWT. About the only other things they might have included are an undo facility and verification for simple data types (dates, numbers, etc.).

To add these features, we must write some code. We'll start by just showing how to grab keystrokes before the characters get entered. To deal with this, we finally have to add an event handler. Note that this is not an `ACTION_EVENT`; it's a `KEY_PRESS`. For this, we have to use `handleEvent()` rather than `action()`.

Here's a whole program, available on the CD, that we'll expand on throughout this section. Note that we've got our single `TextField` object, initialized with `small text`, and sized for about 20 characters. We also provide an `eventHandler()` method to catch `Event.KEY_PRESS` events. Note that returning `false` from our handler causes the `Event.KEY_PRESS` event to be processed by the default handler that's built into the AWT.

Listing 6.1 can be run from the command line or as an applet.

Listing 6.1 Text2.java, Basic textfield keypress handling.

```
import java.awt.*;
import java.applet.*;
import java.util.*;

public class Text2 extends Applet {
    TextField tf;

    public Text2() {
        setLayout(new FlowLayout());
        tf = new TextField("small text",20);
        add(tf);
    }

    public boolean handleEvent(Event e) {
        if (e.id == Event.KEY_PRESS) {
            String s = tf.getText();
            String d;
            int i = tf.getSelectionStart();
            if (e.modifiers > 1 || e.key < ' ') {
                return false;    // let TextField handle these
            } else {    // we check these characters
                d = s.substring(0,i);
                d = d + (char) e.key;
                d = d + s.substring(i);
                tf.setText(d);
                tf.select(i+1,i+1);
            }
            return true;
        }
        return false;
    }

    public static void main(String args[]) {
    Frame x = new Frame("Text2");
    Text2 p = new Text2();
```

```
        x.setLayout(new BorderLayout());
        x.add("North",p);
        x.pack();
        x.show();
    }
}
```

If you run this program, you'll find that it works the same with or without the event handler. We return `false` on characters that we don't want to deal with (backspace, tab, etc.). Normal characters are inserted into the string as they normally would be.

However, when you run this program, you'll find that the on-screen TextField flickers as you type; because we are replacing the entire contents of the object with the call to `setText()`. When we do this, the selection point moves from where we typed to the beginning of the TextField. We then move the selection point back to the typing point with the call to `select()`. This bouncing of the text cursor (selection point) causes the flickering. For this reason, it's much better to avoid catching keypresses if possible. To show this, we'll change our event handler to update the TextField only for those keystrokes we must process ourselves. For example in the following excerpt, we'll convert uppercase characters to lowercase:

```
if (e.modifiers > 1 || e.key < ' ' ||
  (e.key < 'A' || e.key > Z')) {
    return false;     // throw all but upper case back
} else {     // we check these characters
    d = s.substring(0,i);
    d = d + (char)( e.key - 'A' + 'a' ); // make them lower
    d = d + s.substring(i);
    tf.setText(d);
    tf.select(i+1,i+1);
}
```

When you modify this program, you can see that the flickering occurs only when you type an uppercase letter. This greatly reduces the ugliness associated with TextField processing. In any case, it would be nice if the AWT provided an `insertText()` method for TextField that worked with the native windowing system.

A Numeric TextField

The point of all this inserting is to develop a useful class that can process keystrokes specific to our needs. If we enhance the code of **Text2.java** and produce a TextInteger class that inherits from TextField, we've produced a useful class. Here is the procedure.

First, let's add numeric validation to our code. We'll presume that we want to deal with just Integer numbers but we'll be able to adjust that later.

Even though we've tested this code thoroughly on Windows 95, UNIX (Linux), and Macintosh, the hacks we've implemented to get around AWT problems may not work that well on other releases of Java.

The basic premise for allowing or disallowing keystrokes in a numeric TextField looks a lot like the preceding sample. If we want to let the AWT handle a keystroke, we return `false`. If we want to handle the keystroke ourselves, we return `true`. If we want to fail a keystroke and cause an audible alert, we hack into the event object.

The hack we use for an audible alert came from not finding any reasonable method to beep or flash the user on bad keystrokes. For all native windowing systems we've experienced, there is a way to cause an audible or visible alert. The Java AWT doesn't provide one. Of course, you could play a media clip sound file, but that requires multiple threads and doesn't work on a system without a sound card. All normal hardware from teletypes and dec writers on up to PCs and workstations include hardware to beep. We tried several things that might work on some platforms but had problems on others. Our final attempt was to change the keystroke character from whatever bad thing the user typed, to an ASCII bell character (7). This works on all the platforms we've tried. It is ugly and possibly bad form, but it works.

Here's the event handler for `Event.KEY_PRESS` to process integer number input.

```
if (e.id == Event.KEY_PRESS) {
    String s = tf.getText();
    String d;
    int i = tf.getSelectionStart();

    if (e.modifiers > 1 || e.key < ' ') {
        return false;       // let others handle them
    } else if (e.key == '-' || e.key == '+' ) {
        if (i != 0) {       // not in column one
            e.key = 7;      // setting the keystroke to a
bell
            return false; // fail + & -  if not at offset 0
        } else
            return false; // allow them if at front
    } else if (e.key >= '0' && e.key <= '9') {
        return false;       // say digits are fine
    } else {                // all others fail
        e.key = 7;          // setting the keystroke to a
bell
        return false;       // fail this
    }
```

This code seems to work fine, doesn't flicker the displayed TextField, and is small. It leaves most of the editing in the hands of the AWT and the native windowing system but completely manages integer input from the user. We like it!

TextInteger Class

The problem with the preceding event handler is that it's not properly encapsulated. You're certainly free to use it in any container that contains normal TextField objects, but it isn't easily reusable. Since reusability and portability are what AWT is all about, we'll move our code into a class that inherits from TextField. The file **TextInteger.java** on the CD-ROM contains such a class.

First, the appropriate class descriptions are listed in Table 6.3.

Table 6.3 TextInteger Interface

Method	Returns	Notes

`TextInteger()`
`TextInteger(String label)`
`TextInteger(String label, int cols)`
`TextInteger(int value)`
`TextInteger(int value, int cols)`
		There is no constructor with just column width; use `TextInteger("", int cols)` to provide the same function

`intValue()`	Int	Returns zero if invalid or the current value
`isNumberField()`	Boolean	Returns `true` if acting as number field, `false` if acting as TextField
`valueOf()`	Integer	Returns new integer with value or null object if invalid string is in displayed text
`setNumberField(boolean state)`	Void	If state `true`, then acts as number field; if state `false`, then acts as plain TextField
`setText(String label)`	Void	Paint a new text string in the same TextInteger

Note that the TextInteger field allows text strings to be displayed. If a string constructor is used, any text may be displayed. The first time a user types in the field, an audible alert is sounded (using our bell hack), and the entire field is selected. The next keystroke is processed normally (scanning for digits, etc.).

If a `setText()` method resets the field to text, this process is repeated. While this may seem strange at first glance, it allows you to place a hint string in the field initially, to help the user think about what to type.

Another interesting feature of this class is `setNumberField()` and `isNumberField()`. If you pass a `true` argument to a `TextInteger` field, it forces numeric input as already described. If you pass `false`, the field behaves just like a normal TextField. This allows you to instantiate one object and perform both types of input. With the abominable redraw and layout times of the AWT, this feature can make a significant difference in your programming flexibility.

There's very little overhead to use the `TextInteger` class in your code. First, instantiate a `TextInteger` object and add it to your container:

```
TextInteger tn = new TextInteger(10);
add(tn);           // add it to our panel
```

This paints the `TextInteger` field with a 10 column field (when the container is finally painted). The user can interact with the `TextInteger` field at will, and your code can query the object at any time with `valueOf()`, `intValue()`, or even `getText()`. However, it's usually better to wait for the user to press the **Return** or **Enter** key before querying the value of the field. Add the following code to your container's event handler to process the event caused by pressing **Return** (or **Enter**) in the field:

```
public boolean handleEvent(Event e) {
    ...
    if (e.id == Event.ACTION_EVENT && e.target instanceof
TextInteger) {
        TextInteger tn = (TextInteger)e.target;
        if (tn.isNumberField() == true) { // acting number-like
```

```
            int i = tn.intValue());
        } else { // TextNumber acting like TextField
            String s = tn.getText();
            tn.setText("New text!");
        }
        return true;
    }
    ...
}
```

While this class has several limitations (for example, we don't worry about overflow) it is still a useful class. We've implemented several Java applications that use this class (and variations) for real work.

TextArea Class

While single-line input is handled by TextField and custom classes like `TextInteger`, many applications need to display and/or edit larger blocks of text. TextArea is the AWT component that supports this feature. While some platforms have really nice text objects that can support multiple fonts, automatic printing, spell checking, and other features, the AWT sticks with portability at the least common denominator and provides the following basic features.

For practical purposes, there are only a few operational differences between TextField and TextArea. The first difference is that TextArea has an `insertText()` method. Recall that we needed such a beast in the keypress validation example earlier.

For TextField, we had to put up with some update flickering. For TextArea, we can validate the keypress and insert the new text in place to avoid the massive display updates.

A similar method is called `replaceText()`. It can be used to replace a chunk of text (zero or more characters) at any point in the text associated with the text area. This method might be used in a text editor by a search/replace capability.

Other than that, the biggest thing to remember while processing the contents of a TextArea is that text offsets are relative to a string containing the text displayed. Some text may or may not be on-screen but is still part of the text area. Even though the on-screen area is specified in rows and columns, the contents may be thought of as though they are always stored in a single `String` variable. This means that your code must be capable of handling in-line carriage control and probably will need to provide it's own word wrapping and formatting.

Figure 6.3 is a simple example of a 10 row by 30 column TextArea that we'll be using during our editing discussion.

```
Panel p;
TextArea ta = new TextArea("Initial text area " +
                "contents\nfor a 10 by 30" +
                "\nTextArea object.");

p.add(ta);
```

Figure 6.3 AWT Text Area.

Editing a Text Area

Editing within a TextArea is basically the same as editing within a TextField. The insertion methods described previously are useful, but handling keypress events, validating input, and using the other operations we touched on in the TextField section still apply.

Figure 6.4 shows what a `TextArea` looks like after several insertions have been made.

Figure 6.4 AWT edited text area.

The scroll bars are now activated, because we've typed past column 30 and entered more than 10 lines. Even though the contents are now quite extensive, TextArea still treats the whole area as a single `String` object. While this is great for portability, it's probably less than useful for text editing or formatting.

One of the problems with handling a TextArea in a program that is concerned about the visible contents is that there are no methods for accessing the current visible area. `TextArea` doesn't even provide a method to tell us what the offset of the first visible character is. Without this offset, we're pretty much doomed if we try to use TextArea for anything more than simple text entry. Later versions of the AWT probably won't fix this, because the basic interface is set. Hopefully, other development tools will remedy this shortcoming with a new text hierarchy.

Because this book is about how to use the AWT, and we try not to be whiners, we'll give you as much help with TextArea as we can. We'll also provide some work-arounds for dealing with large TextArea objects.

When typing in the text area, the user can perform most of the native cut, copy, and paste operations. However, the AWT doesn't provide specific events for these. What you get is the `KEY_PRESS` and `KEY_RELEASE` events for the native keystrokes. For example, on Windows, a user pressed **Ctrl-V** to paste from the clipboard (notably, **Ctrl-V** is not the paste character on other platforms). This `KEY_PRESS` event reports `event.key = 22`. If you let the inherited handlers manage the insertion (return `false`), you find that potentially several characters (the clipboard contents) were inserted at the selection point reported in the `KEY_PRESS` event. Because the point of the AWT is to be transparently portable to the developer, this functionality stinks.

To demonstrate handling the cut, copy, and paste operations within Java, we'll show the event handling and text operations to manage this activity completely within our code. Note that this code will work on UNIX, but only when you use the Windows edit shortcuts: **Ctrl-X**, **Ctrl-C**, and **Ctrl-V**.

```
// sickening way of faking the clipboard edit keys :(
static final int PASTE_KEY = 22;        // CTRL-V
static final int COPY_KEY = 3;          // CTRL-C
static final int CUT_KEY = 24;          // CTRL-X
String cutbuffer;
...
if ((e.modifiers > 1 || e.key < ' ')) {
    if (e.key == PASTE_KEY) {     // windows
        System.out.println("wants windows paste");
        if (cutbuffer == null) {
            return false;
        } else {
            ta.replaceText(cutbuffer,i,ta.getSelectionEnd());
        }
        return true;
    } else if (e.key == CUT_KEY) {
        System.out.println("wants windows cut");
```

```
            if (i !=  ta.getSelectionEnd()) {
                cutbuffer  = ta.getSelectedText();
                ta.replaceText("",i,ta.getSelectionEnd());
            }
            return true;
        } else if (e.key == COPY_KEY) {
            System.out.println("wants windows copy");
            if (i !=  ta.getSelectionEnd()) {
                cutbuffer  = ta.getSelectedText();
            }
            return true;
        }
        return false;    // let others handle them
    }
```

Managing an Extended TextArea

TextField and TextArea objects (in fact, all components in Java 1.0.x) are implemented in such a way that the native windowing system (via the peer mechanism) is allowed to handle as much user interaction and object maintenance as possible. On most platforms, this means that scroll bar events (among other mouse-related events) are never passed to Java. Thus, we can't modify the visible behavior of the text object; however, we are allowed to handle keyboard events, and mouse movement over the text itself. Other mouse events can't be trapped or managed. Thus, there is no useful way to enhance the capabilities of TextArea (or TextField). To provide enhanced capabilities, we must either modify the Java AWT source directly (possibly in platform specific or native code), or develop a `RealTextArea` object completely from scratch.

Java 1.1.x is supposed to correct this feature. Currently, the only way to see mouse events is to write your own AWT component equivalents and duplicate the effort being put into 1.1.x by JavaSoft.

This new RealTextArea class might use Canvas and other AWT components, or it might be a reimplementation of the existing object, taking better advantage of the capabilities of the native system components. Either way, a RealTextArea class is beyond the scope of this chapter. We'll have to depend on developers of third-party class libraries to provide this and other packages.

CHAPTER 7

Basic Selection Controls

- Buttons
- Checkboxes
- Checkbox Groups
- Checkbox and Checkbox Group Oddities

Almost all windowing systems provide buttons, checkboxes, and checkbox groups (otherwise known as radio buttons). Java provides simple implementations of each of these. Since the primary purpose of all these components is to set or reset the state of an item, they are all bi-state switches. There is no tri-state switch in Java (unless you consider "disabled" a state).

These basic controls are used to choose between two states (hence, bi-state). Clicking (selecting) one of these controls causes a Java event; one of potentially several event handlers in the event chain then becomes responsible for recognizing the selection and acting upon it. Usually the event handler for the control's container is the appropriate handler.

Buttons

Button objects provide the most basic (and most commonly used bi-state controls in the AWT. They are generally labeled with **SUBMIT**, **YES**, **ACCEPT**, **NO**, or other simple one- or two-word messages. Very seldom are AWT Buttons subclassed in a normal application.

A Button is added to a Container object (usually a Panel or a descendant of Panel) and is then said to be contained or owned by the Panel. The event handler for the Panel is normally considered to be responsible for any actions upon the Button.

Figures 7.1 and 7.2 show a Button in the normal and depressed (selected) states. The Button appearance may be quite a bit different than these examples, depending on the platform you are using.

Figure 7.1 Simple Button (not pressed).

Figure 7.2 Simple Button (pressed).

Table 7.1 Button Interface

Method	Returns	Notes
`Button()`		
`Button(String label)`		An empty Button is somewhat unusual, but possible
`getLabel()`	String	What's on the Button right now?
`setLabel(String label)`	Void	Paint a new text string in the same Button; this implies a layout manager relayout

The following example shows the Button shown in the screen images and examples throughout this chapter.

```
public Control1() {
    setLayout(new FlowLayout());
    l = new Label( "TestButton clicked " + i + " times   ");
    add(l);
    b = new Button("TestButton");
    add(b);
    validate();
}
```

Just like many other components we talk about, you can either retain a handle (like we did in *b*) or look the Button up via its text label. You can run the list of components in the container object with `Container.countComponents()`, `Container.getComponent(int)`, and `Button.getLabel()`. If you have a Button whose label changes depending on what the rest of the `Panel` or application is doing, it's usually better to retain a handle as in our first example.

The only useful methods in the Button class deal with changing the text. The Button equivalent to the standard `getText()` and `setText()` methods are `getLabel()` and `setLabel()`. You can also use any of the inherited `Component` methods, but be forewarned that some platforms do not implement the underlying changes yet. For example, changing colors with `setForeground()` works on UNIX but not on Win32 systems. Perhaps this will eventually be corrected, but it probably won't be done soon.

For those developers who are appalled at the lack of jazzy buttons, we've implemented a custom button that provides the same functionality as Button but adds more uniform color and font management as well as allowing a graphic image to be displayed on the button. This `ButtonCanvas` class is discussed in Chapter 11.

Checkboxes

Another common control object in most windowing systems is the checkbox. This object is essentially a bi-state switch that remains in the user-selected (or programmatically set) state.

We will discuss the Choice class in Chapter 10. This class provides a similar service but uses the contents of the cells to select one of many states. The Checkbox is strictly an on/off component and generally depends on other UI objects (typically labels) to indicate what the two states really mean. In our Choice examples, we selected one of many nations. A Checkbox allows the user to select only one group ("us" or "not-us" [them?]). An AWT Checkbox normally has a label (usually describing the function of the object).

While the Button object has a very small interface, Checkbox looks more like a full-featured class. The user interface in Table 7.2 shows that it at least has a `getState()` and `setState()` pair.

Table 7.2 Checkbox Interface

Method	Returns	Notes

`Checkbox()`
`Checkbox(String label)`
`Checkbox(String label,`
`CheckboxGroup group,`
`boolean state)`
		A Checkbox with no label is somewhat unusual, but possible; the third variant automatically adds the Checkbox to a preexisting Checkbox group

`getCheckboxGroup()`	CheckboxGroup	Return the containing CheckboxGroup object, if any
`getLabel()`	String	What is the Checkbox label text?
`getState()`	Boolean	What is the current state of the box?
`setCheckboxGroup` `(CheckboxGroup)`	Void	Move this box to a containing Checkbox group and pass null to remove it from all groups

continued...

Method	Returns	Notes
`setLabel(String label)`	Void	Paint a new text string in the same Checkbox; this implies a layout manager relayout
`setState(boolean state)`	Void	Set the current state of the box

The following excerpt shows a single Checkbox object added to a simple Panel. The event handler sets the label on the left to show how we detect change in the Checkbox state.

```
Checkbox cb1;
public Control1() {
    setLayout(new FlowLayout());
    l = new Label( "Checkbox is xxxxxxx  ");
    add(l);
    cb = new Checkbox("Test Checkbox");
    add(cb);
    validate();
}
public boolean handleEvent(Event e) {
    if (e.id == Event.ACTION_EVENT) {
        if (e.target == cb1) {
            if (((Checkbox)e.target).getState() == true)
                l.setText("Checkbox is ON     ");
            else
                l.setText("Checkbox is OFF    ");
            validate();
            return true;
        }
    ...
```

Our basic Checkbox as it is initially displayed is shown in Figure 7.3. Note that each platform has a different appearance because this kind of control may be represented in several different ways.

Figure 7.3 Simple Checkbox.

Figure 7.4 shows the same Checkbox with the `Checkbox` clicked.

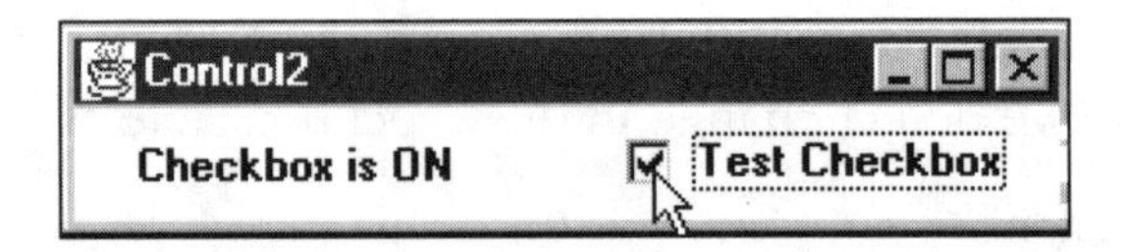

Figure 7.4 Simple Checkbox in ON state.

Checkbox Groups

Since the Checkbox is used to indicate whether a thing is on or off, it's very common to use a group of them to indicate which one of many choices is active. This is the exact functional equivalent of a Choice object with static contents. In the AWT, a group of checkboxes used for a one-of-many control is called a `CheckboxGroup`. Many systems call this kind of control a radio button or other similar name.

Table 7.3 Checkbox Group Interface

Method	Returns	Notes
`CheckboxGroup()`		Creates an empty group
`getCurrent()`	Checkbox	Returns the currently ON box
`setCurrent(Checkbox box)`	Void	Make the passed Checkbox the ON box

Figure 7.5 is an example of a Checkbox group.

Figure 7.5 Simple Checkbox group.

When the user clicks on one of the checkboxes in the group, the generated event can be processed in any of the objects containing the Checkbox. In our case, we handle it in the primary containing parent. Figure 7.6 shows an example image where the first Checkbox has been selected.

Figure 7.6 Simple Checkbox group activated.

The following code excerpt shows the Checkbox- and CheckboxGroup–specific code needed to generate a simple three-item group. Note that we've placed the group in it's own Panel 'p' that uses GridLayout. This causes the Checkboxes to be painted in an appropriate grid.

```
Checkbox cb1,cb2,cb3;
CheckboxGroup g;

public Control3() {
    Panel p = new Panel();     // a grid for the checkboxes
    p.setLayout(new GridLayout(3,1));
    g = new CheckboxGroup();
    cb1 = new Checkbox("USA");
    cb1.setCheckboxGroup(g);     // add it manually
```

```
        // add these automatically
        cb2 = new Checkbox("England",g,true);
        cb3 = new Checkbox("Canada",g,false);
        p.add(cb1);     // add to grid
        p.add(cb2);
        p.add(cb3);
        add(p);         // add grid to parent panel
        validate();
    }

    public boolean handleEvent(Event e) {
        if (e.id == Event.ACTION_EVENT) {
            if (e.target instanceof Checkbox &&
                ((Checkbox)e.target).getCheckboxGroup() == g) {
                if (e.target == cb1) {
                        if (cb1.getState() == true) {
                        l.setText("Hooray for the USA ");
                    }
                } else if (e.target == cb2) {
                    ...
```

Note that the `GridLayout` used to display these is just a convenience and usability feature. It is possible to put Checkboxes in a CheckboxGroup but display them at widely divergent points on the windowing system. It is even possible to put them in different Panels or windows. This might be useful for things like setting a Sex Checkbox in a personal health Panel based on selecting one of **Mr.** or **Mrs.** in an address Panel. Because the normal case of having a one-of-many grouping is much more common, we're limiting our example to that simple case.

Each Checkbox handler in the event-handling code in the previous example merely updates a Label object. In your code, you will want to send a message to whatever code reacts to the Checkbox being set active.

If we were setting up a Panel (say, an address block), we would use the `CheckboxGroup.setCurrent()` method to set the appropriate Checkbox based on the nation reflected in the address.

```
...
String nation = ...;
if (nation == "USA")
    g.setCurrent(cb1);
else if (nation == "Canada")
    g.setCurrent(cb2);
else if (nation == "England")
    g.setCurrent(cb3);
...
```

After the user completes updating the address block, the submission code calls `CheckboxGroup.getCurrent()` to identify what the current nation was:

```
...
String nation = g.getCurrent().getLabel();
// nation is one of "USA", "Canada", or "England"
...
```

One of the interesting ways to use Checkboxes is to selectively `hide()` or `show()` the boxes. For example, let's change the preceding examples to hide the choice of **Canada** if you select **USA**. If you select **England**, we'll show the **Canada** box. Note that as far as the CheckboxGroup is concerned, the Canada box never changes. You can still make it the current choice with `setCurrent()`, and you can change the Label while it's hidden. This is no different from any other AWT component, but the effect is fairly useful.

Here's the event handler code fragment responsible:

```
...
    if (e.target == cb2) {
```

```
            if (cb1.getState() == true) {
                l.setText("Hooray for the USA");
                cb3.hide();
            }
        } else if (e.target == cb2) {
            if (cb2.getState() == true) {
                l.setText("Hooray for " + cb2.getLabel());
                cb3.show();
            }
        } else if (e.target == cb3) {
...
```

Figure 7.7 Checkbox group with hidden Checkbox.

The Checkbox and CheckboxGroup Oddity

If you look closely at the interface tables we've shown for Checkbox and CheckboxGroup, you'll find that it is not really clear how the `CheckboxGroup.setCurrent()` identifies which boxes are in the group.

It turns out that the boxes communicate with the group, rather than the group communicating with the box. Also, the peer objects manage the lowest-level setting and resetting so that there is no public interface required to interoperate between the group and the boxes. The only hidden interface is one `java.awt.*` internal method called `Checkbox.set`

`InternalState`. This method is used by the group to communicate with the current object. It is also used by the box to manage its internal state.

So, even though the interface is slightly obscure, the two classes properly interoperate, with minimum overhead. We think that these classes are among the easiest to work with in the AWT.

CHAPTER 8

Events

- Event interface
- Useful event processing
- Simplified event processing
- Constructing your own events

Event Interface

Events are the primary method for dealing with user input in the AWT. Each event generated by the AWT equates to one Event object. We've been dealing with events throughout this book; the `handleEvent` and `action` methods we use in most example classes are the standard method of processing AWT events. While the examples are understandable even without this chapter, a detailed examination of AWT events is needed to take full advantage of the AWT for full performance and function.

Event processing is by necessity a dynamic, short-duration execution stream. If you add significant execution time to the event path, all event processing will suffer. Learn to use multiple threads or other response-delaying schemes to keep the event execution path short.

Table 8.1 outlines some of the useful methods available to AWT events. Note that the Component class provides most of the useful interface.

Table 8.1 Event Interface

Method	Returns	Notes
	Event Interface	
`Event(Object target,int id, Object arg)`		Use only when constructing events
`Event(Object target, long when, int id, int x, int y, int key, int modifiers)`		
`Event(Object target, long when, int id, int x, int y, int key, int modifiers, Object arg)`		

continued...

continued...

Method	Returns	Notes
`controlDown()`	Boolean	Was the **Ctrl** key down during this event?
`controlDown()`	Boolean	Was the **Ctrl** key down during this event?
`metaDown()`	Boolean	Was the **Meta** key down during this event?
`postEvent(Event evt)`	Boolean	Used to post a constructed event
`shiftDown()`	Boolean	Was the **Shift** key down during this event?
`translate(int dx, int dy)`	Void	Translate this event by `(dx,dy)`
Event-Related Component Interface		
`action(Event evt, Object what)`	Boolean	Action related (user presses **Enter**, etc.)
`gotFocus(Event evt, Object what)`	Boolean	AWT input events focused on this object
`handleEvent(Event evt)`	Boolean	The general event handler
`keyDown(Event evt, int key)`	Boolean	Before the keystroke is echoed
`keyUp(Event evt, int key)`	Boolean	After the keystroke is echoed
`lostFocus(Event evt, Object what)`	Boolean	Events are no longer focused on this object
`mouseDown(Event evt, int x, int y)`	Boolean	Button is now being pressed
`mouseDrag(Event evt, int x, int y)`	Boolean	Mouse is moving with button down
`mouseEnter(Event evt, int x, int y)`	Boolean	Mouse is entering the target object
`mouseExit(Event evt, int x, int y)`	Boolean	Mouse is leaving the target object
`mouseMove(Event evt, int x, int y)`	Boolean	Mouse is moving with no buttons down
`mouseUp(Event evt, int x, int y)`	Boolean	Button is now being released

The AWT event mechanism is very simple to use. The primary detriment to ease of coding is the fact that there are a large number of individual event types for each object. If you have many custom panels or components, keeping track of what event relates to what activity can become complex.

Each event generated by the AWT produces a single Event object. However, you very seldom use an Event method. You do refer to public variables in the Event object and their corresponding enumerated values.

The `Event.target` variable contains the object to which this event is targeted. Typically, this would be something that inherits from a component like a button or a text field. Many mouse events occur over Container objects. In your code, you typically compare `Event.target` to each component you are handling events for

```
public boolean handleEvent(Event evt) {
    if (evt.target == (Button)b)
        ...
```

`Event.evt` is part of the public interface but is used by the AWT to link events into a list. You should not normally deal with or inspect the contents of the other events on the list.

The `Event.arg` object is an arbitrary object tagged onto the event. Depending on the target object, this might be the text label, the state of the object, or another arbitrary status.

`Event.x` and `Event.y` are integers containing the display coordinates of the event. This typically is used with mouse events but is provided for all events. It is especially useful to handlers of containers trying to locate passive components that happen to be under the event location.

For mouse events, developers can use the `Event.clickCount` integer to detect single, double, or triple clicks. This field may or may not behave as you would expect, since the detection of multiple clicks is handled primarily by the native windowing system.

The `Event.id` variable contains the specific event type at hand. The id primarily reflects mouse, keyboard, window, scroll, list, focus, and action events. Two other events (LOAD_FILE and SAVE_FILE) reflect FileDialog events.

The `Event.key` variable contains the specific ASCII keycode or one of the predefined function keys commonly found on keyboards (**Down**, **End**, **Home**, **PgDn**, **F1–F12**, etc.). There are also values predefined for the `Event.modifiers` variable to indicate the state of the **Alt**, **Ctrl**, **Shift**, and **Meta** keys.

The last public variable in an event is the timestamp. `Event.when` can be used to decide whether an event is worth dealing with or for timed input. Most handlers don't bother examining this variable, because actions that occur typically are initiated by the user.

Useful Event Processing

Most of the AWT developer's interactions with events come from a set of methods provided by a component. Since typical AWT events apply to a specific component, it's common to place the event-handling code in the parent container or in the custom class relating to the component. For instance, if you add a standard AWT button to a custom panel, you would manage events for that button in the Java code that supports the custom panel. Here's a very simple example:

```
public class myPanel extends panel {
    Button b;
    myPanel() {
        b = new Button("RESET");
        add(b);
    }
    public handleEvent(Event evt) {
        if (evt.target == b) {
```

```
        // button handling code
    }
    ...
```

Note that we inherit `handleEvent()` from Component (Panel is a subclass of Component). Here we've overridden the base behavior and added a small amount of code to detect events targeted at the button. If the code we add completely handles the event (it usually does), then our code should return `true` to tell the event management code in AWT to dispose of the event.

```
    if (evt.target == b) {
        // button handling code
        return true;
    }
```

If we somehow don't manage to completely process the event or if we don't process the event at all, we should return `false`. The AWT event management code will try to dispatch the event to other handlers until it is processed. If no handler accepts responsibility for processing the event, the base code in Component will quietly dispose of the event.

One interesting twist on the AWT event mechanisms is a result of several different events being produced by what appears to be a single-user action. For instance, when the user moves the mouse over the button above and clicks on it, AWT generates numerous raw events. Depending on the speed at which the mouse is moved (and the native windowing system configuration), one or more Event.MOUSE_MOVE events occur. If the mouse passes over other AWT components (including any otherwise empty areas of a container), Event.MOUSE_ENTER and Event.MOUSE_EXIT events are generated. Finally, the click itself generates Event.MOUSE_DOWN, Event.MOUSE_DRAG, Event.ACTION_EVENT, and Event.MOUSE_UP events.

Since you typically care only about the ACTION_EVENT event, you might be tempted to just let the default handlers process the other events. However, if you do so, the entire event handler list may be traversed just to get to the base code (which disposes of the event). It is much better to dispose of all these extra events right away (if you can). For example, unless your application supports drag and drop or rubberbanding (code you have to write, by the way) you can immediately toss the MOUSE_DRAG events. Also, you can almost always throw away MOUSE_MOVE events, especially if you're dealing with traditional business applications.

To dispose of these extraneous events, you can add code at the top of your handler like:

```
public handleEvent(Event evt) {
    switch(evt.id) {
    case Event.MOUSE_MOVE:
    case Event.MOUSE_DRAG:
        return true; // throw these away
    case ...
    }
```

You must be careful about disposing of events in this way. If an object within your container needs to see an event you have just thrown away (by returning `true`), that contained component will not function properly. You must be aware of what is happening in other portions of your application. If in doubt, just return `false` and let the event dispatcher give other components a chance at the event.

One other common thing is added to many event handlers. The default behavior of `Component.handleEvent` is to call the simplified interface described in the next section. If you develop some small custom handler (like the event culling discussed previously) and neglect to handle the real events that you want to deal with, the events will be improperly handled. The way to work around this is to invoke the original Component method at the tail end of your handler:

```
public handleEvent(Event evt) {
    switch(evt.id) {
    case Event.MOUSE_MOVE:
    case Event.MOUSE_DRAG:
        return true; // throw these away
    case ...
    }
    ...
   return(super.handleEvent(evt));
}
```

This allows the default behavior to occur for every event that you don't specifically dispose of or handle.

Simplified Event Handling

The `Component.handleEvent()` method provides one entry point to handle all event-related activity. If you don't want to customize that behavior, you can use the default behavior inherited from Component to manage the common events (mouse, keyboard, and action). For instance, the Event.ACTION_EVENT events are dispatched by `Component.handleEvent` to a method called `action()`. If your code overrides the default action method, you can avoid worrying about the somewhat intricate handling possible in `handleEvent`. All ACTION_EVENT events that pass through the inherited handler are dispatched to your `action()` method. The arguments to `action()` are somewhat different, but provide the same flexibility.

Other entry points with the same capability as `action()` are: `gotFocus`, `keyDown`, `keyUp`, `lostFocus`, `mouseDown`, `mouseDrag`, `mouseEnter`, `mouseExit`, `mouseMove`, and `mouseUp`. Note that the first argument of all of these methods is the Event object at hand. Additional arguments vary and typically provide either keystroke values, display coordinates where the event occurred, or an object that is involved in the event.

Mouse Events

The AWT generates ix kinds of mouse events. They include

- MOUSE_DOWN—mouse button is now pressed.
- MOUSE_DRAG—mouse move with button down.
- MOUSE_ENTER—mouse entering a component's drawing region.
- MOUSE_EXIT—mouse leaving a component's drawing region.
- MOUSE_MOVE—mouse move with button up.
- MOUSE_UP—mouse button is now unpressed.

Each of these mouse events is specific to a particular (X,Y) position relative to the target object. Note that dragging across a container boundary can cause some slight complexity in calculating position changes because the reported coordinates suddenly switch to the new component. It's useful to keep track of the MOUSE_DOWN and MOUSE_UP event targets, as well as the locations. Having these around allows you to manage drag and drop properly, as well as to simplify the calculation of positions.

Keyboard Events

The primary value of the KEY_PRESS and KEY_RELEASE operations is to verify user input. The AWT provides KEY_PRESS events prior to their being processed by the native windowing system. This allows us to modify the keystroke (say, to convert lower- to uppercase) before echoing the character to the display field. Chapter 6 demonstrated this capability.

KEY_RELEASE is not used as often but can provide us with a hook to examine the contents after the keystroke is displayed. For instance, you might convert the keystroke to uppercase in KEY_PRESS and copy the entire text field in KEY_RELEASE. This is especially useful for fields where multiple threads may be active.

KEY_ACTION is the event generated when one of the special action keys is pressed. The action keys include:

- **Down**
- **End**
- **F1–F12**
- **Home**
- **Left**
- **PgDn**
- **PgUp**
- **Right**
- **Up**

You can of course evaluate the modifiers field for special cases such as **Ctrl-End** and **Alt-F1**.

To provide symmetry with other keyboard events, the KEY_ACTION_RELEASE method allows evaluation after completion of the native windowing system processing of the event.

Focus Events

Focus events are generated as the AWT and the native windowing system decide that a particular component (either a container or active component) becomes the active component. It's often useful to add code to event handlers to record when you have focus. The handler can then quickly decide to ignore events directed at other components, based on not currently having the input focus.

Primarily, choosing to ignore an event based on whether the windowing system is focused on us (a container) would replace code that uses `locate()` to find a contained object to which the event belongs. Instead of

```
if (locate(evt.x,evt.y) == null)
    return false;
...     // one of our contained components
```

which admittedly is one line of source but a significant amount of code to execute each time the handler executes, you can use

```
if (evt.id == Event.GOTFOCUS() || weHaveFocus == true) {
    if (locate(evt.x,evt.y) == null)
        return false;
    ...     // one of our contained components
} else
    return false;
```

This provides a relatively quick way (with no additional method invocation) to ignore events. If the event potentially belongs to this object, the execution falls directly into normal event detection code.

Of course, using focus in this way cannot be universally applied. Operations such as drag and drop don't involve focus events, and objects would need to accept drag-and-drop events (mouse down, drag, and mouse up) whether they had focus or not. Also, some applications may need to track mouse movement or other events, regardless of who has the focus.

Window Events

User interaction with the native windowing system generates window events. For example, Event.WINDOW_MOVE events are generated when the user "grabs" a window and tries to move the window to match personal viewing habits.

The window-related events that the AWT handles are

- WINDOW_DEICONIFY
- WINDOW_DESTROY
- WINDOW_EXPOSE
- WINDOW_ICONIFY
- WINDOW_MOVE

Each of these events is a fairly typical windowing system action. We have generally assumed that you know you're way around windowing systems and are an experienced developer. However, we will touch on each of these events and show how applications may take advantage of them.

Event.WINDOW_ICONIFY and Event.WINDOW_DEICONIFY events are obviously a matched set. Your application can take advantage of the shrunken window syndrome to ease the burden on the event dispatching system, which is similar to using focus. You can also defer painting and updating the contents of windows that are iconified. When the window is restored (it receives a WINDOW_DEICONIFY event), you can then "catch up" by performing a complete update of the window. In situations where output to a window occurs continuously (a status or logging window, for example) this can save a significant amount of processor time and lessen the overall system requirements.

Event.WINDOW_MOVED and Event.WINDOW_EXPOSE events may not be quite as useful to typical applications. Smart developers, especially those developing graphics or imaging code, should immediately realize that a moved window may be partially or completely obscured by either another window or the display screen limits. By updating only the visible portions of the window, you can potentially ease the burden on both your drawing engine and the native windowing system. See Chapter 12 for examples of partially updating custom display components.

The Event.WINDOW_DESTROY is something that should be used in every program that deals with multiple window or frame objects. This event is generated by the windowing system when the user selects the close or destroy action. Your code to handle this should immediately respond by

- generating a dialog window with "Close Window?" or something similar to verify the request and
- cleaning up the contained components, related threads, files, etc., and calling `Window.dispose()` to destroy the window.

Other Action Events

The other AWT events relate to scroll bar objects. Note that these events are not generated by native components in Java 1.0.x versions. Only the AWT ScrollBar class (and descendants of ScrollBar) currently generate these events. Chapter discusses the problems associated with native windowing system scroll bars on TextArea. The five scroll bar events are

- SCROLL_ABSOLUTE
- SCROLL_LINE_DOWN
- SCROLL_LINE_UP
- SCROLL_PAGE_DOWN
- SCROLL_PAGE_UP

Note that the definition of lines, pages, and absolute may vary on each platform, but the AWT always "corrects" these to make sense relative to the ScrollBar object at hand. Horizontal scroll bars also have a terminology problem, which is discussed in Chapter 13.

Constructing Your Own Events

Two other methods—`deliverEvent`, and `postEvent`—are not typically used by developers. Because the base code in Component generally does the right thing, the default behavior is usually not modified.

However, custom components can take advantage of these two methods to take a lower-level set of events and generate one complex event to the containing object. For example, the following code handles a set of mouse events and converts them to a single ACTION event. This particular piece of code is an excerpt from a custom class included on the CD-ROM called **ButtonCanvas.java**.

```
public boolean mouseDown(Event evt, int x, int y) {
    if (evt.target == this)  {
        ...
        return true;
    }
    return false;
}
public boolean mouseUp(Event evt, int x, int y) {
    if (evt.target == this)  {
        ...
        Event e = new Event(this, evt.when, Event.ACTION_EVENT,
            evt.x,evt.y,evt.key,evt.modifiers,(Object)text);
        deliverEvent(e);    // ship off ACTION_EVENT
        return true;
    }
    return false;
}
```

If you look carefully, you'll see that we return `true` for the mouse up and down events that occur over the custom component. This keeps the container object from seeing these low-level events. However, all other events over this component are passed over so that the container can handle them if it desires.

Also, our code obviously doesn't handle the generated ACTION_EVENT event. The `deliverEvent()` method forwards the constructed event to the parent of our custom component (usually a custom container).

Note that the custom component containing these two methods has additional code to animate the component appropriately for the mouseDown and mouseUp events. The drawing components of the custom class **ButtonCanvas.java** are discussed in Chapter 11.

CHAPTER 9

Fonts and Colors

- Font Interface
- Useful Font Processing
- Font and Text Placement
- Automatically Sizing Fonts
- Custom Font Selection Class
- AWT Colors
- AWT Supported ColorModels
- Working with Color

The AWT provides support for multiple fonts and colors. Through the Font, FontMetrics, Toolkit, Graphics, and Component classes, relatively useful font support is available. Color is supported through the Color, Graphics, and Component classes. In this chapter, we will show the basics of Font management, text drawing, and line spacing. We will also discuss how to use and manage color with containers and components. More complex graphic imaging techniques are discussed in Chapter 11.

Font Interface

Table 9.1 outlines some of the useful methods available to manage AWT fonts. Note that the list of fonts is normally obtained from the native windowing system toolkit object. This object provides one of the primary interfaces to the native windowing system.

Table 9.1 Font Interface

Method	Returns	Notes
	Useful Font Interface	
`Font(String name, int style, int size)`		Style is either `Font.PLAIN`, `Font.BOLD`, or `Font.ITALIC`
`equals(Object obj)`	Boolean	Use this to check for a font identical to this one
`getFamily()`	String	Platform-specific font family name
`getFont(String name)`	Static Font	Looks up a font from a system property or null
`getFont(String name, Font font)`	Static Font	Same as above, but return the passed font if the property is not found
`getName()`	String	Returns the name of this font
`getSize()`	Int	The point size
`getStyle()`	Int	Style is either `Font.PLAIN`, `Font.BOLD`, or `Font.ITALIC`
`isBold()`	Boolean	A convenience method to avoid `if (getStyle() == Font.PLAIN)`
`isItalic()`	Boolean	A convenience method
`isPlain()`	Boolean	A convenience method

continued...

Method	Returns	Notes
	Useful FontMetrics Interface	
`bytesWidth(byte datea[],int offset, int length)`	Int	Returns the width (in pixels) of the bytes from offset for length
`charsWidth(byte datea[],int offset, int length)`	Int	Returns the width (in pixels) of the characters from offset for length
`charWidth(char c)`	Int	How wide is this one character?
`charWidth(int c)`	Int	How wide is this one character?
`getAscent()`	Int	How much does a standard character rise above the baseline of the font?
`getDescent()`	Int	How much does a standard character fall below the baseline of the font?
`getFont()`	Font	What is the current font?
`getHeight()`	Int	What is the standard height of this font?
`getLeading()`	Int	What is the standard spacing between lines of this font?
`getMaxAdvance()`	Int	What is the largest gap between characters?
`getMaxAscent()`	Int	What is the largest rise above the baseline for this font?
`getMaxDescent()`	Int	What is the largest fall below the baseline for this font?
`getWidths()`	Int[]	Returns a 256 cell array of the advance widths for the first 256 characters in this font
`stringWidth(String str)`	Int	This is how wide the string would be on screen (in pixels)
	Useful Toolkit Interface	
`getDefaultToolkit()`	Toolkit	Returns a handle to the native windowing system toolkit (this is where much of the peer interface comes from)

continued...

Method	Returns	Notes
`getFontList()`	String fontList[]	Returns an array of strings with the names of the fonts supported by the peer toolkit

Useful Font Processing

Support for specific fonts is not symmetrical across AWT platforms. Each platform selects the fonts to allow and usually does not support all the native fonts installed on a particular machine. Figures 9.1 and 9.2 show the fonts supported on Win32 and Linux by Netscape Navigator 2.02.

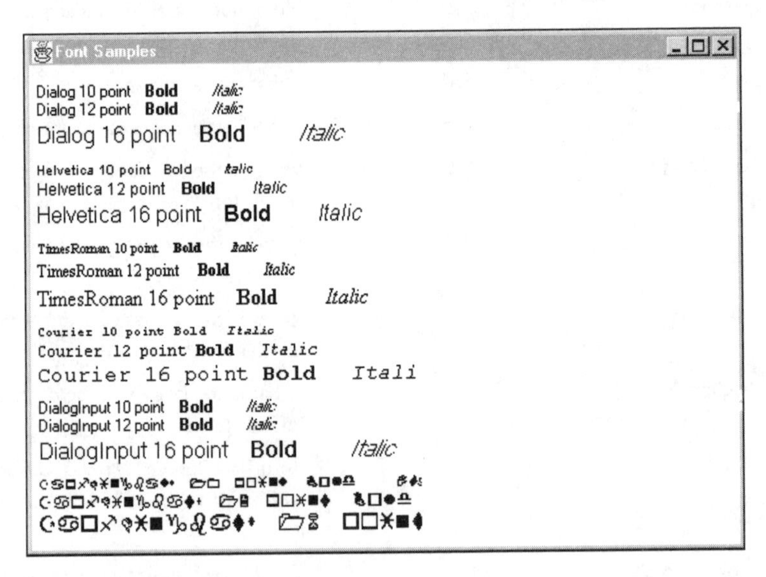

Figure 9.1 Win32 Netscape fonts.

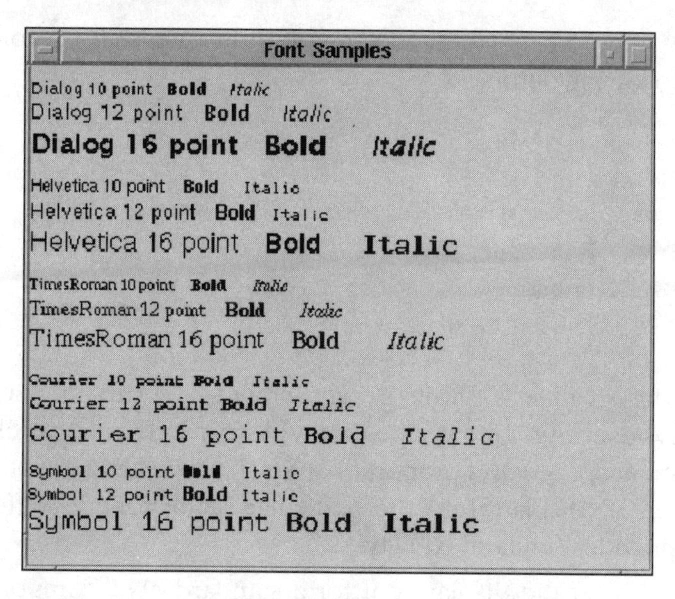

Figure 9.2 Linux Netscape fonts.

Note from the two images that some of the same font names are supported on the platforms shown, but they are rendered in visibly different manners. This is a common occurrence and can cause concern for some users. Ideally, the AWT font support will be updated to support all the fonts installed on the native windowing system, but for now the basic set provided will work for most applications.

To obtain a list of the fonts available to your Java AWT program, use the following code excerpt:

```
Toolkit tk = Toolkit.getDefaultToolkit();
String fontList[] = tk.getFontList();
for (int i=0;i<fontList.length;i++)
    System.out.println("Font " + i + " is " + fontList[i]);
```

When you run the code sample on a Win32 box, you get the following output:

```
Font 0 is Dialog
Font 1 is Helvetica
Font 2 is TimesRoman
Font 3 is Courier
Font 4 is DialogInput
Font 5 is ZapfDingbats
```

This small set of fonts doesn't provide the capability to do real typesetting, but it does provide more than one choice of monospaced and proportional fonts, as well as a set of symbols. On UNIX platforms, the particular set of fonts is different but provides similar flexibility.

To set the display font for a standard AWT component, you can just use the `setFont()` method provided by Component. Note that you must generate a Font object from the names provided by the toolkit. This is easily accomplished by the default font constructor:

```
TextArea ta = new TextArea(10,20);
Font f = new Font("Helvetica",Font.PLAIN,12);
ta.setFont(f);
```

Font and Text Placement

One of the common problems with drawing text (not just with AWT) is associated with *where* to draw text. In systems that deal with lines and columns, placement is simple. On systems that deal with graphics, pixels, and resizable drawing areas, it is more complicated.

While we'll deal with resizing and other issues in Chapter 11, this section will provide the basics of text positioning within a canvas.

Each font has certain characteristics (called metrics) that include the type font (Times Roman, Courier, etc.), the point size, the style (italic, bold, etc.), the height (ascent + descent), the width (advance), and the appropriate line spacing (called leading).

Figure 9.3 shows how each metric is applied to drawing text. The text is Times Roman (normal and italic).

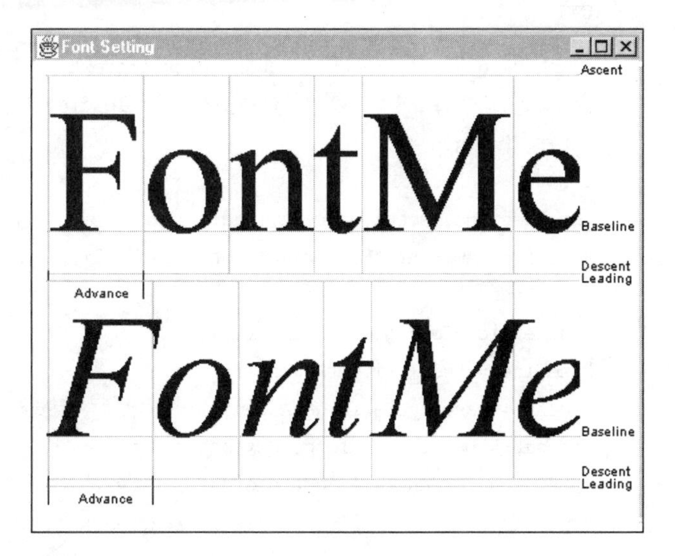

Figure 9.3 FontMetric characteristics.

If you remember learning to write in first and second grade, you can probably recall the Big Chief tablets (or some other similar beginner's tablet). Figure 9.3 is similar to these writing tablets. (You didn't realize that everything important is taught in the first grade, did you?) The line that all characters rest on is called the *baseline*. The line below the baseline is where the bottom of characters like *g*, *q*, or *p* reach to; this is the *descent*. The line above the baseline is where capital letters (and lowercase *L*) reach to; this is the *ascent*. The space between lines is the *leading*, and is designed to make repeated lines of the same type easy to read.

Note that when multiple lines of text are displayed in the same type font, style, and size, the first leading line is in the same place as the second ascent line.

To calculate the spacing between lines, as well as where the baseline should be, start with the following code excerpt. Assume that baseline is already initialized from the previous line of text.

```
Graphics g = ...;           // a graphics context
int top = ...;              // the previous leading line
int leftmargin = ...;       // :)
...
int baseline,ascent,descent,leading;
Font f = new Font("Helvetica",Font.PLAIN,12);
g.setFont(f);
FontMetrics fm = g.getFontMetrics();
baseline = top + fm.getAscent();
ascent = baseline - fm.getAscent();
descent = baseline + fm.getDescent();
leading = descent + fm.getLeading();
top = leading;              // this is where next line can
start
...
g.drawString("text",leftmargin,baseline);
```

Note that the only things we use when drawing (normally) are the baseline and the leading line. The baseline is where we draw this line, and the leading line is where we begin calculating the next line's position. One other useful method is `FontMetrics.getHeight()`. This method returns the normal height of the line and is calculated as ascent + descent + leading. We calculate them separately because you use the intermediate values (all of these involve moving the baseline and resizing the text) for placement of footnotes, superscripts, and subscripts.

Besides line spacing, the spacing between characters on a line is also an important font metric. A manual typewriter spaces the characters uniformly across the line, each centered in a box the same size as all other characters. While this made mechanical typewriters easy to build, it makes reading more tiring. Since *i* is very narrow and *W* is very wide, words like *Willow* have odd gaps between the characters. This kind of uniform spacing is called *monospacing*.

Proportional fonts (like those in newspapers, magazines, and books) adjust the space between characters on a character by character basis. Since *i* is narrow and upright, the white space around it should be less than that in a monospace font. Since *W* and *M* are wide and spread out, the required white space should be the same or greater than that in a monospace font. To demonstrate, here is a sentence in both a monospace font and a proportional font:

`Willow trees weep.`

Willow trees weep.

When the AWT draws a string of characters, it looks at the font metrics for each character to decide how far to move over to begin the next character. This simple form of proportional spacing is easy to implement; it is reasonably correct, and it lends itself to fast drawing. Each character in the font contains an *advance* specific to that character. The `FontMetrics.getWidths()` method returns an array of 256 integers, each containing the width for the character of that value. To find out how wide an *A* is, look in the (int)"A"-th cell of the array. The `String.charAt()` method returns a selected character's integer value, to ease the lookup process. Here's an short code excerpt that makes this more clear:

```
int widths[] = fm.getWidths();
advance = leftmargin + widths[s.charAt(offset)];
```

Note that most printers and some windowing systems provide an additional metric called *kerning*. This is the process of recognizing special sequences of characters that, when taken as a set, have different advance widths than when taken as individual characters. For example, *t* and *h* are treated as a single character when they appear in a word like *their*. When they appear in the word *caught*, they have a different advance. The AWT does not currently support kerning (although it could be implemented in the native windowing system).

One other important thing to note is the effect of special styles such as Bold or Italic upon character placement. Referring to Figure 9.3, the italicized characters all lean past the specified advance point for each character. Some characters actually stretch past the advance point into the space reserved for the next character. This is fine for text that is all one style; however, when an italicized character is followed by a normal character, the characters may touch or overlap slightly. This is a problem solved by some typesetting systems in a manner similar to kerning; others carry separate advance widths for each style. With the AWT, you just have to put up with it or add space yourself.

Automatically Sizing Fonts

In dealing with the AWT, you should not just pick a font size. It's often best to use a font specified as a system property; they are typically set to match the user's requirements. See the PrintProperties program in the Examples Appendix. However, in other situations, it's wise to size the font to match the container space available. For instance, a title or heading should be sized to show it's prominent status. It is easy enough to calculate the best font size for a particular set of components and to use the calculated size in an organized manner. For example, the following code calculates a point size based on what will fit in the current size of a component.

```
Graphics g = ...;
String s = ...;
Dimension d = size();
sizedDraw(g,s,d);       // go pick correct size and draw
...
public void sizedDraw(Graphics g, String s,Dimension d) {
        FontMetrics fm;
    boolean fits = false;
    int points = 64;    // maximum size we'll draw
    Font f = g.getFont();;
    g.setFont(f = new Font(f.getName(),f.getStyle(),points));
    fm = g.getFontMetrics();
    while(fits == false) {
        if ((fm.getHeight() <= d.height) && (fm.stringWidth(s)
<= d.width)) {
            fits = true;
        } else {
            points—;    // drop pointsize by 1
            g.setFont(f = new Font(f.getName(), f.getStyle(),
points));
            fm = g.getFontMetrics();
        }
    }
    g.drawString(s,0,(d.height-fm.getMaxDescent()));
}
```

Custom Font Selection Class

This section of the chapter discusses letting users select the display font, style, and size. It is common practice to provide a simple menu or choice box in production applications to perform this operation. We will present a custom FontSelect class that can be easily added to your own code.

Figure 9.4 shows the FontSelect component in use:

Figure 9.4 Custom FontSelect component.

As shown in Table 9.2, the interface to this object is very simple: a single constructor, one method to get the current font selection, two methods to set the font selection, and a single event generated for each user interaction with the FontSelect object.

Table 9.2 FontSelect Interface

Method	Returns	Notes
`FontSelect()`		Creates a font selection Panel
`getSelectedFont()`	Font	Returns a Font object that implements the selected font, style, and size from the font selection Panel
`setSelectedFont(Font f)`	Void	Sets the font selection Panel to match the passed-in Font object
`setSelectedFont(String name, int style, int size)`	Void	Sets the font selection Panel to match the passed-in Font parameters

FontSelect generates an ACTION_EVENT event each time the user selects a Choicebox in the font selection Panel. The Event.arg field is a Font object that matches the selection. The developer may choose to implement an event handler interface or merely use the get-and-set programmatic interface to deal with font selection.

The FontSelect class is provided on the CD-ROM. However, to show what is involved, we will walk through the entire class and provide commentary.

```
import java.awt.*;
public class FontSelect extends Panel {
        static int sizes[] =
{6,7,8,9,10,11,12,13,14,15,16,18,20,22,24,28,32,48,64 };
        Choice nameList,styleList,sizeList;
        Font currentFont;
        static String fontList[] = null;
```

FontSelect is based on Panel. This allows us to add font selection to any layout easily. There are three Choice objects—one for each of name, style, and size. The class also maintains the font selection in a Font object called currentFont. The list of fonts supported by the windowing system are stored as an array of strings in fontList. Finally, the various font sizes (in points) are stored in an array, ready to be added to the sizeList choicebox.

```
        public FontSelect() {
                int i;
                setLayout(new FlowLayout());
                if (fontList == null) {
                        Toolkit tk = Toolkit.getDefaultToolkit();
                        fontList = tk.getFontList();
                }
```

The list of fonts supported by the AWT on any particular platform are obtained from the `toolkit` object. `getFontList()` returns an array of strings. We place these in `fontList`, but never refer to them again. A fully productized version of the class would use `fontList` to validate programmatic changes to the font name.

```
        nameList = new Choice();
        styleList = new Choice();
        sizeList = new Choice();
        for(i=0;i<sizes.length;i++)
                sizeList.addItem("" + sizes[i]);
        sizeList.select(6);     // hopefully this is
12 point
```

The `sizeList` is initialized with string versions of the sizes array contents. Note that we caused implicit conversion from `int` to `String` (suitable for `addItem()`) by appending the int to a null string. This is a short and easy way to perform this common operation.

```
        styleList.addItem("Normal");
        styleList.addItem("Bold");
        styleList.addItem("Italic");
        styleList.addItem("Bold+Italic");
        styleList.select(0);
```

We enter the built-in styles: plain (we call it normal), bold, italic, and bold + italic to the `styleList` `Choicebox` and select **normal** as the default.

```
        add(nameList);
        add(styleList);
        add(sizeList);
        for(i=0;i<fontList.length;i++)
                nameList.addItem(fontList[i]);
    }
```

Each of the three Choiceboxes are added to the Panel (we set it to `FlowLayout` earlier). We also populate the font name Choicebox with the fontList strings obtained from the toolkit earlier.

```
public boolean action(Event evt, Object arg) {
Event e;
```

This is a standard `action()` method; each choice box action event is handled here. Other `ACTION_EVENT` events (pressing **Return**, etc.) over the panel are just passed on to the parent container. We also define an `Event` variable for later use.

```
        if (evt.target == nameList) {  // selected a new
                                          font
                System.out.println("selected " +
                (String)arg);
                currentFont = new
                Font(nameList.getSelectedItem(),

styleList.getSelectedIndex(),

sizes[sizeList.getSelectedIndex()]);
        } else if (evt.target == styleList) {
                System.out.println("selected " +
                (String)arg);
                currentFont = new
                Font(nameList.getSelectedItem(),

styleList.getSelectedIndex(),

sizes[sizeList.getSelectedIndex()]);
        } else if (evt.target == sizeList) {
                System.out.println("selected " +
                (String)arg);
                currentFont = new
                Font(nameList.getSelectedItem(),

styleList.getSelectedIndex(),
```

```
sizes[sizeList.getSelectedIndex()]);
            } else
                  return false;
```

Each of the Choice objects is handled in much the same way. We compare the event target to each box in turn. If it doesn't match any of the three Choiceboxes, we return `false` to pass the event on to other handlers.

The `nameList` box stores the values in usable form (Helvetica, Courier, etc.). For the `styleList` box, we take the selection index and use it directly to match the enumerated styles. Note that `bold + italic` has the numeric value three (3) but is really the logical OR of `Font.BOLD` and `Font.ITALIC`. For the `sizeList` box, we use the index as an offset into our `sizes[]` array. We could also convert the text of the selection into an integer and use that. We felt like a simple array lookup might be more efficient but didn't bother to verify it. Either method works fine.

After we obtain the three Font components (name, style, and size), we construct a new Font object in `currentFont`. This font is used by `getSelectedFont()` and other methods.

```
e = new Event(this, evt.when, Event.ACTION_EVENT,
evt.x,evt.y,evt.key,evt.modifiers,(Object)currentFont);
deliverEvent(e);    // ship off ACTION_EVENT
        return true;    // flush the choice's event
}
```

Next, we construct a new Event object. This event is also an `ACTION_EVENT`, but establishes the font selection panel as the target. We also set the `event.arg` field to the just created Font object. When the event is accepted by a parent container, the container can just use the passed Font object directly, without making a call back to the FontSelect object. After delivering the event, we dispose of the original event (one of the Choicebox action events) by returning `true`.

```
        public Font getSelectedFont() {
                return currentFont;
        }
```

The `getSelectedFont()` method allows any code with a handle to the font selection panel to find out what is currently selected in the Panel. Normally, the parent container would find out via the `ACTION_EVENT` generated previously.

```
        public void setSelectedFont(Font f) {
                setSelectedFont(f.getName(), f.getStyle(),
f.getSize());
        }
        public void setSelectedFont(String name, int style, int
size) {
                int i;
                Font cf;
                nameList.select(name);
                styleList.select(style);
                for(i=0;i<sizes.length;i++) {
                        if (size == sizes[i])
                                break;
                }
                if (i < sizes.length)
                        sizeList.select(i);     // select the
appropriate one
                else {
                        int sl[] = new int[sizes.length+1];
                        for(i=0;i<sizes.length;i++)
                                sl[i] = sizes[i];
                        sl[i] = size;
                        sizes = sl;
                        sizeList.addItem("" + size); // add to
choices
                }
                cf = new Font(name,style,size);
```

```
            if (cf != null) // don't replace unless valid
                    currentFont = cf;
            else
                    System.out.println("bad font");
    }
```

These two routines provide a way for your code to set the selection inside the font selection Panel. You can either pass a valid Font object in or pass the component pieces (name, style, and size). If the size is not listed in the current sizeList box, it is appended to the existing list of sizes. Note that the mechanics of extending an array are fairly elaborate.

```
    public Insets insets() {
            return new Insets(10,10,10,10);
    }
    public void paint(Graphics g) {
            Dimension d = size();
            g.drawRect(0,0,d.width -1,d.height-1);
    }
}
```

The insets and paint methods are here merely to make the component look better. Insets are covered in Chapter 14 and the `paint()` method is covered in Chapter 11.

Font management in the AWT is somewhat primitive compared to the native support available on most platforms, but it is capable enough to implement the basics of rich text and typesetting. Hopefully, additional capability will appear over time.

AWT Colors

We now take up the subject of color. Since color support across native windowing systems can vary wildly, the AWT tries to take an approach that is easily supported on any platform. There are simple `setForeground()` and `setBackground()` methods that allow you to easily manipulate components that operate in bicolor modes. Most of the AWT-provided components are managed with these two color methods.

When drawing images directly (within a graphics context), you use the `setColor()` method. This is supported with very simple drawing methods for rectangles, lines, text, fill, etc.

AWT-Supported Color Models

Most video displays today support one of two basic color models. Many other models are also available, but every video adapter supports one of these two basic methods. The first and most common model is the pseudo-color model. This is supported by most X window servers and by pretty much every single PC on the face of the planet. Basically, a pseudo-color display allows 256 distinct colors at one time (a single byte per pixel). Each of the 256 color cells displayed may come from a much larger palette (typically 256K or 16M colors). At any one time, the native windowing system is using a handful (or more) of the 256 color cells. This typically leaves around 200 to 240 cells for applications. During execution, an application can change colors in a cell without having an impact on any displayed windows or images, as long as no more than 256 unique colors are needed at one time.

For the vast majority of applications, this is never a problem. On most systems, black, white, and a few shades of gray are all that is ever used. However, those users who are color happy or who display numbers of graphical images (clipart, photos, games, etc.) will occasionally see odd colors in windows that are partially obscured. Typically, the windowing system will temporarily "steal" color cells from idle or background applications and give them to the current application. X servers are notorious for this, especially when running XV or other imaging programs that have private colormaps.

On high-end computer systems, another color model is used. Some high-end PCs and many UNIX workstations support the true color model. While there's nothing especially "true" about the colors displayed, this color model provides for many more colors at a time. Instead of 256 colors from a palette of 256K, true color may support 32,768 different colors, or even 16,777,216 colors, at a time. Basically, each pixel is either 16 or 32 bits long (instead of 8 bits). The video adapter breaks up the pixel into red, green, and blue components (usually in even portions of 5 or 8 bits) that are converted directly into the analog signals sent to the video display. Some adapters also provide support for an alpha or transparency channel.

As we said earlier, the AWT tries to support both color models equally well. The physical characteristics of a particular video adapter are well hidden by the AWT, and the act of setting and getting colors use a high-level model that is possible to implement on any typical display. The `Color` class provides this color model.

In any case, for most purposes, the AWT completely hides the hardware model used by the native windowing system. You normally deal only with colors through the `Color` class.

Color Class Interface

The Color class provides several simple methods. We outline these in Table 9.3 and then go into some depth on the commonly used methods.

Table 9.3 Color Interface

Method	Returns	Notes
`Color(float r, float g, float b)` `Color(int rgb)` `Color int r, int g, int b)`		Each constructor has the same range of colors but receives them in various formats
`brighter()`	Color	The returned color is brighter by some color model specific amount
`darker()`	Color	The returned color is darker by some color model specific amount
`equals(Object obj)`	Boolean	Is the passed object a color that has the same RGB component?
`getBlue()`	Int	Gets the blue component of this color object
`getColor(String name)`	Static Color	Looks up the "name" in the system properties and converts the property into a color
`getColor(String name,Color c)`	Static Color	Looks up the "name" in the system properties and converts the property into a color; if the property doesn't exist, returns the passed color
`getColor(String name,int rgb)`	Static Color	Looks up the "name" in the system properties and converts the property into a color; if the property doesn't exist, returns a color that matches the passed int (in RGB format)
`getGreen()`	Int	Gets the green component of this color object
`getHSBColor(float h, float s, float b)`	static Color	Returns a color that represents the passed hue, saturation, and brightness
`getRed()`	Int	Get the red component of this color object
`getRGB()`	Int	Returns a 32-bit color where all components are in the range 0–255, red is in bits 16–23, green in 8–15, and blue is in 0–7

continued...

Method	Returns	Notes
`HSBtoRGB(float h, float s, float b)`	Int	Same as `getHSBColor()`, except returns the color as an int in RGB format
`RGBtoHSB(int r, int g, int b, float hsbvals[])`	static float[]	Converts the passed integer color components to HSB form; if hsbvals is null, creates a new array of floats for the result; if a float array is passed for hsbvals, updates the passed array with the hue, saturation, and brightness

In addition to operating on the individual color components as most of the Color-provided methods do, there are 13 static Color objects that are predefined to common colors:

- black
- blue
- cyan
- dark gray
- gray
- green
- light gray
- orange
- pink
- red
- white
- yellow

It is very common for AWT applications to use only these predefined colors. In fact, most business applications will not use more than a handful of these 13 colors.

Working with Color

Since display objects that inherit from Component typically display only in two colors (say, black text on a white background), the AWT provides the `setForeground()` and `setBackground()` methods to set the two colors. Occasionally, disabled Components "lowlight" the foreground color (say, changing text from black to gray). This is usually transparent to the developer and is part of the natural behavior of the Component.

For Components that inherit from Canvas, the concept of foreground and background is blurred. All drawing on a canvas is done via the graphics context associated with a canvas (or a bounded rectangle of the canvas). The drawing primitives provided by Graphics all draw in the "current" color (i.e., the color set by the most recent call to `setColor()`). Alternatively, some of the primitives will require a second color; `setXORmode()` is an example.

Basic color usage is very simple; however, we want to provide a couple of examples that may be useful. The first example, in Figure 9.5, just uses an event to set the background color of a Panel.

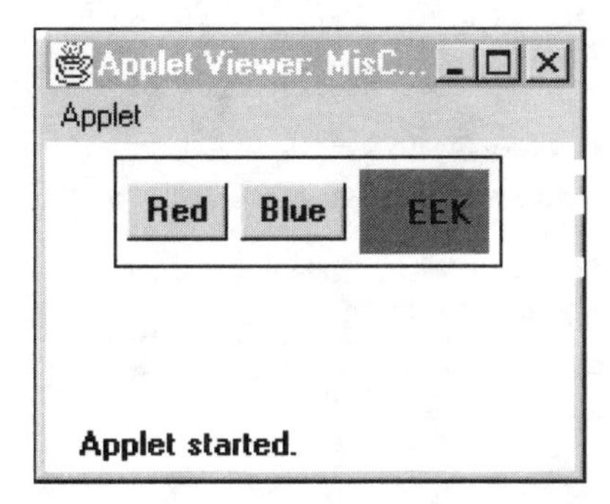

Figure 9.5 Setting the background color.

On normal platforms, the background of both the Panel and the embedded Label change colors from red to blue as the appropriate button is clicked. However, on Win32 platforms, the Label object doesn't change colors until the Panel is re-laid out or the Label is obscured by another window. This behavior is irritating. Presumably, the folks responsible for commercial Java products will fix this bug in their ports of the AWT.

```
class ColorTest extends Panel {
        Button red,blue;
        Panel testPanel;
        Label l;
        ColorTest(){
                add(red = new Button("Red"));
                add(blue = new Button("Blue"));
                add(testPanel = new Panel());
                testPanel.add(l = new Label("EEK"));
                show();
        }
```

We create an outer Panel with two buttons and a subpanel with a Label. Initially, the background of all Components is white.

```
        public boolean action(Event evt, Object arg) {
                if (evt.target == red) {
                        testPanel.setBackground(Color.red);
                } else if (evt.target == blue) {
                        testPanel.setBackground(Color.blue);
                } else
                        return false;
                testPanel.repaint();
                return true;
        }
}
```

When we click on the **Red** button, we set the background color of the subpanel to red. This is what produced the image in Figure 9.5. Obviously, clicking on the **Blue** button produces the same image, with the red background replaced by blue. Note that we used the predefined Color objects for red and blue. An alternative would have been to say

```
Color myred = new Color(255,14,14); // slightly off-red
testPanel.setBackground(myred);
```

Setting the foreground color is essentially identical. Try replacing `setBackground` with `setForeground` to change the text color (text is drawn in the foreground color).

Because more complex color management is limited almost exclusively to custom classes that are based on Canvas and Graphics objects, we defer discussion of `setColor` to Chapter 11.

CHAPTER 10

Menus and Choosing

- Menus
- Choices

Building on what we've learned about frames, dialog windows, and layout managers, we'll use this chapter to talk about what the AWT provides in the way of menus. We'll also mention choices at the end of this chapter. An example of a simple menu appears in Figure 10.1.

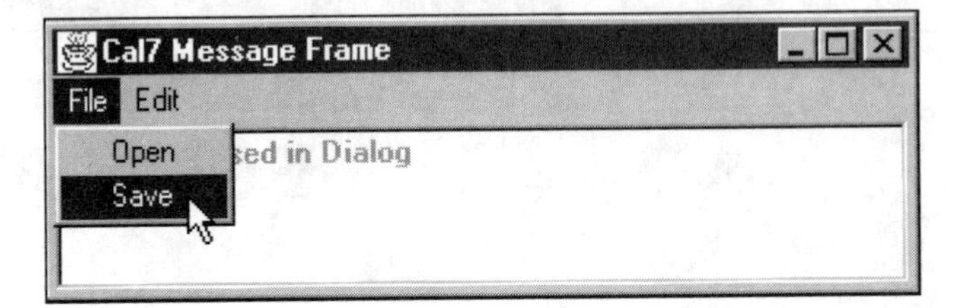

Figure 10.1 Simple menu.

Much of the usefulness of menus can also be provided fairly easily via Buttons, Checkboxes, and Lists. We'll show examples of these components in later chapters. For now, though, we'll stick to the windowing manager-based world and talk about menus.

NOTE

AWT menus can be attached only to instances of Frame. Panel instances (as in applets) cannot have menus. Generally you cannot work with menus in a useful way in Java applets.

Menus

Table 10.1 outlines some of the useful methods available to AWT menus. We will demonstrate the use of each of these in this chapter.

Table 10.1 Menu Interface

Method	Returns	Notes
	Useful MenuBar Interface	
`MenuBar()`		Add these to Frames only
`add(Menu m)`	Menu	Add a menu object
`countMenus()`	Int>	How many menu objects currently?
`getHelpMenu()`	Menu>	Returns null if `setHelpMenu()` hasn't been called

continued...

Method	Returns	Notes
`getMenu(int i)`	Menu>	Get the *i* th menu object
`remove(int index)`	Void>	Remove a menu at the index
`remove(MenuComponent m)`	Void>	Remove a particular menu object
`setHelpMenu(Menu m)`	Void>	Designate a particular menu as the Help menu
	Useful Menu Interface	
`Menu(String label)` `Menu(String label, boolean tearOff)`		If tearOff is `true`, some platforms allow tear-off menus
`add(MenuItem mi)`	MenuItem	Add an entry in a menu
`add(String label)`	Void	Implicitly create a menu item with this label
`countItems()`	Int>	How many items in this menu?
`addSeparator()`	Void>	Just a little white space
`getItem(int i)`	MenuItem>	Return the *i* th item
`remove(int index)`	Void>	Remove the item at the index
`remove(MenuComponent item)`	Void>	Remove a particular item
	Useful MenuItem Interface	
`MenuItem(String label)`		A single totally plain menu item
`disable()`	Void	Disable and usually lowlight the menu item
`enable() enable(boolean cond)`	Void	Enable and restore the visual state of the item
`getLabel()`	String	Get the text currently on the menu item
`isEnabled()`	boolean	Is this item currently enabled?
`setLabel(String label)`	Void	Put a new text label on the item
	Useful MenuComponent Interface	
`getFont()`	Font	Not often used
`getParent()`	MenuContainer	May need to be used with a cast
`setFont(Font f)`	Void	Not often used

Building Menus

To create the menu shown in Figure 10.1 we used the code in Listing 10.1.

Listing 10.1 Basic menu.

```
class Message extends Frame {
    Menubar menubar;          // the Menu Bar itself
    Menu menu1,menu2;          // two drop down menus
    TextField l;              // just some component for the Frame

    Message() {
        setTitle("Cal7 Message Frame");
        setLayout(new BorderLayout());
        l = new TextField("no change yet to input TextField!",36);
        l.disable();
        l.setForeground(Color.black);
        add("Center",l);
        pack();

        menubar = new Menubar();
        setMenuBar(menubar);
        menu1 = new Menu("File");
        menubar.add(menu1);
        menu1.add(new MenuItem("Open"));
        menu1.add(new MenuItem("Save"));

        menu2 = new Menu("Edit");
        menubar.add(menu2);

        pack();
        show();
    }
}
```

The Guts of Basic Menus

The simple menu example shown in Figure 10.1 easily handles much of the menu interaction required by typical applications. The Menubar object provides the basic framework for menus; a Menu object corresponds to each entry on the menubar. Each Menu object contains zero or more MenuItem objects that are linked to specific actions in the application.

Menus can be attached only to instances of Frame. The Frame class provides `setMenuBar()` and `remove()` methods to deal with attaching and removing menus.

Under normal use, selection of a menu item is detected in the `Event.ACTION_EVENT` handler. The simplest way to identify a particular menu click is just to compare the `Event.target` object to each MenuItem object in turn.

For instance, to hook the **OPEN** menu item to an open `FileDialog` window, try the following:

```
MenuItem open;          // The OPEN menu item
public boolean action(Event event, Object arg) {
  if (event.target instanceof MenuItem) {
    if (event.target == open) {
      FileDialog fd = new FileDialog((Frame)this,
        "Cal8 Open FileDialog",FileDialog.LOAD);
      fd.show();
      // code to open the file
      return true;
    }
    ...     // other MenuItems
  }
  ...
}
```

An alternative (but inferior) way to determine which menu item we're dealing with is to examine the `arg` object passed into `action()`. Convert `arg` to a String (either explicitly by assignment or implicitly in an if statement) and compare it to the text you placed on each MenuItem. For instance, here's the same comparison using `arg` comparison.

```
    boolean action(Event event, Object arg) {
        if (event.target instanceof MenuItem) {
            if (arg == "Open") {// implicit conversion of the label
to string
                // this is the OPEN menu item.
            }
        }
        return true;
    }
```

The Menu class also provides a small group of methods to obtain menu items by index. The `countItems()` method returns the total number of menu items in a particular Menu object. The `getItem()` method returns the `MenuComponent` at a particular index. Note that where submenus are involved, you must check whether the returned component is a MenuItem or Menu object.

While menus can be interrogated by index, there is no functionality provided in AWT for leaving placeholders in the menubar. If a menu is removed from the menubar, the remaining menus slide over to fill the gap. There is also no capability for adding a menu between other menus. The only reasonably nice solution is to instantiate another menubar, add the menus in the new order, and run `Frame.remove(oldmenu)` and `Frame.setMenuBar(newmenu)` to show the new menu. Depending on the platform, some superfluous window redrawing may occur.

Submenus and Proper Event Handling

While the simple menus already described do provide enough capability for most applications, the AWT does provide for a few variations. The first extension we will discuss involves nested menus. Java calls this feature a submenu, and it is commonly used by applications that provide several variations of a single operation. For example in Figure 10.2, we show a submenu with menu items of **England**, **USA**, **Canada**, and **Australia**. This could be used to select a particular character encoding or perhaps a nation-specific dictionary.

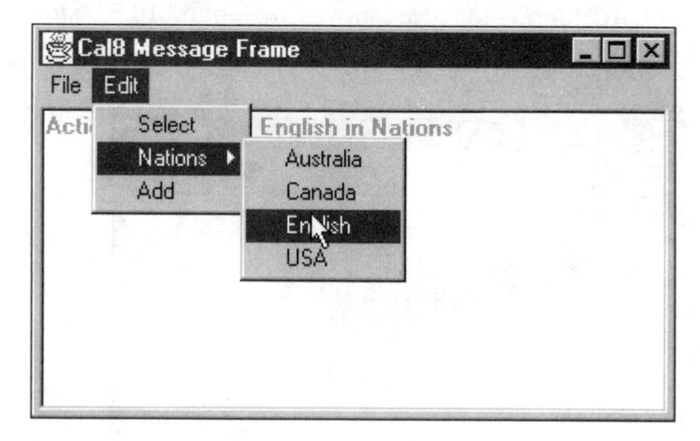

Figure 10.2 Submenu.

To add a submenu, merely call the `Menu.add()` method with the new menu object you've created for the submenu. Then use the same techniques we've already learned and add the menu items to the submenu.

```
Menu encoding = new Menu("Nations");
...
menu2.add(new MenuItem("Select"));
menu2.add(new MenuItem("Add"));
menu2.add(encoding);          // the submenu
encoding.add(new MenuItem("Australia"));
```

```
encoding.add(new MenuItem("Canada"));
encoding.add(new MenuItem("England"));
encoding.add(new MenuItem("USA"));
```

In our example, the user can click on any of the four nations. Our program handled each menu selection, but there was no feedback on which of the particular menu items was on or off. What we'd like to see is a positive indication of which nation is the current nation. The AWT provides a special subclass of MenuItem called CheckboxMenuItem (notice that the *b* in box is lowercase). If we substitute the Checkbox menu items for the standard menu items as shown in Figure 10.3, each click will flip the state of the Checkbox between `true` and `false`.

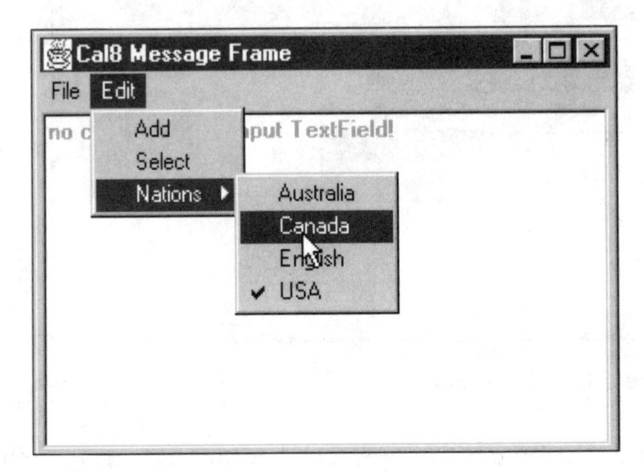

Figure 10.3 CheckboxMenuItem.

While this allows us to see what state each MenuItem is in, it doesn't let us treat a group of MenuItems as a one and only one group. Because you can be in only one of the four nations at a time, we show the following code fragments to demonstrate one way of doing this. You'll probably want to develop a custom class to handle, but for our purposes we'll just show you the not so object-oriented method. First, we'll create an array of four CheckboxMenuItems with the nations as labels;

we'll then add them to the submenu. Note that we also set **USA** as the default for regional purposes; the default state of CheckboxMenuItem is `false`.

```
encoding = new Menu("Nations");
menu2.add(encoding);

encoding.add(new CheckboxMenuItem("Australia"));
encoding.add(new CheckboxMenuItem("Canada"));
encoding.add(new CheckboxMenuItem("England"));
encoding.add(new CheckboxMenuItem("USA"));
((CheckboxMenuItem)encoding.getItem(3)).setState(true);
```

Note the last line of this excerpt. Because `setState()` is a CheckboxMenuItem method and `getItem()` returns a generic MenuComponent we cast the result of the `getItem()` call to the appropriate class to keep the Java compiler happy.

When the submenu is selected, the four choices are displayed, with **USA** checked `true`. To make sure that only one of our four nations is selected at a time, we'll add some code to `action()` to reset the other boxes. Note that we could have used a constant of 4 and an array of nations to contain the items. Using the MenuComponent method `getParent()` and the Menu methods `countItems()` and `getItem()` means that our code doesn't really need to know or care how many menu items actually exist.

```
if (mi instanceof CheckboxMenuItem) {
    int i,j,count;
    Menu parent = (Menu)mi.getParent();
    count  = parent.countItems();    // number of cells
    for (i=0;i < count;i++) {
        if (parent.getItem(i) == (CheckboxMenuItem)mi) {
            for(j=0;j< count;j++) { // check others
                if (j != i) {
((CheckboxMenuItem)parent.getItem(j)).setState(false);
```

```
                    // tell someone
                }
            }
        }
    }
}
```

Note that we've repeated our use of a cast to convince the compiler to accept the call to `setState()`. We have no real problem doing this, since we grew up with assembly language and C, but purists might want to work out how to get rid of the cast.

Help Menus

Most platforms support a special menu type for on-line help. The AWT `MenuBar` class allows a program to designate one menu on the menubar as the help menu. Calling `MenuBar.setHelpMenu()` causes the passed Menu object to become the designated help menu. The `getHelpMenu` method returns the `Menu` object that was previously designated the help menu. If there isn't a help menu, the `getHelpMenu` method returns `null`.

On a few platforms, the help menu looks just like all the other menus. However, some windowing systems place the help menu at one end of the menubar, to make it more distinctive. Some platforms may also have a keyboard shortcut to activate the help menu. Otherwise, help menus behave just like normal menus.

Tear-Off Menus

AWT menus can also be designated as tear-off menus. Depending on the platform, a tear-off menu can hang around on the screen separate from the rest of the menubar. To create a tear-off menu, the AWT provides a menu constructor with an optional `boolean tearOff`. If `tearOff` is `true`, the menu qualifies as a tear-off menu.

Figure 10.4 is an example of our nations submenu operating as a tear-off.

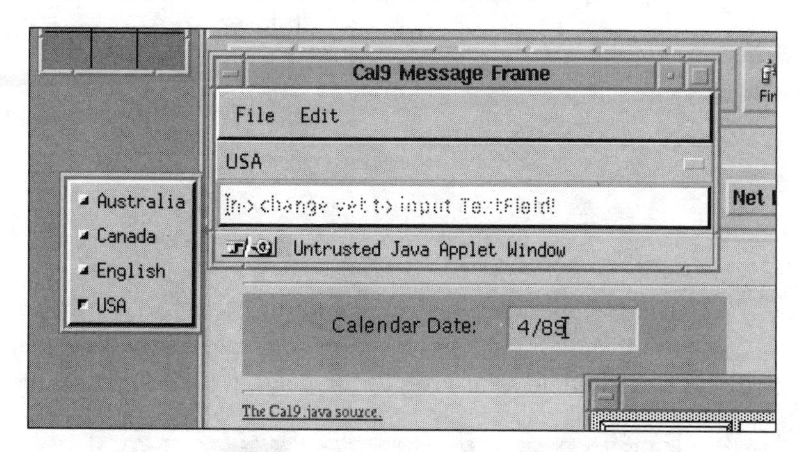

Figure 10.4 Tear-off menu.

On Windows 95 (and NT), tear-off doesn't work. Because Microsoft doesn't support tear off menus in the native windowing system, the AWT exception-to-the-rule mechanism kicks in again and implements tear-off menus on UNIX.

Disabling and Enabling Menu Items

Often, applications don't allow certain operations until other operations have been performed. One of the most common is to not allow saving before the document has been modified. To add this feature, use the `disable()` method to turn off those menu items that are not valid. On the platforms we're aware of, the disabled menu items are usually lowlighted. Once your code has something that is capable of being saved, you would call the `enable()` method on the **SAVE** menu item. If the user then clicks on the item, your `action()` method will receive the event as we've discussed.

Menu Cosmetics

Two last menu capabilities are strictly cosmetic. The `Menu.addSeparator()` method allows us to add a platform-dependent separator between menu items. We'll add the separator between our normal Edit menu items and the nations item, as shown in Figure 10.5.

```
menu2.add(new MenuItem("Select"));
menu2.add(new MenuItem("Add"));
menu2.addSeparator();
menu2.add(encoding);          // the submenu
```

The other menu feature is setting the font with `setFont()`. Because we don't discuss fonts until later in the book (and menus with multiple fonts are silly anyway), we'll ignore this method.

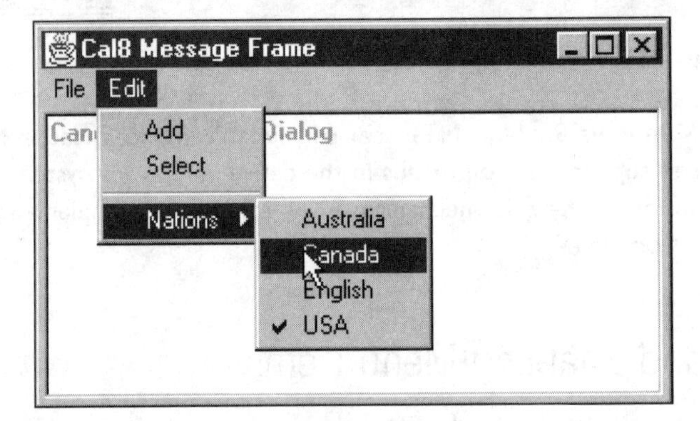

Figure 10.5 Menu separator.

Choices

As we've seen, the AWT supports traditional menus relatively well. There are certainly a few hiccups in the various platform implementations, but most features are available. However, one of the common problems found in application programming is not addressed by menus (on any platform).

Often there are things going on in a window that almost fit into a menu. For instance, the nations submenu works fine if we're setting the language to be used by an application. However, if we really want to select the origin or destination of a trip, we wouldn't put the choices in a menu. The AWT implements a class called Choice that provides similar capabilities.

We'll talk about Choice in this chapter, rather than later, because it can be used to implement simple menu-like behavior in a panel. Since applets use panels almost exclusively, Choice is as close as AWT will let us get to menus in WWW browsers. If you're desperate to have a real menu, you'll have to create a frame outside of the browser window and do things there. However, that's definitely not the most user-friendly method.

Table 10.2 Choice Interface

Method	Returns	Notes
Useful Choice Interface Choice()		Creates an empty choice box; use addItem() to populate
addItem(String item)	Void	
countItems()	Int	Useful for interrogating the Choice contents
getItem(int index)	String	From 0 to countItems() -1
getSelectedIndex()	Int	Tells which item is selected by number
getSelectedItem()	String	Returns the selected item's text
select(int pos)	Void	Make a particular cell the default
select(String str)	Void	Highlight the first cell with text equal to str

Creating a Choice in a Panel (or Window) is similar to creating a menu. First, instantiate the Choice object, add it to the container, and then invoke addItem() for each item in the list of Choices. Because Choices inherit from Components, all the normal colors, fonts, and other neat features work fine.

```
Choice choice = new Choice();
```

```
choice.addItem("Australia");
choice.addItem("Canada");
choice.addItem("England");
choice.addItem("USA");
choice.select("USA"); // set the default nation
```

Unfortunately, the AWT allows you to populate only the Choice object with text strings. For WWW use, it would be nice to support embedded images in each item. We hope that Java GUI-builders will one day provide such a class (if we don't get to it first).

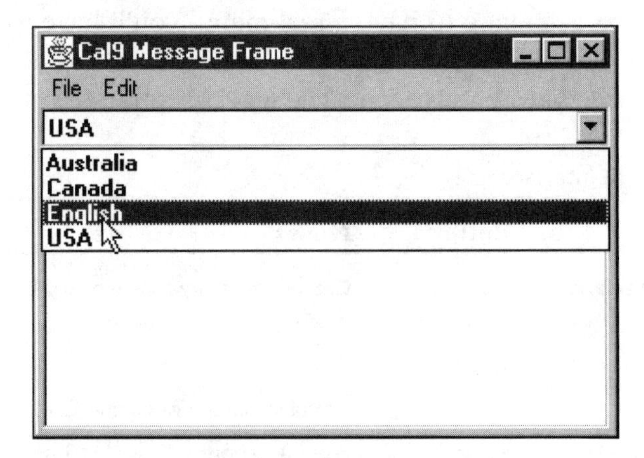

Figure 10.6 Basic choice box.

One interesting tidbit associated with the methods for this class is that a `select(String str)` method exists. Since you can have as many items as you want and the contents are irrelevant, what happens if you have more than one item with the same text contents? The current implementation selects the first matching cell. However, the API doesn't specify this. Hopefully, it will never matter to you.

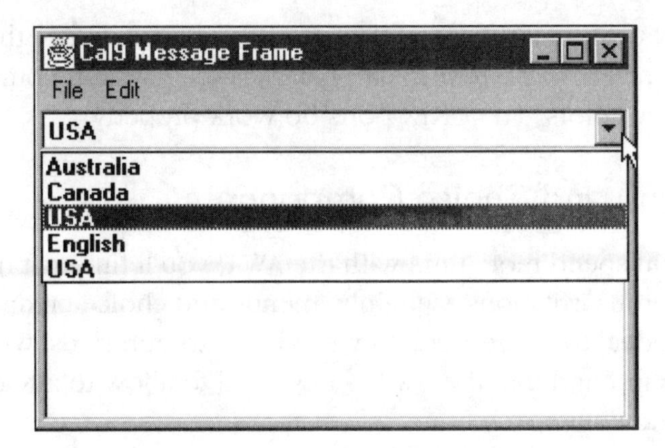

Figure 10.7 Choice.

To handle the events associated with `Choice`, the code looks much like any other `Event.ACTION_EVENT` handler. We've once again used a cast to keep the compiler convinced about the appropriateness of the method we use. Note that `getSelectedItem()` returns a String with the contents of the item.

```
    if (event.target instanceof Choice) {
        setText("The new Nation is " +
((Choice)event.target).getSelectedItem());
        return true;
    }
```

While you can't set individual items to specific fonts or colors easily, you can specify the attributes of the `Choicebox` as a whole. For instance,

```
        choiceMenu = new Choice();
        choiceMenu.setBackground(Color.red);
        choiceMenu.setForeground(Color.cyan);
        choiceMenu.addItem("Australia");
        choiceMenu.addItem("Canada");
```

Of course, on Windows we've already discovered that AWT can't make some of the native windowing system components change colors. The UNIX ports do work properly.

Missing Menu and Choice Components

As you spend more time with the AWT, you'll find that there are numerous irritations. Certainly, menus and choice boxes leave a great deal to be desired. As we say this to ourselves, we should keep in mind that the AWT is designed to allow totally portable programming.

Some of the Win32 UI features are not supported by AWT; for instance, multiple selections don't work in the choice box (or much of anywhere else). Also, tear-off menus aren't part of Win32, so the AWT just lies and leaves the menu attached (disappearing when you release the mouse button).

The other "feature" that is slightly irritating is the lack of menu support in applets. While most of today's applets don't really need menus and it would require intimate knowledge of the implicit window created by each browser, we'd still like to see it added.

CHAPTER 11

Drawing

- Drawing Interface
- Useful Drawing Interface
- Drawing Examples
- Graphics Primitives
- Double-Buffered Drawing
- A Fun Drawing Example
- Moiré Drawing Example

Drawing Interface

The AWT provides two classes (Graphics and Component) that Java programs can use to draw graphics and text. The Component class has been used throughout the book, because it also provides the base for all of the GUI classes we've discussed (except Menus). In this chapter we'll focus on the Graphics class: what it provides, how it is used, and what it's limitations are. We'll show examples of mixing text, line graphics, and images. We'll also provide a glimpse into a couple of really nice Java applets that make extensive use of the drawing capabilities of the AWT.

We have already talked about drawing text within a graphics context in Chapter 9. In this chapter, we will assume you have read Chapter 9.

Useful Drawing Interface

Table 11.1 outlines some of the useful methods used when drawing text, line graphics, and images. Most of this interface is provided by the Graphics class.

Table 11.1 Drawing Interface

Method	Returns	Notes
	Graphics Interface	
`graphics()`	Private abstract	Graphics is an abstract class. We'll focus on its use in Panel and Canvas objects.
`clearRect(int x, int y, int width, int height)`	Abstract void	Clears the specified rectangle to the background color
`clipRect(int x, int y, int width, int height)`	Abstract void	Sets a clipping rectangle in this context

continued...

Method	Returns	Notes
`copyArea(int x, int y, int width, int height, int dx, int d y)`	Abstract void	Copies a rectangle to a new location based on the offset
`create()`	Abstract graphics	Creates a new graphics context that is identical to the current context
`create(int x, int y, int width, int height)`	Graphics	Creates a new graphics context that is translated by x and y and is sized by width and height
`dispose()`	Abstract void	Releases resources in the native windowing system and the component peer
`draw3DRect(int x, int y, int width, int height, boolean raised)`	void	Draws a raised (highlighted) 3D rectangle
`drawArc(int x, int y, int width, int height, int startAngle, int arcAngle)`	Abstract void	Draws an arc centered on (x,y) that is `width` wide and `height` tall
`drawBytes(byte data[], int offset, int length, int x, int y)`	void	Draws text that is the graphic representation of the selected character values in `bytes[]`
`drawChars(char data[], int offset, int length, int x, int y)`	void	Draws text that is the graphic representation of the selected character values in `data[]`
`drawImage(Image img, int x, int y, Color bgcolor, ImageObserver observer)`	Abstract boolean	Draws image at (x,y); transparent pixels are drawn in the `bgcolor`
`drawImage(Image img, int x, int y, ImageObserver observer)`	Abstract boolean	Draws image at (x,y); transparent pixels leave destination pixels as they were

continued...

Method	Returns	Notes
`drawImage(Image img, int x, int y, int width, int height, Color bgcolor, ImageObserver observer)`	Abstract boolean	Draws image inside the rectangle, scaling if necessary; transparent pixels are drawn in the `bgcolor`
`drawImage(Image img, int x, int y, int width, int height, ImageObserver observer)`	Abstract boolean	Draws image inside the rectangle; transparent pixels leave destination pixels as they were
`drawLine(int x1, int y1, int x2, int y2)`	Abstract void	Draw a line from (x1,y1) to (x2,y2) in this context's clipping rectangle
`drawOval(int x, int y, int width, int height)`	Abstract void	Draws a circle or ellipse that fits in the rectangle described by (x,y) that is `width` by `height`
`drawPolygon(int xPoints[], int yPoints[], int nPoints)`	Abstract void	Draws lines through the array of points
`drawPolygon(Polygon p)`	void	Draws a polygon that is specified by the argument
`drawRect(int x, int y, int width, int height)`	void	Draws a rectangle bounded by (x,y) and (x+width,y+height)
`drawRoundRect(int x, int y, int width, int height, int arcWidth, int arcHeight)`	Abstract void	Draws a rectangle as in `drawRect()` but with rounded corners
`drawString(String str, int x, int y)`	Abstract void	Draws text that is the graphic representation of the selected character values in `str`
`fill3DRect(int x, int y, int width, int height, boolean raised)`	void	Same as `draw3DRect()` but filled with the current color

continued...

Method	Returns	Notes
fillArc(int x, int y, int width, int height, int startAngle, int arcAngle)	Abstract void	Same as drawArc() but filled with the current color
fillOval(int x, int y, int width, int height)	Abstract void	Same as drawOval() but filled with the current color
fillPolygon(int xPoints[], int yPoints[], int nPoints)	Abstract void	Same as drawPolygon() but filled with the current color
fillPolygon(Polygon p)	void	Same as drawPolygon(Polygon p) but filled with the current color
fillRect(int x, int y, int width, int height)	Abstract void	Same as drawRect() but filled with the current color
fillRoundRect(int x, int y, int width, int height, int arcWidth, int arcHeight)	Abstract void	Same as drawRoundRect() but filled with the current color
finalize()	void	Makes sure dispose() is called when the last reference to the context is removed
getClipRect()	Abstract e Rectangl	Returns the rectangle that bounds the clipping rectangle
getColor()	Abstract Color	Gets the current drawing color for this context
getFont()	Abstract Font	Gets the current drawing font for this context
getFontMetrics()	FontMetrics	Gets the current font metrics for this context
getFontMetrics(Font f)	Abstract FontMetrics	Gets the font metrics that would be used in this context, if the passed font were the current font

continued...

Method	Returns	Notes
`setColor(Color c)`	Abstract void	Sets the current drawing color for this context
`setFont(Font font)`	Abstract void	Sets the current font for this context
`setPaintMode()`	Abstract void	Sets the paint mode to write in the current color
`setXORMode(Color c1)`	Abstract void	Sets the paint mode to XOR; pixels in the current color are changed to the passed color, other pixels are changed unpredictably, but can be restored by drawing them again (typical XOR operation)
`translate(int x, int y)`	Abstract void	Sets the current origin to (x,y) in the coordinate system in place when this context was created
	Point Interface	
`Point(int x,int y)`		Creates a point object with (x,y) coordinates
`equals(Object arg)`	boolean	If the argument is a point and the coordinates are equal to this object's (x,y), then returns true
`move(int x,int y)`	void	Replaces this point's coordinates with (x,y)
`translate(int dx,int dy)`	void	Moves this point to (x+dx,y+dy)
	Rectangle Interface	
`Rectangle(), Rectangle (Dimension d), Rectangle(int width, int height), Rectangle(int x, int y, int width, int height), Rectangle(Point p), Rectangle(Point p, Dimension d)`		Various forms of creating a rectangle

continued...

Method	Returns	Notes
add(int newx,int newy)	void	Resizes this rectangle to the smallest rectangle that contains the point and the previous rectangle
add(Point p)	void	Resizes this rectangle to the smallest rectangle that contains the point and the previous rectangle
add(Rectangle r)	void	Resizes this rectangle to the smallest rectangle that contains the both the original rectangle and the passed rectangle
equals(Object arg)	boolean	If arg is a rectangle that has the same bounds as this rectangle, returns true
grow(int h, int v)	void	Grows the rectangle by 2*h in width, and 2*v vertically. The result is a resized rectangle, centered on the previous location
inside(int x,int y)	boolean	Is this point inside the rectangle
intersection (Rectangle r)	Rectangle	Returns the rectangle that is the intersection of the object and the passed rectangle
intersects(Rectangle r)	boolean	Do these two rectangles intersect?
isEmpty()	boolean	Is the width or height <= 0?
move(int x,int y)	void	Relocates this rectangle to (x,y)
reshape(int x,int y, int width,int height)	void	Basically, recreates the rectangle with the new size and position
resize(int width, int height)	void	Replaces the size of the rectangle
translate(int dx,int dy)	void	Moves the rectangle to new coordinates (x+dx,y+dy)
union(Rectangle r)	Rectangle	Returns the smallest rectangle that completely encloses this object and the passed rectangle

continued...

Method	Returns	Notes
	Polygon Interface	
`Polygon(), Polygon(int xpoints[], int ypoints[], int npoints)`		Creates a polygon
`addPoint(int x,int y)`	void	Adds a point to the polygon
`getBoundingBox()`	Rectangle	Returns the smallest rectangle that encloses the list of points in the polygon
`inside(int x, int y)`	boolean	Is the point within the bounds of the polygon as defined by the list of points
	Dimension Interface	
`Dimension(), Dimension (Dimension d), Dimension (int width, int height)`		Creates an object that can be used wherever bounding width and height are needed.

Many of the `Graphics` methods are defined as abstract; note that all these methods are implemented somewhere in the component, its peer, or the native windowing system. Under normal circumstances, you may use all of these methods.

The primitive objects (`Rectangle`, `Point`, `Dimension`, and `Polygon`) make their bounding coordinates public as integer values. This can improve performance (as well as make the code more readable) since you can say `Point.x` or `Dimension.width` in expressions.

`Point` provides `x` and `y` coordinates. `Dimension` provides `width` and `height`. `Rectangle` provides `x`, `y`, `width`, and `height`. `Polygon` provides `npoints`, `xpoints[]`, and `ypoints[]`.

Drawing Examples

With all the methods already listed, you might think that drawing in Java is complicated. The truth is, it's easy to draw simple line objects; the complex part is understanding how to deal with multiple graphics contexts, clipping, and translation, while still producing an application that doesn't flicker, perform poorly, or take forever to load. While we can't go into the detail that all these topics really deserve, this chapter does cover the basic principles.

Just for fun, we're going to use an image produced for Chapter 9 as a drawing example. Figure 11.1 demonstrates fonts, colors, text drawing, and simple line drawing. It also demonstrates clipping and sizing of objects.

Figure 11.1 Drawing example.

There are numerous drawing activities demonstrated in this example image. First, there is the obvious `drawString()` operation. Supporting the text, there are calls to get and set the font and font metrics. There are also calls to construct a new graphics context with a different clipping region. There are calls to draw the light gray lines showing the advance for each character and the metrics for the particular font, style, and size. Finally, there are a set of `drawString()` and `drawLine()` operations to annotate the larger text image appropriately.

We're going to present the entire program that produced the image in Figure 11.1. As we walk through the code with you, we'll try to mention alternatives to each concept and talk about some performance-related issues.

First, we have the normal AWT import and constructors. Notice that we're subclassing `Frame`, so this example won't work as an applet. The Frame receives a title based on the string passed to the constructor.

```
import java.awt.*;
public class FontPicture extends Frame {
    FontPicture() {
        this("");
    }

    FontPicture(String s) {
        super(s);
    }
```

This is the main program. It creates a new `FontPicture` frame and gives it a size that's reasonably large (640 x 400 pixels).

```
    public static void main(String args[]) {
        FontPicture f = new FontPicture("Font Setting");
        f.resize(640,640);
        f.show();
    }
```

The `paint` method is where all the real work is done. In double-buffered drawing schemes, most of the work is done in the `update()` method. We're doing a static drawing here, so we do everything in `paint()`

```
public void paint(Graphics g) {
    int i,j;
    Dimension d = size(); // the size of the Frame
    FontMetrics fm;       // a place for the primary
                          // font's font metrics
    Font f;               // a place for the primary font
    Font annotation;      // a second font, for the
                          // annotations
    FontMetrics afm;      // metrics for the annotations
    Graphics g2;          // a graphics context for the
                          // clipped primary text
    int advances[];       // the character advances for fm
    int points = 128;     // a huge font to start with
    int leftmargin = 10;  // left margin is 10 pixels from
                          // edge of frame
    int topmargin = 10;   // top margin is 10 pixels from
                          // top edge
    int rightmargin;      // we'll calculate the right
                          // margin
    int baseline;         // we'll calculate each baseline
    int advance;          // the pixel width of the string
    int c;                // contains one character for
                          // charWidth()
    String s;             // will be "FontMetrics"
    String comments[] = {"Ascent",
                          "Baseline",
                          "Descent",
                          "Leading",
                          "Advance"};  // this is the
                                       // annotation text
    Toolkit tk = Toolkit.getDefaultToolkit();
    String fontList[] = tk.getFontList();  // the list of
                                           // fonts
```

After we allocate all the variables and initialize most of the static ones, we begin to calculate the annotation placement and the margins.

```
baseline = topmargin;  // start at the top of the page
annotation = new Font("Helvetica",Font.PLAIN,10);
g.setFont(annotation); // set the annotation text
afm = g.getFontMetrics();
rightmargin = d.width-1 afm.stringWidth(comments[1]) 20;
```

Next, we create a new graphics context and set the clipping rectangle width to `TT>rightmargin-leftmargin`. This allows us to draw without regard to size. We know that anything drawn will be automatically clipped at the edges of the `g2` graphics context. The annotations are drawn into the `g` graphics context associated with the Frame, while the main text in `s` ("FontMetrics") will be drawn into the `g2` context.

```
g2 = g.create();      // a second graphics area
g2.clipRect(leftmargin-1,0,rightmargin,d.height-1);
```

Now that we've decided how much room we have, we need to pick a font that fills the `g2` clipping rectangle. Our code uses a for loop that uses only values 0 and 2 (corresponding to `Font.PLAIN` and `Font.ITALIC`). We originally used all four type styles (plain, bold, italic, and bold-italic), but the image was too big and complicated for our fonts and colors example.

We use `fontList[2]` which is "Times Roman" on Win32 and UNIX, but the code will run no matter what font is used. We start with `points` equal to 128 (huge!) and get the character widths (advances) with a call to `fm.getWidths()` (remember that `fm` is the primary font, not the annotations font `afm`). `getWidths()` returns a 256 cell array of `ints` that contains the width of each character (of the first 256 characters in your font).

```
for(j=0;j<3;j+=2) {
```

```
f = new Font(fontList[2], j, points);
g2.setFont(f);
fm = g2.getFontMetrics();
advances = fm.getWidths();
s = "FontMetrics";
```

Now we calculate the baseline for this font, style, and size. The first time through, the baseline is set to the top margin. We always add the ascent to the previous baseline to get the drawing location for this line.

```
baseline += fm.getAscent();
```

Next, we set the color to light gray and draw the annotation line for the baseline, the ascent, the descent, and the leading. These are the light gray horizontal lines on the example image. Note that we use the new graphics context, with the width set to the width of the frame; the lines are actually wider than the context and are clipped automatically by the graphics context. This example would be better if we used the width of the graphics context, but we wanted to show that clipping really works.

```
g2.setColor(Color.lightGray);
g2.drawLine(0,baseline,d.width-1,baseline);
g2.drawLine(0,baseline-fm.getAscent(),
    d.width-1,baseline-fm.getAscent());    // top
g2.drawLine(0,baseline+fm.getDescent(),
    d.width-1,baseline+fm.getDescent());   // bottom
g2.drawLine(0,baseline+fm.getDescent()+fm.getLeading(),
    d.width-1, baseline+fm.getDescent()+ fm.getLeading());
    // spacing
```

After the horizontal lines are drawn, we need to set the basic advance. Since we're always left adjusting text in this example, the left margin works fine for a starting point. We then draw a line up the left margin, that is the height of the line (the total height is obtained with `getHeight()`, or by adding advance, descent, and leading). We then use a for loop to walk through each character in the string `s` ("FontMetrics") and draw a vertical line at the advance position of the character. The advance is found by taking the advance position of the previous letter in the string and adding this character's advance. The vertical annotation line reaches from the ascent to the descent of this line of text.

```
advance = leftmargin;     // picked a left margin
g2.drawLine(advance,baseline-fm.getAscent(),
advance,baseline+fm.getDescent());
for(i=0;i<s.length();i++) {
    c = s.charAt(i);     // get the first character
    advance+= advances[c];
    g2.drawLine(advance,baseline-fm.getAscent(),
    advance,baseline+fm.getDescent());
}
```

At this point, we've drawn the entire grid of light gray annotation lines for this particular line of text. We now need to draw the primary text. First, we set the color to black (it was light gray) and call `drawString()` to draw the text "FontMetrics" starting at `(leftmargin,baseline)` in the `g2` graphics context.

```
g2.setColor(Color.black);
g2.drawString(s,leftmargin,baseline);
```

The image in Figure 11.1 has been resized to fit in the pages of this book. If you run the example on your system, the entire string "FontMetrics" is drawn.

The first time through the `j` loop, we annotate the ascent line with the string "Ascent". We don't add this annotation on other lines, since the leading line of this text line is the same as the ascent line of the next. We then draw the other annotations ("Baseline", "Descent", and "Leading") Note that we draw all these annotations onto the original graphics context, which is the same size as the frame. If we had used `g2` instead of `g`, all of our text would have been clipped, since the origin of the string (`rightmargin+10`) is outside the `g2` context. The text of the annotations is obtained from the `comments[]` array.

```
if (j==0)
    g.drawString(comments[0],rightmargin+10, baseline-
            fm.getAscent());
g.drawString(comments[1],rightmargin+10,baseline);
g.drawString(comments[2],rightmargin+10,
            baseline+fm.getDescent()-2);
g.drawString(comments[3],rightmargin+10,
            baseline+fm.getDescent()+fm.getLeading()+2)
            ;
```

We now will draw the single "Advance" marks that show the width of the first character of each line. The x location of the right-hand side of the first character is equal to the left margin plus the width of the character.

```
advance= leftmargin + advances[s.charAt(0)];
```

Next we draw the small black tick mark at the left margin below the character. Then we draw the string "Advance" centered between the left margin and the advance of the first character. Finally, we draw the right-hand tick mark at the advance of the first character (also the left margin of the second character).

```
g.drawLine(leftmargin,baseline + fm.getDescent() +
    fm.getLeading() + afm.getHeight(),leftmargin,
    baseline + fm.getDescent()-2);
g.drawString(comments[4],((advance-
afm.stringWidth(comments[4]))/2) + leftmargin,
     baseline + fm.getDescent() + fm.getLeading() +
     afm.getHeight());
g.drawLine(advance,baseline + fm.getDescent() +
    fm.getLeading() + afm.getHeight(),advance, baseline
    + fm.getDescent()-2);
```

The last thing we do is advance the baseline to match with what we believe to be the next line's ascent line. Remember that the baseline + the descent + the leading it the same as the ascent line of the next line. When we iterate through the `j` loop, we'll advance the baseline to match the metrics of the next line of text. This way, each line can have different fonts, styles, and sizes and still appear properly spaced.

```
            baseline += fm.getLeading() + fm.getDescent();
        }
    }
```

The last little bit of code causes the frame to be sized to 400 x 120 pixels. You would want to calculate this number in most applications, and in fact, our main program resized the frame once, to 640 x 400. Our examples are contrived; you will want to think through your presentation and appropriately compute your sizing.

```
    public Dimension minimumSize() {
        return new Dimension(400,120);
    }
    public Dimension preferredSize() {
        return new Dimension(400,120);
    }
}
```

We hope that the preceding example gave you a fair amount to consider. Nothing we did was that complicated, but we did show you the basics of all drawing in the AWT. We talked about multiple overlapping graphics contexts, multiple colors, and multiple primitive drawing operations. The remaining drawing primitives are covered in the next section.

Graphics Primitives

If you look through the list of methods provided by the Graphics class, you'll find that a large number deal with drawing primitive shapes. The shapes available directly through `Graphics` include:

- line
- rectangle
- polygon
- ellipse (oval)
- circle
- arc (circular or elliptical)
- 3D rectangle
- rounded rectangle

Each of the primitives, which cover an area (except for line), also have a filled variant. The filled versions paint the entire covered area of the object. Figure 11.2 is an example image containing each of the AWT primitives.

We will go through the guts of the example code that generated Figure 11.2 in the following paragraphs. Here is the complete program (an application, not an applet) so you can recognize where the code excerpts we detail fall in the program.

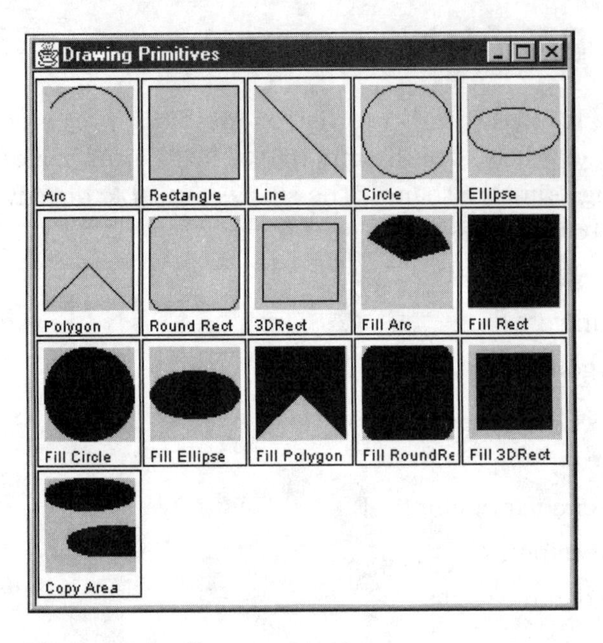

Figure 11.2 Drawing primitives.

```
import java.awt.*;
public class DrawingPrim extends Frame {
    static final int ARC=0;
    static final int RECT=1;
    static final int LINE=2;
    static final int CIRCLE=3;
    static final int ELLIPSE=4;
    static final int POLYGON=5;
    static final int ROUNDRECT=6;
    static final int THREEDRECT=7;
    static final int FILLARC=8;
    static final int FILLRECT=9;
    static final int FILLCIRCLE=10;
    static final int FILLELLIPSE=11;
    static final int FILLPOLYGON=12;
    static final int FILLROUNDRECT=13;
```

```
static final int FILLTHREEDRECT=14;
static final int COPYAREA=15;
static String comments[] = { "Arc", "Rectangle", "Line",
"Circle",
        "Ellipse", "Polygon", "Round Rect", "3DRect",
        "Fill Arc", "Fill Rect", "Fill Circle", "Fill
        Ellipse",
        "Fill Polygon", "Fill RoundRect", "Fill 3DRect" ,
        "Copy Area"};
static final int CELLSPERROW = 5;
int width,height,offset,voffset;
Font commentary;
FontMetrics cfm;
static final Toolkit tk = Toolkit.getDefaultToolkit();
static final String fontList[] = tk.getFontList();
DrawingPrim() {
    this("");
}
DrawingPrim(String s) {
    super(s);
    height = 60;     // some generic size for the primitive //
                     to draw in
    width = 60;      // some generic size for the primitive //
                     to draw in
    offset = 70;     // how far apart each primitive is (in //
                     the frame)
    commentary = new Font("Helvetica",Font.PLAIN,10);
    setFont(commentary);     // for our annotations
    voffset = offset + 30;   // initial distance between
                             // rows
}
public static void main(String args[]) {
    DrawingPrim f = new DrawingPrim("Drawing Primitives");
    f.resize(f.preferredSize().width,
    f.preferredSize().height);
     f.show();
}
```

```
public void paint(Graphics g) {
    int i,j;
    int vrow = 0;
    Dimension d = size();
    g.setFont(commentary);
    cfm = g.getFontMetrics();
    voffset = height + cfm.getHeight() + 10;
    g.drawRect(0,0,d.width-1,d.height-1);
    for(i=0;i<comments.length;i++) {
        Graphics g2;
        int top;
        if ((i!=0) && ((i%CELLSPERROW) == 0))
            vrow++;
        top = 5 + (voffset*vrow);
        g2 = g.create(((i-(CELLSPERROW*vrow))*offset)+7,
                       top+5,
                       width,height+cfm.getHeight()+5);
        g.drawRect(((i-(CELLSPERROW*vrow))*offset)+2,top,
                       offset-2, height+cfm.getHeight()+7);
        g2.setColor(Color.black);
        g2.drawString(comments[i],0, height+cfm.getAscent()+3);
        g2.setColor(Color.lightGray);
        g2.fillRect(0,0,width,height);
        g2.setColor(Color.black);
        switch(i) {
        case LINE:
            g2.drawLine(0,0,width-1,height-1);
            break;
        case RECT:
            g2.drawRect(0,0,width-1,height-1);
            break;
        case ARC:
            g2.drawArc(0,0,width-1,height-1,15,135);
            break;
        case CIRCLE:
```

```
        g2.drawOval(0,0,width-1,height-1);
        break;
    case ELLIPSE:
        g2.drawOval(0,height/4,width-1,height/2);
        break;
    case POLYGON:
        {
        int xp[] = { 0,width-1,width-1,width/2,0,0};
        int yp[] = { 0,0,height-1,height/2,
        height-1,0};
        Polygon p = new Polygon(xp,yp,xp.length);
            g2.drawPolygon(p);
        }
        break;
    case ROUNDRECT:
        g2.drawRoundRect(0,0,width-1,height-1,20,20);
        break;
    case THREEDRECT:
        g2.draw3DRect(5,5,width-11,height-11,true);
        break;
    case FILLARC:
        g2.fillArc(0,0,width-1,height-1,15,135);
        break;
    case FILLRECT:
        g2.fillRect(0,0,width-1,height-1);
        break;
    case FILLCIRCLE:
        g2.fillOval(0,0,width-1,height-1);
        break;
    case FILLELLIPSE:
        g2.fillOval(0,height/4,width-1,height/2);
        break;
    case FILLPOLYGON:
        {
            int xp[] = { 0,width-1,width-1,width/2,0, 0};
```

```
                        int yp[] = { 0,0,height-1,height/2,
                        height-1,0};
                        Polygon p = new Polygon(xp,yp,xp.length);
                        g2.fillPolygon(p);
                    }
                    break;
                case FILLROUNDRECT:
                    g2.fillRoundRect(0,0,width-1,height-1,20,20);
                    break;
                case FILLTHREEDRECT:
                    g2.fill3DRect(5,5,width-11,height-11,true);
                    break;
                case COPYAREA:
                    g2.fillOval(0,0,width-1,height/3);
                    g2.copyArea(0,0,width-1,height/3,width/4,
                    height/2);
                    break;
                default:
                    System.out.println("too many" + i);
                    break;
            }
        }
    }
    public Dimension minimumSize() {
        int rows = (comments.length + CELLSPERROW)/CELLSPERROW;
        return new Dimension(CELLSPERROW*offset+10, rows*voffset);
    }
    public Dimension preferredSize() {
        int rows = (comments.length + CELLSPERROW)/CELLSPERROW;
        return new Dimension(CELLSPERROW*offset+10, rows*voffset);
    }
}
```

We'll skim through most of the startup code, since the `paint` method is where everything important happens. Note that we used a frame for our example. You may use a panel or applet and accomplish the same thing (with small changes here and there).

We first establish a series of constants for use as switch constants. There is one constant per primitive drawing cell in Figure 11.2.

```
static final int ARC=0;
static final int RECT=1;
...
```

Next, we initialize a static array of strings with the titles for each of the primitive drawing cells. We then allocate variables to contain the width, height, horizontal offset, and vertical offset for each drawing cell. We also initialize a CELLSPERROW constant so that all the drawing cells don't end up in one row.

The last group of variables are related to font handling. Note that the font, toolkit, and font list are initialized in the constructor. The font metrics are established in the `paint` method.

The constructor for the class performs all the instance-related setup. First, we call the frame constructor (`super(s)`) to set the title and set up the native resources. Next, we set the height and width to 60 pixels. The cell offset (the distance between individual primitive drawing origins) is 70 pixels. We also set the commentary or annotation font to 10 point Helvetica. Finally, we set the vertical offset temporarily to 100.

The next piece of code is `main()`. This instantiates the frame and resizes it to the best approximation of an appropriate window. It also calls `show()` to display the frame.

When we enter the `paint` method, we are passed a graphics context that covers the entire frame. With this context, we can draw anywhere in the entire frame. The size of the frame (and context) is from `(0,0)` to `(size().width,size().height())`. We obtain this range with a call to `Frame.size()` and place the result in a `Dimension` object. We tend to use `d` for the name of the object; feel free to follow a different convention.

```
public void paint(Graphics g) {
    int i,j;
    Dimension d = size();
```

Next, we set the font for this graphics context. We could have set the font in the constructor but chose to keep it close to the painting, in case we wanted to reuse some of this code for a later example. Note that we did create the font (in commentary) in the constructor, so we just use it here. After we associate a font with this context, we call getFontMetrics() to get the current font metrics. The height of a line of text is added to the height we set in the constructor. We also added a little white space (10 pixels) to give us more room. We will use voffset to calculate the vertical spacing between rows of drawings and to calculate the size of the frame.

```
    g.setFont(commentary);
    cfm = g.getFontMetrics();
    voffset = height + cfm.getHeight() + 10;
```

Next, we use this original graphics context to draw a rectangle at the edge of the frame. Note that you can't see this in the image; if our Container were a Panel, the rectangle would delineate the boundary of our drawing samples.

```
    g.drawRect(0,0,d.width-1,d.height-1);
```

To make size and position calculations easier, we chose to create a new graphics context for each cell of the image. The call to g.create() creates a copy of our original context, with the origin moved to our new offset (i*offset+7,vrow) and the size set to the predefined width and height. Note that i is used to produce the offset as well as to select which primitive will be drawn. Suffice it to say that it counts up and causes each sample primitive drawing to be shifted across the frame. The calculations with vrow and CELLSPERROW are used to develop short rows of cells, rather than one huge horizontal row. The new context is stored in `g2`; the original context is still valid in `g`. We also surround the drawing area with a rectangle that is just outside the drawing area defined by `g2`.

```
for(i=0;i<comments.length;i++) {
    Graphics g2;        // a working context
    int top;            // the top of the drawing
    top = 5;            // offset for whitespace
    if ((i!=0) && ((i%CELLSPERROW) == 0))
        vrow++;
    top = 5 + (voffset*vrow);
    g2 = g.create(((i-(CELLSPERROW*vrow))*offset)+7,top+5,
                        width,height+cfm.getHeight()+5);
    g.drawRect(((i-(CELLSPERROW*vrow))*offset)+2,top,
                        offset-2,height+cfm.getHeight()+7);
```

Now we get into the drawing for each primitive. First, we set the color to black and draw an annotation below the primitive drawing area. Note that we use the new graphics context, and the baseline is simply the height of the primitive space plus the ascent of the current font metric plus 3 pixels of white space.

```
        g2.setColor(Color.black);
        g2.drawString(comments[i],0, height+cfm.getAscent()+3);
```

We set the color to light gray and draw a filled rectangle in that color. This is used to set the background to something that contrasts with the foreground. We then reset the drawing color to black to prepare for the drawing primitive.

```
        g2.setColor(Color.lightGray);
        g2.fillRect(0,0,width,height);
        g2.setColor(Color.black);
```

Now we get down to the primitives themselves. If you remember, we used `i` as a counter to generate the offset. We also used it as a switch to select which primitive to draw in which box. The constants ("ARC", "LINE", etc.) are defined at the top of our class. We'll quickly look at each call.

Remember that we constructed a new graphics context that was sized and positioned so that each primitive has an equal sized cell to draw in. If we were using separate Panel objects and a GridLayout for the various primitive cells, we wouldn't have to create a separate context (each Panel has it's own context with it's own origin and size). The disadvantage to separate Panels in a grid is that we would have to have a custom subclass for each primitive (or do even uglier things) to get them painted properly. Since we don't normally paint one single primitive in a component, it makes sense to learn how to manipulate the context to clip and scale our drawing. In any case, having a context sized and positioned to match the drawing at hand allows us to use simple parameters, like `(0,0)` and `(width-1,height-1)`.

Lines are drawn from `(0,0)` and `(width-1,height-1)` as two end points. Rectangles are drawn starting at (0,0) for a width of `width-1` and height of `height-1` . While these two formats look the same in this example, it's pretty clear that they do different things when the origin is not at (0,0).

```
switch(i) {
case LINE:
    g2.drawLine(0,0,width-1,height-1);
    break;
case RECT:
    g2.drawRect(0,0,width-1,height-1);
    break;
```

Circle and ellipsoids are both variants of AWT ovals. The parameters to `drawOval` are essentially a bounding box for an ellipse. If the deltaX (x1 - x2) is equal to deltaY (y1 - y2) then the oval will be a circle; if deltaX is less than deltaY, then the oval will be a vertical ellipse; if deltaX is more than deltaY, then the oval is a horizontal ellipse (as in the example in Figure 11.2).

```
case CIRCLE:
    g2.drawOval(0,0,width-1,height-1);
    break;
case ELLIPSE:
    g2.drawOval(0,height/4,width-1,height/2);
    break;
```

Arcs are another variant of oval; however, instead of a complete circle or ellipse, arc draws a segment specified by a starting angle (where 0 is due east or 3 o'clock) and continuing counterclockwise for the appropriate arc angle. Our example starts at 15 degrees and covers a 135 degree arc, ending at 170 degrees (northwest).

```
case ARC:
    g2.drawArc(0,0,width-1,height-1,15,135);
    break;
```

For polygons, the single Polygon parameter is produced from a list of X coordinates and Y coordinates. While you can add points one coordinate pair at a time, that's considerably less efficient. Also, there is no constructor that uses an array of Point objects; we presume that this is just another example of the AWT being obtuse. Also, note that the array of points can contain coordinates outside the clipping region of the context. The lines to these points are clipped appropriately. The only oddity in `drawPolygon()` is that it doesn't automatically close the drawing. While this may be useful for some applications, it certainly isn't the normal case. Be sure to close your polygons by repeating your starting coordinates in the last cell of the Polygon object. Note that there is no "get" method for a Polygon object; you have to retain the list of points somewhere else if you think you may want to change them.

```
case POLYGON:
    {
        int xp[] = { 0,width-1,width-1,width/2,0, 0};
        int yp[] = { 0,0,height-1,height/2,
        height-1,0};
        Polygon p = new Polygon(xp,yp,xp.length);
        g2.drawPolygon(p);
    }
    break;
```

A rounded rectangle just has an arc width and arc height parameter that is used to generate the rounded corners. Since width and height are separate (rather than just an arc radius), you can have asymmetrical rounded corners (useful for outlining wide text boxes, for instance).

```
case ROUNDRECT:
    g2.drawRoundRect(0,0,width-1,height-1,20,20);
    break;
```

`draw3DRect` is a relatively crude attempt at raised and lowered rectangles. It is typically used to emulate button behavior or to highlight a particular component. It works, but the effect is not quite as pronounced as other 3D components. Our example insets the 3D effect from the normal drawing cell (that's the 5's and 11's in the following example).

```
case THREEDRECT:
    g2.draw3DRect(5,5,width-11,height-11,true);
    break;
```

The filled variants of all the calls we've already gone through (except `drawLine()`) have the same parameters. The filled area is drawn in the same color as the outline color (in other words, it's a solid fill). If you want to outline the drawing, you should probably try to fill the object one pixel smaller than the desired size and then use the unfilled variant to draw the outline in a different color. If you draw both colors the same size, the final appearance is the same, but there is usually an update flicker. Even if you are double buffering, you are still wasting compute time drawing extra pixels.

```
case FILLARC:
    g2.fillArc(0,0,width-1,height-1,15,135);
    break;
case FILLRECT:
    g2.fillRect(0,0,width-1,height-1);
    break;
case FILLCIRCLE:
    g2.fillOval(0,0,width-1,height-1);
    break;
case FILLELLIPSE:
    g2.fillOval(0,height/4,width-1,height/2);
    break;
case FILLPOLYGON:
    {
        int xp[] = { 0,width-1,width-1,width/2,0, 0};
        int yp[] = { 0,0,height-1,height/2,
        height-1,0};
        Polygon p = new Polygon(xp,yp,xp.length);
        g2.fillPolygon(p);
    }
    break;
case FILLROUNDRECT:
    g2.fillRoundRect(0,0,width-1,height-1,20,20);
    break;
case FILLTHREEDRECT:
    g2.fill3DRect(5,5,width-11,height-11,true);
    break;
```

The last primitive we will cover is the `copyArea()` method. This method provides an easy way to duplicate any given area of space. In our example, we draw a flat ellipse in the top half of the cell and copy the top third of the cell into the bottom right-hand corner of the cell. Note that the destination is clipped properly.

```
case COPYAREA:
    g2.fillOval(0,0,width-1,height/3);
    g2.copyArea(0,0,width-1,height/3,width/4,
    height/2);
    break;
```

The default case is just to let us know whether we broke the constants or comments array. It's purely debugging and doesn't really have any purpose in a production object. We left it in because it shows the value of traditional debugging tools. The Java-approved alternative is to add exception handling around the entire switch (or selected portions) to catch the exceptions and croak more gracefully.

```
default:
    System.out.println("too many");
    break;
}
}
}
```

These are the standard sizing methods. Note that we use CELLSPERROW to calculate the size, along with `offset` and `voffset`. We started out with literal constants sprinkled around and gradually replaced the more useful ones with named constants.

```
public Dimension minimumSize() {
    return new Dimension(CELLSPERROW*offset+10,
    (comments.length/CELLSPERROW)*voffset+0);
}
public Dimension preferredSize() {
```

```
        return new Dimension(CELLSPERROW*offset+10,
        (comments.length/CELLSPERROW)*voffset+0);
    }
}
```

After going through this example (along with Chapter 9), you should have a reasonable grasp of simple drawing with the AWT. Personally, our most common use of the drawing primitives is to draw a simple rectangle around each major panel in our applications. It also helps to show off Checkbox groups and other grouped features (similar to the FontSelect class we showed earlier).

Double-Buffered Drawing

For simple drawings like the ones we've already talked about, the style we've shown is fine. However, as most of you realize, drawing things onscreen is a fairly slow operation. If you draw lots of things, you end up with the most dreaded feature of computer graphics: flickering. One of the traditional methods used to overcome this problem is one you are probably already familiar with: Buy a faster computer! Of course, we all know that's not possible in the majority of cases, and eventually you'll need your own chilling tower to cool your really fast computer system.

The other traditional method of avoiding image flicker is to use a technique called *double buffering*. What this means is that you draw your screen into an offscreen buffer (with it's own graphics context[s]). When you've completed your drawing, you then "blit" the complete image to the screen. All modern video games use this technique, since it is very effective at hiding the oddities associated with animations.

Double buffering is equally effective at avoiding the flickering associated with initial drawing, resizing, repainting or hiding component objects, etc. Your code can be as inefficient as you want when it's drawing into the offscreen buffer. The only thing you have to be careful with is the final painting operation onto the screen.

Adding double buffering to any Java component is simple. Primarily, you create an image space (the offscreen buffer) the same size as the onscreen component. You also obtain the graphics context associated with that Image object. Once you've done this, all that is required is to call the `paint()` method, passing the offscreen graphics context instead of the onscreen context. The `paint` method does all it's drawing into the offscreen image and returns. You then call `drawImage` in the displayed graphics context to copy the offscreen image onto the screen in one smooth operation.

Here's a simple excerpt that shows you what's involved:

```
import java.awt.Graphics;
import java.awt.Image;
public class xxx extends yyy {
    private Image offScreenImage;
    private Graphics offScreenGC;
    public void update(Graphics g) {
        if (offScreenImage == null) {
            offScreenImage = createImage(size().
            width,size().height);
            offScreenGC = offScreenImage.getGraphics();
            offScreenGC.setColor(getBackground());
            offScreenGC.fillRect(0,0,size().width,size(). height);
            offScreenGC.setColor(getForeground());
        }
        paint(offScreenGC);
        g.drawImage(offScreenImage,0,0,null);
    }
    ...
}
```

We'll quickly step through each line to make sure you understand what is going on. First, we import the two classes involved in double buffering. You will always have other imports (usually **java.awt.***) in your code. We also pick an imaginary class name. This excerpt works for any class based on Component:

```
import java.awt.Graphics;
import java.awt.Image;
public class xxx extends yyy {
```

Next, we define the offscreen image (the second buffer) and the graphics context that will be associated with the buffer.

```
    private Image offScreenImage;
    private Graphics offScreenGC;
```

The `update()` method is the only method we have to modify. Often, you do not even override this method in single-buffer drawing. The graphics context passed into `update` is the context associated with the displayed component. (At least normally, somebody above you could have done something strange and passed you their offscreen buffer to draw in.)

```
    public void update(Graphics g) {
```

When we call `update()` the first time, offScreenImage is null (remember that we only defined the Image object earlier). If our code detects that there is not an offScreenImage yet, we call `createImage()` (inherited from Component) to build one the same size as our onscreen context.

```
        if (offScreenImage == null) {
            offScreenImage = createImage(size().width,size().
            height);
```

Once we have an image, we can call `getGraphics()` to obtain the context for the image space.

```
        offScreenGC = offScreenImage.getGraphics();
```

One of the things that you have to perform manually in double buffering is to draw the background of offscreen images (at least in Java 1.0.x). Here we set the drawing color to our own background color, filled the entire image with that color, and then reset the drawing color to our foreground color.

```
        offScreenGC.setColor(getBackground());
        offScreenGC.fillRect(0,0,size().width,size(). height);
        offScreenGC.setColor(getForeground());
    }
```

Now we finally get to painting our image. All that is required is to call our previously existing, fully flickering `paint` method. Of course, we don't pass the onscreen graphics context. We pass our private offscreen context. The paint routine draws like crazy and populates the image object with whatever is appropriate for this point in time.

```
    paint(offScreenGC);
```

Now that the image is painted, all we have to do is get it onto the screen. We call `drawImage()` to block copy the completed image to the onscreen graphics context. Since the image is complete, we pass `null` for an image responder.

```
    g.drawImage(offScreenImage,0,0,null);
}
```

That's really all there is to simple double buffering. Other than these modifications, you don't have to do anything to your code. Of course, if you add double buffering to every component you are duplicating effort. Your container will call each contained component with it's offscreen context, and each component will create another buffer. This means that you make a lot of redundant calls to `drawImage` as you work from one component to another. In this case, you might be better off to teach only your containers to double buffer and to override the code that paints the contained components.

A Fun Drawing Example

We're now going to talk about one of the best Java applets we've seen. For rail fans, the ChooChooCad applet produced by Corey Trager is definitely cool. While Corey would be the first to admit that his applet is not a real train simulation, it provides an opportunity to have the same kind of fun you had with your first train set (in our case, that was many, many years ago). Corey had the foresight to release his code for any use; we're taking advantage of his goodwill and will pick apart sections of the code to show off some important aspects of drawing with Java.

We're not going to talk about how to use ChooChooCad. To be brutally honest, it's more fun to use it than it is to explain it. Suffice it to say, grab ChooChooCad off the CD-ROM, and run it with Appletviewer or Netscape. After that, you're on your own.

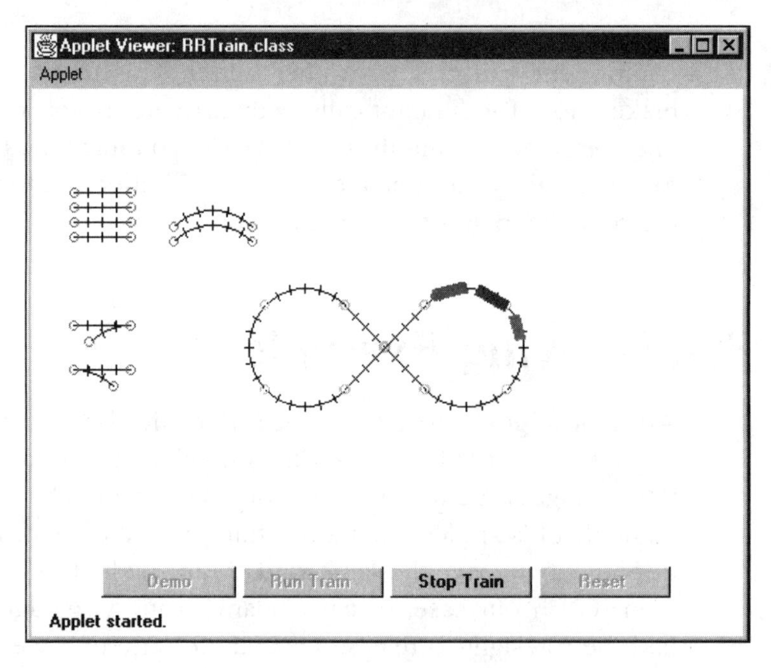

Figure 11.3 Corey Trager's ChooChooCad.

One of the better features of Corey's code is that he went to a lot of trouble to encapsulate the functionality of the individual railroad components. His track sections are composed of interconnecting circles, individual ties, and a single line delineating the rails. As you can see, his track looks a lot like the symbol used on maps for railroads. Since Corey's background is in CAD systems, this was all pretty natural for him.

We'll outline a few of the interesting things in Corey's code next. Our interest is primarily in how he deals with grabbing, moving, and snapping track into place. With the modularity that Corey built into his code, just examining the mouse event handlers gives you enough information to decide how he goes about his business.

```
public boolean mouseDown(Event evt, int x, int y) {
    // see if we've grabbed hold of a track
    transformMode = Track.NOT_GRIPPED;
    boolean gripped = tc.tryToGrip (x,y);
```

On mouse down events, we start by saying we haven't grabbed a track (yet). `transformMode` is used to maintain the state of the internal track movement code. The collection of track pieces is maintained in `tc`. Calling `tryToGrip` with the location of the mouse down event instigates a scan of the track collection, looking for a piece of track that falls under the mouse. The definition of "under" is determined by two classes that we will not go through in detail, TrackCollection and Track. Basically, Corey looks for every section of track that is close to where the mouse event occurred (within Track.GRIP_RANGE pixels). `TrackCollection.tryToGrip()` keeps the section of track closest to the mouse event location that is less than GRIP_RANGE pixels away.

```
    if (!gripped) {
        pick = noPick;
    }
```

If there was no track section grabbed by `tryToGrip()`, we reflect that for the mouse drag and mouse up events by setting `pick=noPick`.

```
    else
    {
        // We've grabbed a track

        grippedTrack = tc.getGrippedTrack();
        transformMode = grippedTrack.transformMode;
        pick = grippedTrack;
        Track thisTrack = grippedTrack;
```

If we grabbed a section of track, we remember which piece and what kind of transformation we're doing.

```
            // Detach this Track from any neighbor and detach
            // the neighbor
            // from this Track
            // In other words, free up the snap points
            thisTrack.detach();
```

Next, we remove this section from any neighbors it might have.

```
            // Move or rotate the track - depending on
            // where we gripped it
            if (transformMode == Track.TRANSLATE_MODE)
                thisTrack.move(x, y);
            else {
                thisTrack.rotate(x, y);
            }
        }
```

As Corey's comments note, we call either move or rotate, depending on where we grabbed the track section. If we grabbed either end of the track section, then we rotate the section. If we grabbed near the middle, we are in TRANSLATE_MODE and will move the section.

```
        repaint();
        return true;
    }
```

Finally, we repaint the entire Panel; this approach is not particularly efficient, but for this class of program, it's okay. The overall paint process is double buffered, so at least things don't flicker. If there are a lot of track sections, moving track does become unbearable.

```
// Mouse Drag
    public boolean mouseDrag(Event evt, int x, int y) {
        if (pick == noPick)
            return true;
        else
```

When a mouse drag occurs, we first check to see if we have a section of tracked grabbed (or picked out, depending on your terminology). If no, we just dispose of the event. Nobody else will ever see it, but that's okay for this version. If you had other classes or threads running (say, a scenery class, or an automobile thread), you would want to return false and let the other folk try and handle the event.

```
        if (transformMode == Track.TRANSLATE_MODE)
            ((Track)pick).move(x, y);
        else {
            ((Track)pick).rotate(x, y);
        }

    repaint();
    return true;
}
```

Things are pretty simple in `mouseDrag()`. We just look at what mode we're in and continue to either move or rotate the section as appropriate.

```
// Mouse Up
    public boolean mouseUp(Event evt, int x, int y) {
        if (pick == noPick)
            return true;
        else
```

Once again, we throw this event away if we don't have a track section grabbed.

```
            // See if we're near another track
            snap ((Track) pick);
```

Since we're releasing the track with this event, we snap the section to adjacent sections. If there are no nearby sections (within SNAP_DIST pixels), we just drop the track where we are. This is just like throwing a section of track on the floor with your train set. At least this way you don't end up losing the section under the couch.

```
        pick = noPick;
        repaint();
        return true;
    }
```

After we've snapped the track into place (or dropped it on the floor), we forget which piece it was and just repaint the panel that contains the whole drawing space.

The act of snapping is something that most applications can make use of when dealing with drawing or drag-and-drop functionality. The high level code to snap track sections depends on the TrackCollection and Track class to do all the useful work.

Essentially, Corey traverses the array of track sections and translates the end points of the track section (along with all the design features like ties) to match up with the adjacent sections. There is quite a bit of code involved in this in ChooChooCad, and we're going to leave the details for you to work through from the source listings in the back of the book.

All in all, a review of Corey's code shows proper encapsulation of function, with a reasonable approach to the class hierarchy. His image drawing is double buffered but suffers from repainting every object (every rail, every connection point, and every tie) each time any change is made. While this is fine for a free applet like ChooChooCad, a production Java program should make every attempt to minimize drawing time.

In any case, ChooChooCad is a lot of fun, and a cheap way to dig into the basics of CAD systems. Much of Corey's code can be reused in any similar real world simulation; Geographic Information Systems, inventory tracking, security system monitoring, etc. We like it!

Moiré Drawing Example

For a simpler example of drawing in applets, we'll present a very simple, slightly optimized moiré pattern generator. Figure 11.4 shows the applet as it is nearing the end of a rotation.

Figure 11.4 Moiré drawing example.

We'll walk through this example program, and point out where we've made some small performance enhancements. We definitely have kept the program small, and we've made certain design compromises that would require a redesign of the end-point calculations if you wanted to do anything other than a counterclockwise rotation.

```
import java.awt.*;
import java.applet.*;
public class Moiré  extends Applet implements Runnable {
    Thread thread;
```

We are going to implement threads, so we don't block the CPU. We haven't talked much about threads, since they don't have a lot to do with the AWT except during animations (which this example probably qualifies as). In any case, moiré is an applet which implements the applet life-cycle and the runnable thread interface.

```
static final int LINE_SKIP=4;
```

The LINE_SKIP constant is just how far we move the outer end point along whatever axis is currently moving.

```
private Image offScreenImage;
private Graphics offScreenGC;
```

The applet implements double buffering using the scheme we talked about earlier in this chapter.

```
Line lines[] = new Line[32];
int x,y;      // the outer end point
int a,b;      // the inner end point
int yskip,xskip;  // which way to move the outer end point
int nextLine;     // which line to draw next
```

Figure 11.4 shows 31 visible lines. Our line array contains 32 lines. As we draw the 32nd line, we erase the first, so that only 31 show at any one point. Also, `nextLine` is used to select the next cell of the array to redraw (in a new location). One small optimization is to avoid redrawing all 32 lines each time `update()` is called.

```
public void init() {
    x = 0;                      // start at upper left
    y = 0;
    a = size().width/2;     // inner end point at center
    b = size().height/2;
    yskip = LINE_SKIP;
```

```
        xskip = 0;
        nextLine = 0;
    }
```

This is the standard applet life-cycle `init()` method. We do most of the initialization here. The outer end point `(x,y)` is set to `(0,0)`. The inner end point `(a,b)` is set to the center of the panel. We also set `yskip` positive, indicating that we're counting up. By setting `xskip` to zero, we keep the X coordinate stable for now. We also set the next line to be changed to cell zero (`lines[nextLine]`).

```
    public void run() {
        while(thread != null) {
            repaint();
            sleep(50);     // short delay 1/20th sec
        }
    }
```

This is more applet life-cycle stuff. Primarily we just perform a call to `repaint()`. The `sleep` method is implemented within this class. The loop just paints, sleeps 50 milliseconds, and sleeps again.

```
    public void start() {
        offScreenImage = null;
        thread = new Thread(this);
        System.out.println("Start thread = " + thread);
        thread.start();
    }
```

This is part of the `runnable` interface. We fire up a new thread here and call its `start()` method to begin. The thread object's `start()` method calls our `run()` method.

```
    public void stop() {
        System.out.println("Stopped thread");
```

```
        thread = null;
    }
```

When you set garbage collect on a thread, it is terminated. `stop()` is called on in a browser when you leave the web page associated with the applet. Our stop method kills the working thread, effectively putting our applet to sleep until the browser returns to our Web page.

```
    public void update(Graphics g) {
        if (offScreenImage == null) {
            offScreenImage = createImage(size().width,size().
            height);
            offScreenGC = offScreenImage.getGraphics();
            offScreenGC.setColor(getBackground());
            offScreenGC.fillRect(0,0,size().width,size(). height);
            offScreenGC.setColor(getForeground());
        }
        paint(offScreenGC);
        g.drawImage(offScreenImage,0,0,null);
    }
```

This is the same double-buffering code as our example earlier in the chapter. The only thing we do different at all is throw this buffer away when our start method is called by the browser. This way we always clear the background and start with the current line drawn. It doesn't fix all update problems, but it is a practical (and cheap) optimization.

```
    public void sleep(int millisecs) {
        try {
            Thread.sleep(millisecs);
        } catch(InterruptedException e){}
    }
```

This is a thread-based sleep routine. We just toss any InterruptedException and pretend that we did sleep for the delay specified.

```
public boolean handleEvent(Event e) {
    if (e.id == Event.WINDOW_DESTROY)
        System.exit(0);
    return false;
}
```

Here is more standard stuff; we use the window destroy event to kill off our entire applet. Of course, this can't really happen when the applet is running inside a browser. In an application or an applet that has a separate frame outside the HTML page, this is the correct behavior.

```
public void paint(Graphics g) {
    int i,j;
    Dimension d = size();
    if (nextLine >= lines.length)
        nextLine = 0;
    i = 0;
```

This is normal stuff to see in a `paint()` routine. About the only odd thing is the code involving `nextLine`. Instead of drawing all 32 lines on each call to `paint()`, we just draw the two lines that change (`lines[nextLine]` and `lines[(nextLine+1)% lines.length]`). The first line is drawn in the foreground color, and the other is drawn in the background color. These two lines correspond to the leading and trailing lines of the image at any one time. The other lines don't change, and we don't even repaint them into the double buffer.

The following lines of code are definitely nonoptimal. They provide only for a counterclockwise rotation of the pattern, and they move only one end point of each line drawn. Obvious optimizations involve an object-oriented end point scheme where you can specify the pattern you want, instead of this fixed pattern.

```
if (yskip>0) {
    if (y < (d.height - LINE_SKIP)) {
        y += LINE_SKIP;
    } else {
        yskip = 0;
        y = d.height;
        xskip = LINE_SKIP;
    }
} else if (yskip == 0) {
    if (xskip>0) {
        if (x <= (d.width - LINE_SKIP)) {
            x += LINE_SKIP;
        } else {
            x = d.width;
            xskip = 0;
            yskip = -LINE_SKIP;
        }
    } else {
        if (x > LINE_SKIP) {
            x -= LINE_SKIP;
        } else {
            xskip = 0;
            x = 0;
            yskip = LINE_SKIP;
        }
    }
} else if (yskip < 0) {
    if (y > LINE_SKIP) {
        y -= LINE_SKIP;
    } else {
        yskip = 0;
        y = 0;
```

```
            xskip = -LINE_SKIP;
        }
    }
```

Again, feel free to tweak this code as much as you want. We agree that it stinks, but we didn't feel the need to improve it for this example.

```
    lines[nextLine] = new Line(x,y,a,b);
    lines[nextLine].setBackground(getBackground());
    lines[nextLine].setForeground(getForeground());
```

Here is where we create each new line. We also set the background and foreground colors for each one, since somebody might want to change colors every so often. That's a place where you can make another optimization.

```
    try {
        lines[nextLine].drawLine(g);
        lines[(nextLine+1)%lines.length].clearLine(g);
    } catch (nullPointerException e) {}
```

The 32 lines in the array are gradually replaced over time because `nextLine` is incremented from zero to `lines.length` and reset. Because the first 31 times through paint, `lines[(nextLine+1)%lines.length]` is null, we catch the null pointer exception and silently drop it on the floor. Notice that we draw the new line we created previously and clear the line at the trailing edge of the pattern; this causes the sweeping pattern visible in Figure 11.4.

```
//        System.out.println("drawing " + nextLine + " from "
//        + lines[nextLine]);
        nextLine++;
    }
```

We left in the commented call to `println`, so you could see how to examine the points you're generating. If you change these end point calculations, you'll need this call to verify that your new scheme works. We also increment `nextLine` so we'll draw the next leading edge line in the `lines[]` cell that we just erased with `clearLine()`.

```
    public Dimension minimumSize() {
        return new Dimension(128,128);
    }
    public Dimension preferredSize() {
        return new Dimension(512,512);
    }
}
```

Normally, our standard sizing routines don't do much if you are running within a browser, since the HTML tags set the window size in a static way.

Throughout the example, we maintained end points for each line in an array called `lines[]`. We'll show you this class, not because it is great but because it makes for a reasonable way to contain the coordinate pairs for each line. If you think about how `Polygon` keeps track of the coordinates (as an "x" array and "y" array), we believe that you'll agree that an array of objects is perhaps cleaner. Of course, the array of integers is probably faster, but not nearly as clean. It also doesn't allow us to encapsulate the other operations like drawing and color management. If you were to expand this (as in Corey Trager's ChooChooCad applet) to support scaling and more sophisticated rendering (line styles, tick marks, etc.), you would definitely want to maintain this object-oriented style. If you are really concerned about performance, you should be working in C or Fortran anyway.

Note that Line inherits only from Object. You could inherit from Component, but that makes for a fatter object, and lines don't generally need much special rendering. If you were to enhance the class as we discussed in the previous paragraph, it would make sense to inherit from Component (or perhaps even Canvas).

```
class Line {
    int x1,y1,x2,y2;
    Color cf,cb;
    Line() {
        x1 = y1 = x2 = y2 = 0;
    }
    Line(int xp1,int yp1, int xp2,int yp2) {
        x1 = xp1;
        y1 = yp1;
        x2 = xp2;
        y2 = yp2;
    }
```

The lines don't really have a head and tail; other than that, we always use them the same way in our example. You could extend this class to support drawing circles and arrows on the head and tail, among other things.

```
    public void setEndPoints(int xp1,int yp1, int xp2,int yp2) {
        x1 = xp1;
        y1 = yp1;
        x2 = xp2;
        y2 = yp2;
    }
```

This can be used to replace the end points on the same line. Our example program chose to destroy each object and create a new one as it worked around the pattern area. An obvious enhancement would be to use the constructor on the first pass through the array, and use `setEndPoints()` after that. You could also avoid the repeated calls to `setForeground` and `setBackground`.

```
public void setForeground(Color c) {
    cf = c;
}
public void setBackground(Color c) {
    cb = c;
}
```

Both of these methods help each line maintain it's own sense of color. The constructor will use black and white for the foreground and background, if you don't change them here.

```
public void drawLine(Graphics g) {
    g.setColor(cf);
    g.drawLine(x1,y1,x2,y2);
}
```

This method is used to draw the line on the leading edge of the pattern by our example program. It just draws the line in the foreground color.

```
public void clearLine(Graphics g) {
    g.setColor(cb);
    g.drawLine(x1,y1,x2,y2);
}
```

This method is used to erase the line on the trailing edge of the pattern by our example. You could use it to draw in the background color for other applications.

```
public int[] getEndPoints() {
    int p[] = new int[4];
    p[0] = x1;
    p[1] = y1;
    p[2] = x2;
    p[3] = y2;
    return p;
}
```

This is just a way to get the end points back from an object. We wouldn't want to have to keep an external array of coordinates, would we?

```
    public String toString() {
        return "Line(" + x1 + "," + y1 + "," + x2 + "," + y2 + ")";
    }
}
```

The `toString()` method is provided for debugging; we used it during debugging by calling `println` from our paint routine.

We've gone over several drawing examples in this chapter. Although we've totally ignored bit-mapped images and the ever-popular Java animation applet, don't be too distraught. Chapter 14 will discuss images and animations in detail.

CHAPTER 12

Lists

- List Interface
- Useful List Processing
- Using Lists for Text

List Interface

The AWT provides the List class to allow selection of one of many choices. The Choice class provides similar behavior in a pop-up list, with the added feature of always showing the currently selected item. However, Choice does not allow multiple items to be selected concurrently. List also provides the ability to reorder items, ensure that certain items are visible, and selectively allow or disallow multiple selections.

Table 12.1 outlines some of the useful methods available to AWT Lists. Note that the Component class provides most of the useful interface.

Table 12.1 List Interface

Method	Returns	Notes
	List Interface	
`List()` `List(int rows, boolean multipleSelections)`	Void	Pass `true` if you want to allow multiple selected items
`addItem(String item)`	Void	Add at end
`addItem(String item, int index)`	Void	Add in slot index
`allowsMultipleSelections()`	Boolean	Does this list currently allow multiple selections?
`clear()`	Void	Empty the list
`countItems()`	Int	How may items total?
`delItem(int position)`	Void	Remove a particular item
`delItems(int start, int end)`	Void	Remove a group of items
`deselect(int index)`	Void	Unselect item in slot index
`getItem(int index)`	String	Return a string containing the text of item index
`getRows()`	Int	How many rows are visible?
`getSelectedIndex()`	Int	Index of first selected item

continued...

Method	Returns	Notes
getSelectedIndexes()	Int[]	Array of indexes for each selected item
getSelectedItem()	String	String of first selected item
getSelectedItems()	String[]	Array of strings for text of each selected item
getVisibleIndex()	Int	The last thing made visible (as opposed to scrolled off screen)
isSelected(int index)	Boolean	Is this element selected?
makeVisible(int index)	Void	Make this item visible, not necessarily at any particular position on screen
minimumSize()	Dimension	For layout purposes
minimumSize(int rows)	Dimension	For layout purposes
preferredSize()	Dimension	For layout purposes
preferredSize(int rows)	Dimension	For layout purposes
replaceItem(String newValue, int index)	Void	Instead of delete and insert
select(int index)	Void	Make this item selected
setMultipleSelections (boolean v)	Void	Enable or disable multiple selections, affects operation of select()

Useful List Processing

List objects are one of the standard objects used in all business applications. While very similar to Choice, AWT's implementation of List drops the selected item box and provides a simple list of items. List can also support multiple selections, which is a standard windowing system function (although supported differently on individual platforms).

Figure 12.1 shows a list box, with one selected item.

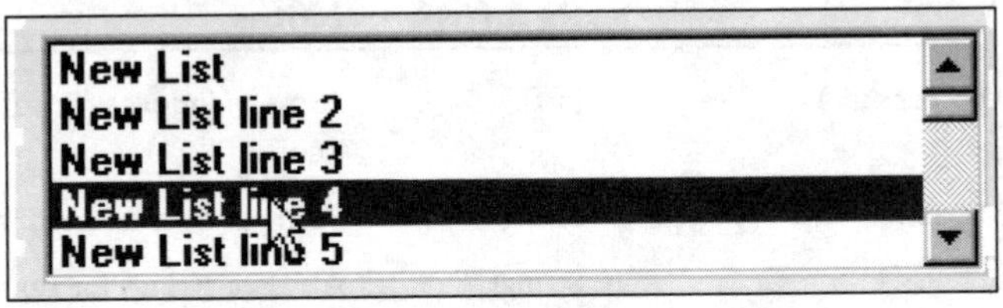

Figure 12.1 Standard list object.

Here is the code used to generate Figure 12.1. Note that items can be added, deleted, and replaced at any time, whether the List is displayed or not.

```
list = new List(5,false);
...
list.addItem("New List        ");
for(i=2;i<20;i++)
    list.addItem("New List line " + i));
...
```

To detect the selection of the line in this image, the container (a panel in this case) should include code in the event handler. `Event.LIST_SELECT` and `Event.LIST_DESELECT` events pass an integer in `Event.arg`, which contains the index of the list element involved.

```
int selection;
List list;
...
public boolean handleEvent(Event evt) {
    if (evt.target == list) {
        switch (evt.id) {
        case Event.LIST_SELECT;
            selection = ((Integer)evt.arg).intValue();
        default:    // eat all list events
            return true;
        }
    }
    ...
```

Note that if you've enabled multiple selections, the `getSelectedIndex()` method returns -1 to indicate that more than one item is selected. You should call `getSelectedIndexes()` to obtain an array of index values. The `length` public variable of the Array built-in type contains the number of elements in any array. We use it here to run through the list returned by `getSelectedIndexes()`.

```
if (evt.target == list) {
    if (evt.id == Event.LIST_SELECT) ||
        evt.id == Event.LIST_DESELECT) {
        String s;
        int i;
        int select[] = list.getSelectedIndexes();
        if (evt.id == Event.LIST_SELECT)
            s = "Selected " + evt.arg;
        else
            s = "DeSelected " + evt.arg;
            for(i=0;i<select.length;i++) {
                if (i>0)
                    s = s + ", ";
                s = s + select[i];
            }
        }
        ta.appendText(s + "\n");
        return true;
    }
}
```

The list box in Figure 12.2 shows the results of running the preceding code and selecting several items. Note that the output of this code is displayed in the Text Area at the bottom of the window.

New List
New List line 1
New List line 2
New List line 3
New List line 4
New List line 5
New List line 6
New List line 7

Selected 0
Selected 2 Items currently selected are:0, 2
DeSelected 0
Selected 3 Items currently selected are:2, 3
Selected 4 Items currently selected are:2, 3, 4
Selected 5 Items currently selected are:2, 3, 4, 5
DeSelected 4 Items currently selected are:2, 3, 5

Figure 12.2 Multiple selection list object.

Using Lists for Text

The List class provides some of the behavior we asked for the TextArea discussion in Chapter 6. Primarily, we're talking about the capability to tell what lines of the list are visible and what is on a particular line. The particular methods we are thinking about are

- `addItem()`
- `countItems()`
- `delItem()`
- `getItem()`
- `getRows()`
- `getSelectedIndex()`
- `getSelectedItem()`
- `getVisibleIndex()`
- `makeVisible()`
- `replaceItem()`
- `select()`

While it would be considered nontraditional, these methods let us use a List object to replace a TextArea when you need to know what lines are currently displayed. Of course, List is an output-only object. It has no concept of a cursor, and you cannot perform any of the normal text selection (other than the obvious "select an entire item in the list" capability).

However, the AWT generously delivers the keyboard events that occur when the List object has the focus. Low performance code can be developed to update a List item's contents with the keystrokes received. Here's a short excerpt of `keyDown()` that updates the selected row with the current keystrokes.

```
public boolean keyDown(Event evt, int key) {
    if (evt.target == list) {
        String s;
        int i;
        if (list.getSelectedIndex() < 0) {
            list.select(list.getVisibleIndex());
        }
        i = list.getSelectedIndex();
        s = list.getSelectedItem();
        list.replaceItem(s+(char)key,i);
        list.select(i);
    }
    ...
}
```

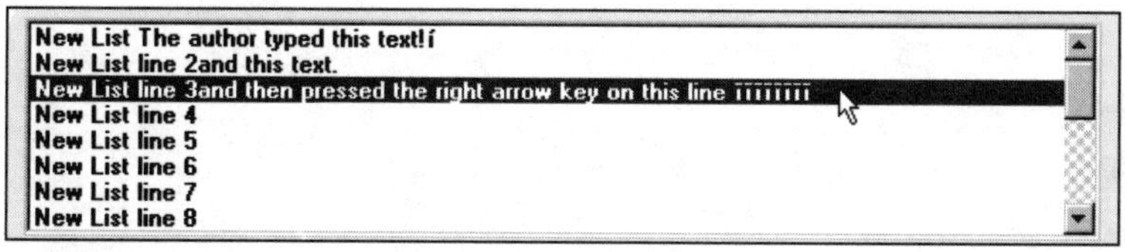

Figure 12.3 List used for echoing text.

This example doesn't maintain a current cursor position; it just appends the keystroke to the existing text. It also returns `false` to the native windowing system, so all the cursor movements still work. Obviously, you could add code to maintain a cursor position for typing as well as to interpret **Backspace**, **Delete**, and **Left/Right Arrow** keys. Anything you don't handle yourself should be left to the default behavior.

The other tidbit that you'll need to make List work reasonably for text is to make sure that the layout manager sizes the List object to the width you desire. Because you cannot specify a width at creation time, you can override the `preferredSize()` method or put the List in a layout with another component of the appropriate width. Our examples used BorderLayout with a TextArea in the "south" zone and List in the "center" zone. because TextArea allows you to specify a width at creation time, things work out OK.

CHAPTER 13

Scrollbars

- Scrollbar Interface
- Useful Scroll Bar Processing
- Using Scroll Bars to Produce a Color Panel

Scrollbar Interface

The AWT provides Scrollbar to allow selection of one of many choices. Table 13.1 outlines some of the useful methods available to AWT scroll bars. Note that the Component class provides most of the useful interface.

Table 13.1 Scrollbar interface.

Method	Returns	Notes
	Scrollbar Interface	
Scrollbar(), Scrollbar(int orientation), Scrollbar(int orientation, int value, int visible, int minimum, int maximum)		Orientation is either horizontal or vertical; value is starting value; visible is the page size; minimum and maximum are the reporting range for the ends of the bar
getLineIncrement()	Int	How much is each "click" worth?
getMaximum()	Int	What is the largest value the scroll bar will report?
getMinimum()	Int	What is the smallest value the scroll bar will report?
getOrientation()	Int	Either horizontal or vertical
getPageIncrement()	Int	How much is a page movement worth?
getValue()	Int	What is the current value of the bar?
getVisible()	Int	How big is the handle (in line increments)?
setLineIncrement(int value)	void	Each click of the up/left, right/down buttons moves the current value this far
setPageIncrement(int value)	void	Each click of the page up/left right/down moves the current value this far
setValue(int value)	void	Set the handle at this value
setValues(int value, int visible, int minimum, int maximum)	void	Reset the scroll bar to reflect the bounds passed in

The default orientation is vertical. Also, Win32 variants of ScrollBar don't work very well; they sometimes report out of range values and spontaneously unset the current value.

Useful Scrollbar Processing

Scroll bar objects are one of the standard objects used in most business applications.

Figure 13.1 shows two sample scroll bars, one in the vertical alignment and the other a horizontal bar (currently in the act of paging right).

Figure 13.1 Standard scroll bar objects.

Here is the code used to generate the image in Figure 13.1. Note that the vertical scroll bar used the default constructor. To make the bar behave reasonably, you must call `setValues()` method to initialize the current value, the visible page increment, and the minimum and maximum values.

```
add("Center",new Button("Scrollbars"));
add("East",sb1 = new Scrollbar(Scrollbar.VERTICAL));
sb1.setValues(0,1,1,8);
add("South",sb2 = new Scrollbar(Scrollbar.HORIZONTAL,
0,16,0,512));
```

The decision to use the default versus the more complete constructors should be made based on what the application requirements are. Note that many times the application will not even display the scroll bar until the associated component contains more entries than will fit in the visible region. Using `hide()` and `show()` to display the scroll bars when needed and `enable/disable()` to allow interaction with them, gives you the flexibility needed for most application requirements.

In some releases of the AWT, scroll bar objects are unreliable. We believe that you should use other components if you can still meet the user interface requirements.

Event handling for Scrollbar is fairly easy. There are only a few scroll bar-related event id's:

- SCROLL_ABSOLUTE
- SCROLL_LINE_DOWN
- SCROLL_LINE_UP
- SCROLL_PAGE_DOWN
- SCROLL_PAGE_UP

Each of these events passes the new current value of the Scrollbar in the **evt.arg** field. For simple scroll bar use, it's easy to message the containing object with the new value.

For more complex interactions, it may be necessary to report the current value, the page increment, the specific scroll action (`SCROLL_LINE_DOWN`, etc.), and possibly the metakeys that are pressed during the scroll operation.

Using Scrollbars to Produce a Color Panel

One very common use for scroll bars in any windowing system is to generate a simple color picker. Figure 13.2 shows a custom color picker that we'll go through in the next few pages.

Figure 13.2 shows three vertical scroll bars; each of these corresponds to a particular component of the chosen color. In the time-honored tradition, the leftmost is red, the middle is green, and the rightmost is blue. Next to each scroll bar is a custom canvas that is painted with the color corresponding to the current value of the scroll bar. The leftmost canvas is the sum of the three components and displays the chosen color.

Note that the green component is in the midst of a SCROLL_PAGE_DOWN event on a Win32 box.

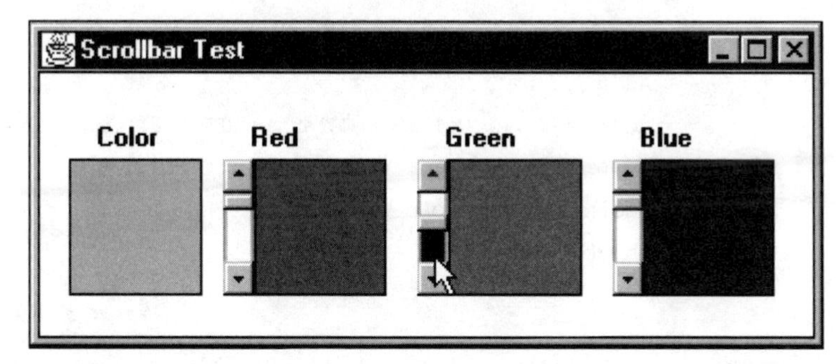

Figure 13.2 Color Picker with scroll bars.

When you run this program on a system that displays few colors (like this book), the effect is less than enticing. On a true color display, you quickly learn to generate the color desired. A useful color picker would let you drag and drop colors from and to the color well(s) on this Panel. Since our example is designed to demonstrate event handling for scroll bars, we've left out this fundamental feature.

We will quickly run through the basic code to generate the color Panel. Each scroll bar and it's associated canvas are encapsulated in a custom class called Colorbar. Since Colorbar contains both a scroll bar and a color canvas, it inherits from the Panel (rather than the scroll bar). We also encapsulated the canvas in a custom class `ColorCanvas`, which just knows how to paint itself in it's current color. To set up the color Panel, we first create a subpanel that contains the color well (the chosen color) and a title:

```
public void init() {
    Panel p = new Panel();
    p.setLayout(new BorderLayout());
    p.add("North",new Label("Color"));
    p.add("Center",color = new ColorCanvas());
    p.show();
```

Next, we set the color picker to `FlowLayout()`, add our color well, and add the custom Colorbar components.

```
        setLayout(new FlowLayout());
        add(p);
        add(red = new Colorbar(Colorbar.RED,1,8));
        add(green = new Colorbar(Colorbar.GREEN,1,8));
        add(blue = new Colorbar(Colorbar.BLUE,1,8));
        show();
    }
```

The next useful piece of code handles the events generated by each Colorbar object. Note that we don't care which of the components changed, we just collect their current values and repaint the color well appropriately:

```
    public boolean handleEvent(Event evt) {
        if (evt.target == red || evt.target == green || evt.target
        == blue) {
            if (evt.id == Event.ACTION_EVENT) {
                color.setBackground(new Color(red.getValue(),
                    green.getValue(),
                    blue.getValue()));
                color.repaint();
            }
            return true;
        }
        return false;
    }
```

That's all there is to using the Colorbar objects. They have a slightly larger interface in the implementation included on the CD, but our example (and probably yours) doesn't need anything more than what we've shown.

Our example walkthrough hasn't event mentioned a scroll bar yet, and as far as using the class off the CD, we don't need to. However, since this chapter is on using scroll bars, we'll show you the insides of the Colorbar class now.

```
Colorbar(int colorComponent, int v, int visible) {
    int r = 0;
    int g = 0;
    int b = 0;
    value = v;
    type = colorComponent;
```

The constructor receives three arguments: a color component flag, the initial value for the component, and a parameter that is used to designate the page size for the scroll bar.

The component flag is one (or more) of RED, GREEN, or BLUE. This flag tells the color bar which of the three color guns should be adjusted when the scroll bar moves or the current value is set with `setValue()`.

The initial value is used to set the color bar at a particular level when the object is first created. Normally this would be 255 (the brightest value).

The page size would normally be matched to the number of unique shades that can be generated in each color component. For instance, a 16-bit high-color display (on a PC) normally provides 5 bits per component (32 shades). The visible field would be set to 256/32 or 8. This way, paging up and down through the scroll bar would cause a visible color shift for each movement. On a 24-bit display, there are 256 shades per component, and a page motion would move by one bit (a single shade step).

```
        setLayout(new BorderLayout());
        add("West",sb = new
Scrollbar(Scrollbar.VERTICAL,v,visible,0,255));
        add("Center",canvas = new ColorCanvas());
        add("North",new Label(colorNames[type]));
```

We set the color bar to the good old BorderLayout. The scroll bar is placed vertically on the left, with the appropriate initial value, page increment, and a range from 0 to 255. Since this is the range that the AWT supports for Color components, we use it here so we don't have to scale values. However, since vertical scroll bars work from 0 (at the top) to 255 (at the bottom), the world is upside down. Human nature likes big values to be at the top of the bar (like in a bar graph), so our code will occasionally flip the values (for import and export), as well as color display to the ColorCanvas.

```
        if ((type & RED) != 0)
            r = 255-value;
        if ((type & GREEN) != 0)
            g = 255-value;
        if ((type & BLUE) != 0)
            b = 255-value;
        canvas.setBackground(new Color(r,g,b));
        canvas.repaint();
        repaint();
    }
```

We start by setting the component (perhaps more than one) to the current value. Note that this is one of those places where we flip the value. We also set the color of the ColorCanvas object to the resultant value and repaint everything.

```
    public int getValue() {
        return 255-value;
    }
    public void setValue(int v) {
        value =  255-v;
        sb.setValue(v);
        repaint();
    }
```

Here is where we set and get the current value of Colorbar. We always use the internal view of the color, since there are a couple of AWT bugs that might give us the wrong value. We also flip the value here, and set Scrollbar to the appropriate value.

```
public boolean handleEvent(Event evt) {
    Event e;
    if (evt.target == sb) {
        switch (evt.id) {
        case Event.SCROLL_LINE_DOWN:
        case Event.SCROLL_LINE_UP:
        case Event.SCROLL_PAGE_DOWN:
        case Event.SCROLL_PAGE_UP:
        case Event.SCROLL_ABSOLUTE:
            break;
        default:
            System.out.println("idono:" + evt.id);
            return false;
        }
```

The event handler is straightforward. We take every scroll event targeted at the Scrollbar associated with our component. Everything else is disposed of appropriately, by returning false.

```
        value = ((Integer)evt.arg).intValue();
        repaint();
```

Here we just get the integer value of Scrollbar and repaint ColorCanvas with the new color.

```
        e = new Event(this, evt.when, Event.ACTION_EVENT,
                evt.x,evt.y,evt.key,evt.modifiers,new
                Integer(255-value));
        deliverEvent(e);    // ship off ACTION_EVENT
        return true;
    }
    return false;
}
```

Finally, we create a new ACTION_EVENT to inform our parent that the selected color has changed and pass the flipped value along in **e.arg**. Since we've now handled the original scroll event properly, we dispose of it by returning true. If the event is not one of the scroll bar events we want, we pass it on to our parent(s).

The Colorbar object gets repainted every time there is a scroll bar event. The following code is used to paint the ColorCanvas object with the current color. Note that we use the `type` instance variable to decide which color component(s) we are dealing with. We also don't bother with retaining the old color object, but just make a new one.

```
public void paint(Graphics graphics) {
        int r = 0;
        int g = 0;
        int b = 0;
        if ((type & RED) != 0)
                r = 255-value;
        if ((type & GREEN) != 0)
                g = 255-value;
        if ((type & BLUE) != 0)
                b = 255-value;
        canvas.setBackground(new Color(r,g,b));
        canvas.repaint();
}
```

The other custom class we use in this example is ColorCanvas. This is just a simple class that produces a fixed size canvas.

```
class ColorCanvas extends Canvas {
        Color color;
        ColorCanvas() {
                color = new Color(255,255,255);
        }
        ColorCanvas(Color c) {
                setBackground(c);
        }
```

We provide a `setBackground()` method to pass the new color in. We also provide a `getBackground()` for symmetry, but don't use it in our example as an external method.

```
public Color getBackground() {
        return color;
}
public void setBackground(Color c) {
        color = c;
        repaint();
}
```

The paint() method obtains the background color and draws a filled rectangle one pixel smaller than the canvas. An outline rectangle is drawn around the filled area, in the foreground color (usually black), to make ColorCanvas more easily detected.

```
public void paint(Graphics g) {
        Dimension d = size();
        g.setColor(getBackground());
        g.fillRect(1,2,d.width-2,d.height-2);
        g.setColor(getForeground());
        g.drawRect(0,0,d.width-1,d.height-1);
}
```

Finally, there are the obligatory size methods. We don't allow any resizing at all, so they are very simple.

```
public Dimension minimumSize() {
        return new Dimension(32,16);
}
public Dimension preferredSize() {
        return new Dimension(64,64);
}
```

CHAPTER 14

Bits and Pieces

- Insets
- Resizing Windows
- Embedding Layouts
- Loading Images
- Displaying Images

We've touched on many topics in this book without really giving them more than a cursory examination. This chapter will go into more detail about a handful of topics that are not necessarily AWT classes but that are definitely style issues. Using the AWT containers and layout managers, you often end up with GUI layouts that are not quite pleasing. We'll talk about these bits and pieces in this chapter.

Insets

We have used insets several times in this book. When you override the `Container.insets()` method, you are instructing the AWT to provide a margin around your container. The inset is used mostly by the Layout Manager to calculate sizing and positioning for contained objects. The Layout Manager will fit everything inside the insets you provide to it. The most common use of the inset space is to provide white space around a set of components to make them stand out as a group or just to provide more pleasing balance to a window. Remember that the insets indicate the distance from the border of the container to the contained objects. Effectively, you are setting the margins for your container. The space between the top, left, right, and bottom inset and the border of the container would be considered the margin.

For instance, `Insets(20,10,10,1)` would cause the Layout Manager to leave a 20 pixel top margin, 10 pixels on the left and right, and only 1 pixel at the bottom. We've started using a standard inset of 10 pixels for most of our containers, but you should follow your environment's guidelines for code of your own.

The method can be implemented very simply:

```
public Insets insets() {
        return new Insets(10,10,10,10);
}
```

This produces a new Insets object every time insets is called. If you want to enhance performance, and the specific constant insets will always be appropriate, you can instantiate a private object in the constructor and always return that object. Also, the four values allow you to vary the inset width on each of the top, left, bottom, and right.

You will often combine the inset with a simple border. In the container `paint()` method, you can call `drawRect()` to draw a simple pixel wide border around the container. The border is at the outside of the container, and contained components will be inset from the line by the active inset amount.

```
public void paint(Graphics g) {
        Dimension d = size();
        g.drawRect(0,0,d.width-1,d.height-1);
}
```

Of course, just as on paper, you can draw in the margins of your container. You can use things other than `drawRect` to give the special effect you desire. A custom container might draw a shadow or other 3D effect that consumes all the space between the container border and it's inset. You are definitely not limited to lines, either. You can draw images, text, or any other graphic component in the margin of your container.

Figure 14.1 shows an example of both of these features from Chapter 9.

Figure 14.1 Container insets and border.

Resizing Windows

One of the issues that we tripped over repeatedly when we were learning about the AWT was what it took to resize containers properly. One of the most common problems was that of creating a Frame, setting its Layout Manager, adding components, and then displaying the frame. Here's an example of what we started out with:

```
...
Frame f = new Frame("FrameTest.java Demo");
f.setLayout(new BorderLayout());
f.add("Center",new Button("Button"));
f.add("North",new Label("Can you see me?"));
f.show();
...
```

When you run this form of code, you get the not-so-useful display shown in Figure 14.2.

Figure 14.2 Not-so-useful frame.

If you then use the mouse to resize the Frame, you get the display shown in Figure 14.3.

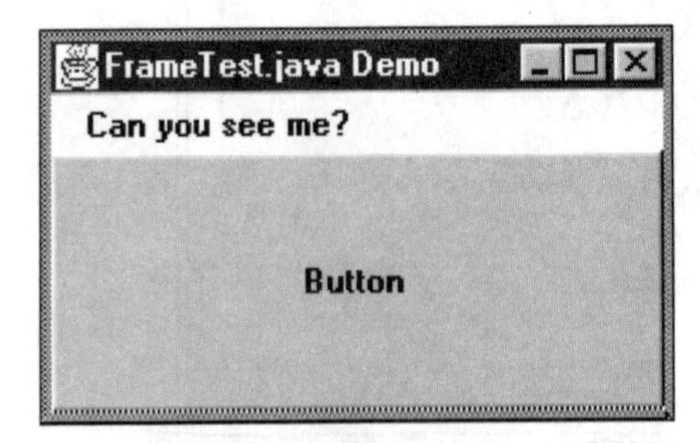

Figure 14.3 More-useful frame.

So, we're properly populating the display, we're just not sizing it correctly. At first, we tried using `resize`.

```
...
Frame f = new Frame("FrameTest.java Demo");
f.setLayout(new BorderLayout());
f.add("Center",new Button("Button"));
f.add("North",new Label("Can you see me?"));
f.resize(250,140);
f.show();
...
```

Calling `resize` works, but you have to pass constant values to resize. Since it's decidedly inconvenient to hand calculate the width and height for every program you write, we thought we might be able to use the `preferredSize` methods of each component, but then we thought, "This is stupid, we're obviously not doing something important." After running through the Frame class API, we realized there was the `pack` method. `Frame.pack` "causes the subcomponents of this window to be laid out at their preferred size".

```
...
Frame f = new Frame("FrameTest.java Demo");
f.setLayout(new BorderLayout());
f.add("Center",new Button("Button"));
f.add("North",new Label("Can you see me?"));
f.pack();
f.show();
...
```

Of course, this takes care of our resize problem. Calling `pack` basically calls the `layout` method, which causes the Layout Manager to query each contained components' `preferredSize` methods, add in any inset that the container requires, and calculate the appropriate size. The `pack` method then causes the Window to be sized to fit the entire laid out contents.

One important thing to note, is that `pack` is a Window method. You can call this method only for frames and windows in your application. If you are running in the premanufactured window inside an applet viewer or web browser, you cannot call `pack`. For Panel-based resizing problems, you can call `validate`; this performs the same kind of layout operation.

Embedding Layouts

One of the things you repeatedly stumble over with the AWT is the need to lay out components easily. While the provided layout managers, along with other more sophisticated third-party managers (PackerLayout is included on the CD, as an example layout manager) can work out your layout successfully, we tend to stick to using the three simplest layout managers.

For instance, our FontSelect class uses `FlowLayout`. Our example shown in Figure 14.1 shows a FontSelect panel embedded in the North position of a `BorderLayout`. The Center position contains the TextArea, and we could easily add another FlowLayout container in the South position to provide status and other message space without requiring us to spend much time managing the layout. It's also easy to put a single column GridLayout in the East and West positions of the `BorderLayout`. You might fill the single column GridLayout with buttons or other small components.

Of course, you can replace the TextArea with another Panel, and repeat the nesting process. However, if you get too many layers, things can get fairly ugly when painting and resizing.

Figure 14.4 provides an example of stacked layouts using the basic layout managers that provide a fully functional layout, without ever learning anything more complicated than `BorderLayout`.

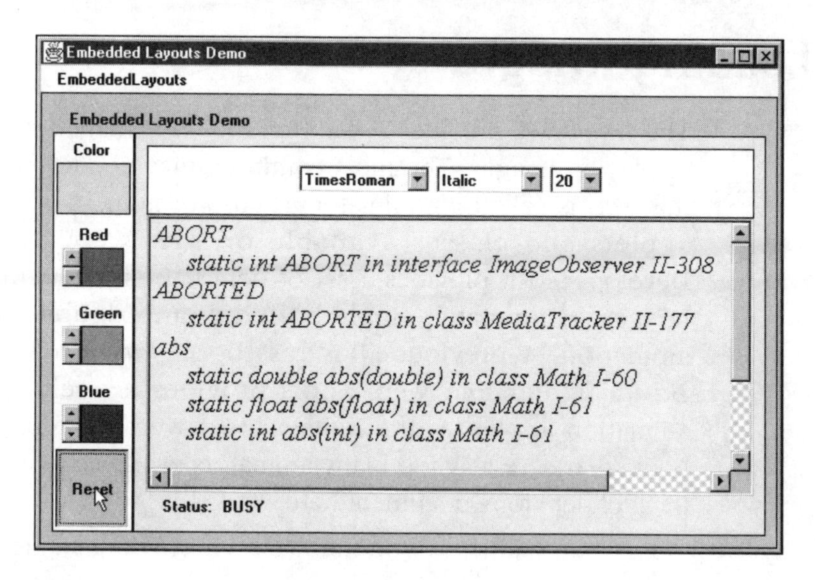

Figure 14.4 Embedded container layouts.

By the way, there are actually nine separate panels and layout managers active in Figure 14.4. They are the `FontSelect` panel, which uses `FlowLayout`, and the ColorPanel, which uses GridLayout. Each color cell uses `BorderLayout`. The yellow embedded panel (the font selector, the text area, and the status line) uses BorderLayout and is in the Center region of the light gray BorderLayout panel, which is itself contained in the Center region of the `BorderLayout` associated with the outermost Frame.

You should realize that we use GridBag and other layout managers when required, but we don't normally consider them for simple applications. It's up to you to understand what the application UI will require and make the tough choices up front. Be forewarned though, it can be hard to switch from stacked simple layout managers to a single layout manager. You should try to understand your real needs before spending much time in development.

Loading Images

The Java AWT provides several classes to manage loading and displaying images. The most common image code you see on the Web is called an animator. There are numerous animation applets and classes available on the WWW. The Java Developer's Kit provides a set of demo applications that draw images using static, single-buffered, and double-buffered animation. A previous MIS:Press book *Java Programming Basics* by Pencom Web Works provides a freely available animation applet. At the moment that we are preparing this book, there are way too many animators available to even keep track of, let alone document here.

First, we will show you the basics of drawing single images. In fact, two of the classes we developed earlier actually did everything you need to know to draw an image into a graphics context.

```
if (image != null) {
        g.drawImage(image,xloc,yloc,getBackground(),this);
}
```

This call simply draws the "image" object at (xloc,yloc) in the graphics context `g`. Any transparent pixels are drawn in the background color of the component, and "this" object is notified when the image is drawn. Even though this is a very standard way of drawing images, there are numerous other ways to call `drawImage`. We'll talk about them a little later.

Of course, before you can draw an image, you have to obtain one. Because Java is very biased toward supporting the WWW, the AWT provides a full-featured set of dynamic image loaders. The following code excerpt shows both local and network-based image loading.

```
    if (inAnApplet) {
            image = getImage(getCodeBase(), "./clss1312.gif");
  } else {
    image = tk.getImage("./clss1312.gif");
     }
```

If the image is stored locally on the machine (typical for applications) you use the default Toolkit object to load the image file. The `Toolkit.getImage` method receives one parameter (the filename) and begins loading the image file into a new Image object. The preceding example shows a simple GIF image file. The AWT also provides integral support for jpeg images.

If the image is to be obtained from the network, the `Applet.getImage` method should be used. You pass the directory containing the image (as a URL) along with the base filename (the same GIF as before). The HTTP server on the other end of the Applet connection should process the HTTP request for the image URL just like any other WWW HTTP request. Note that there is no requirement that the HTTP server be a full-fledged WWW server, it just must support the basic operations required to pass the image. If you were developing a large distributed imaging system, you might provide a custom image server that could only serve images, or otherwise differentiate itself from a standard web server.

After starting the image load as already shown, you can proceed to other work. If the image is loaded locally by the toolkit, it will usually load immediately. If the image must be obtained from a web server, there may be a substantial (perhaps infinite!) delay before the image arrives. The AWT provides two methods for dealing with image-loading delays. We chose to use the very simple MediaTracker method.

```
tracker = new MediaTracker(this);
tracker.addImage(image,0);
```

MediaTracker provides for checking the status of the image-loading process for as many images as you need. The preceding example shows the case of waiting on a single image.

First, you must create a new MediaTracker instance. The MediaTracker constructor is passed an object that is normally where the image will eventually be painted. Note that this doesn't absolutely mean that the parameter is the actual graphics context or component, but it usually is. For our purposes, we'll assume that this is the case. After the MediaTracker is instantiated, you would add the images to be tracked by calling `MediaTracker.addImage()`. There are two forms of `addImage`; the first receives only the Image object and a unique id that you will use later as a reference ID when working with the tracker. The second form of `addImage` also receives a width and height that will be used to scale the image as it loads. According to the MediaTracker class documentation, images managed with lower ID's receive some preferential treatment while loading. It's not clear how you can impact the server to deliver them any differently, but there are potential local optimizations that might be done. Note that the image doesn't begin loading the instant you call `addImage`. Until you call a `status` or `wait` method, the image-loading process remains pending.

The MediaTracker can be run in it's own thread or in the main tread. If you are loading images that must completely load before you can do anything else, you might wait in the main thread. If you can do other useful work before worrying about the image, you would probably use multiple threads via the Runnable interface.

Our example uses the main thread, since we load only a single image and are willing to wait for it to finish loading.

```
System.out.println("waiting");
try {
        tracker.waitForID(0);
```

```
} catch (InterruptedException e) {
}
System.out.println("not waiting");
```

Essentially, if you call one of the `MediaTracker.wait`*xxx* methods you just block until the image loads, or something "bad" happens. Our example waits for a single image, referenced by the id we passed into `addImage`. When the image finishes loading, `waitForID` returns, and we can be assured that the image is ready to display. If there is an error (fairly common when the networked version of `getImage` is used), the MediaTracker throws an exception, and we can try and deal with it. Depending on what your application requirements are, you might try loading the image from an alternate source or just fake something up internal to your app. One obvious alternative is to follow the HTML <IMG> tag's lead and just use `drawText` to render an alternate text string into an image object.

MediaTracker also provides `checkAll` and `checkID` methods that give you the capability to check on and initiate the load status of images. You can use these methods to check on the load status of important images and alter the application activity depending on what the status is. For instance, an animation program might render frames faster or slower depending on how fast the images are being received from the server. You might even decide to pause the animation or skip some frames and wait for special sync frames to arrive. This is much the way some MPEG-viewers operate.

The `statusID` and `statusAll` methods provide yet another way to begin the loading of images queued up in MediaTracker. However, their primary purpose is to give you an indication of the current status of images being tracked.

For tracking image loading where you need more precise information than MediaTracker provides, we suggest you investigate the ImageObserver interface. We personally use

MediaTracker because we believe that it provides sufficient capability for normal application image loading. If you are truly concerned about animations and other complex image-loading processes, we suggest you look at one of the many animation applets available over the web. The Java Links appendix will give you several starting points for your search.

Displaying Images

While the basic `drawImage` call shown previously covers the vast majority of cases you'll come across, there are several other incantations you can use to draw Image objects.

There are four different overloaded `drawImage` methods in Graphics. Figure 14.5 shows the results of each method. Our descriptions are in the same order as the images.

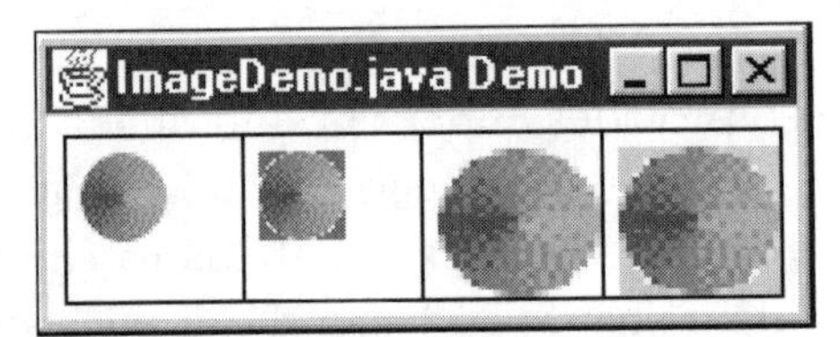

Figure 14.5 Four basic drawImage methods.

First, we'll show you the least complicated call:

```
if (image != null) {
        g.drawImage(image,xloc,yloc,this);
}
```

This causes the image to be drawn lifesize (no scaling is applied), with the upper left corner of the image positioned at (xloc,yloc) in the current graphics context clipping rectangle. If any errors or events occur while the image is being rendered, they are ignored (potentially leaving the image in some strange display state). If the image contains transparent pixels, the destination pixels are left as they were before the drawImage call was made.

Next we'll show you the image-loading call we used in the previous section:

```
if (image != null) {
        g.drawImage(image,xloc,yloc,getBackground(),this);
}
```

This call draws the image scaled normally (100%) with the upper left corner of the image positioned at (xloc,yloc). If the image has transparent pixels, those pixels in the destination graphics context are drawn in the color passed to drawImage. Our example passes the background color of the container we're drawing in. This is different than the previous call, where the destination pixels were left alone.

Both of the methods we just discussed draw the image at a one-to-one ratio. Each pixel in the source image is drawn directly into the destination graphics context. While this works for the vast majority of cases, there are situations where the source image needs to be scaled (up or down) to fit into a particular region of the destination graphics context. Two variations of drawImage provide width and height parameters to be used in scaling the destination image. Regardless of the source image size, the destination image is rendered to the size specified in the width and height. This example leaves the transparent pixels as they were before the call to drawImage.

```
if (image != null) {
        g.drawImage(image,xloc,yloc,width,height,this);
}
```

The next example draws the transparent pixels in light gray. All pixels other than the transparent pixels are drawn in the source pixel color.

```
if (image != null) {
        g.drawImage(image,xloc,yloc,
        width,height,Color.lightGray,this);
}
```

If something interesting happens while an image is being drawn, the AWT image-drawing code notifies `this.imageUpdate`. For most of your code, you can just pass `this` as the image observer. The default behavior implemented by Component is usually sufficient to get the image drawn. If your application is using incremental drawing, you may need to implement your own `imageUpdate` method. When the `imageUpdate` method is called, it receives a small block of status information:

- `Image img`—the image being referenced
- `int infoflags`—the logical OR of the following bits, each of which indicates that the related information is available
- WIDTH
- HEIGHT
- PROPERTIES
- SOMEBITS
- FRAMEBITS
- ALLBITS
- ERROR
- ABORT
- `int x`—the X location of the image
- `int y`—the Y location of the image
- `int width`—if `(infoflags&WIDTH)`, then this is the width of the image
- `int height`—if `(infoflags&HEIGHT)`, then this is the height of the image

Summary

You should now know enough about the Java AWT to take full advantage of it's capabilities to develop useful business applications, as well as sophisticated applets.

APPENDIX A

Java Programming Examples

This appendix contains the complete source to several of the example programs in this book, as well as to a couple of other applets that we didn't have space to discuss.

Small Examples from Book

This section gives many of the small example programs, so you can refer to them while reading the description in the book chapter.

LabelCanvas.java

You can use this class as a basis for developing your own "flowery" labels. By adding images, borders, etc., you can spiff up your applications with a common style and emphasis to labels.

```
/*
* This is a Label object that is based on Canvas.  It duplicates
* the AWT Label class, but allows you to add your own "flowery"
extensions
* such as borders, background images, etc.
*/

import java.awt.*;
/*
* a pure Java label
*/
class LabelCanvas extends Canvas {
    String text;
    Color c;
    Font font;
    Dimension preferredSize;

    LabelCanvas() {
        this("");
    }
    LabelCanvas(String l) {
        text = l;    // remember the text
    }
```

```
    /*
    * this draws the text
    */
    public void paint(Graphics g) {
        Dimension d = size();
        FontMetrics fm;
        int x;
        int y;
        fm = g.getFontMetrics();
        g.setColor(getBackground());
        /*
        * add your own flowery extensions here
        */
//        g.drawRect(0,0,d.width-1,d.height-1);
        g.setColor(getForeground());
        x = (d.width - fm.stringWidth(text))/2;
        if (d.height > preferredSize.height)
            y = (d.height-preferredSize.height)/2 +
            fm.getMaxDescent()+1;
        else
            y = fm.getMaxDescent()+1;
        g.drawString(text,x,d.height-y);
    }
    public Dimension minimumSize() {
        int x,y;
        FontMetrics fm = getFontMetrics(getFont());
        x = fm.stringWidth(text) + fm.getMaxAdvance();
        y = fm.getLeading() + fm.getAscent() + fm.getDescent();
        preferredSize = new Dimension(x,y);
        return preferredSize;
    }

    public Dimension preferredSize() {
        return minimumSize();
    }
```

```
    public void setFont(Font f) {
        super.setFont(f);
        resize(preferredSize());
    }
}
```

ButtonCanvas.java

This class provides a button equivalent that provides both a text and image label on the button. You can use this class as a basis for developing your own "flowery" buttons.

```
/*
* This is a custom button developed on top of Canvas, rather than
on Button
* It provides Button functionality with an Image and Text Label.
*/

import java.awt.*;
import java.awt.image.*;

/*
* a pure Java button
*/
public class ButtonCanvas extends Canvas {
    Color stableColor;
    String text;
    Font font;
    Dimension preferredSize;
    boolean state = true;
    Image image = null;
    int imageWidth, imageHeight;

    ButtonCanvas() {
        this("");
    }
    ButtonCanvas(String l) {
```

```
        text = l;     // remember the text
    }
    ButtonCanvas(String l,Image i) {
        text = l;     // remember the text
        image = i;     // remember the image
    }

    /*
    * this draws the text
    */
    public void paint(Graphics g) {
        Dimension d = size();
        FontMetrics fm;
        int x;
        int y;
        fm = g.getFontMetrics();
        g.setColor(getBackground());
        g.draw3DRect(0,0,d.width-1,d.height-1,state);

        if (image != null) {
            g.drawImage(image,6,6,getBackground(),this);
        }

        g.setColor(getForeground());
        if (state == false)
            g.drawRoundRect(4,4,d.width-9,d.height-9,5,5);
        x = (d.width - (imageWidth + fm.stringWidth(text)))/2;
        if (d.height > preferredSize.height)
            y = (d.height-(preferredSize.height-fm.getHeight()))/2
            + fm.getMaxDescent()+4;
        else
            y = fm.getMaxDescent()+4;
        g.drawString(text,x+imageWidth,
        (d.height+fm.getHeight())/2);
    }
    /*
    * min and preferred are always same
```

```
*/
public Dimension minimumSize() {
    int x,y;
    int h,w;
    FontMetrics fm = getFontMetrics(getFont());
    x = fm.stringWidth(text) + fm.getMaxAdvance() + 8;
    y = fm.getLeading() + fm.getAscent() + fm.getDescent() + 8;
    if (image != null) {    // add in image size
        imageHeight =image.getHeight(this);
        imageWidth =image.getWidth(this);
        if ((imageHeight+10) > y)
            y = imageHeight + 10;  // 2 pixels all around
        x = x + imageWidth + 10;
    }
    preferredSize = new Dimension(x,y);
    return preferredSize;
}

public Dimension preferredSize() {
    return minimumSize();
}

/*
* tell parent, and adjust for us
*/
public void setFont(Font f) {
    super.setFont(f);
    resize(preferredSize());
}

/*
* show button in depressed state
*/
public boolean mouseDown(Event evt, int x, int y) {
    if (evt.target == this)  {
        state = false;
```

```
            repaint();
            return true;
        }
        return false;
    }
    /*
    * show button in normal state and create new
    * ACTION_EVENT for our container
    */
    public boolean mouseUp(Event evt, int x, int y) {
        if (evt.target == this)  {
            state = true;
            repaint();
            Event e = new Event(this, evt.when, Event.ACTION_EVENT,
                evt.x,evt.y,evt.key,evt.modifiers,(Object)text);
            deliverEvent(e);    // ship off ACTION_EVENT
            return true;
        }
        return false;
    }

    /*
    * weird fakeout for disable/enable
    */
    public void setForeGround(Color c) {
        stableColor = c;
        super.setForeground(c);
    }

    public Color getForeGround() {
//          super.getForeground();
        return stableColor;
    }

    public void enable() {
        super.setForeground(stableColor);
```

```
        super.enable();
        repaint();
    }

    public void disable() {
        stableColor = super.getForeground();
        super.disable();
        super.setForeground(Color.gray);
        repaint();
    }
}
```

TextInteger.java

This class provides a simple text field that does input verification for integers. You can use this class as a basis for developing your own numeric fields.

```
import java.awt.*;
import java.applet.*;
import java.util.*;

/*
* TextInteger is an integer input field
* it can behave as a normal TextField, if need be,
* but... it is designed to validate integer input of the
* form:
*         +nnnn
*         -nnnn
*         nnnn
* Different constructors modeled on TextField
* with some additional methods:
*     int intValue()
*  Integer valueOf()
*  boolean isNumberField() -- if false, behave like TextField
```

```
*  void setNumberField(boolean state)-- if false, is behaving like
TextField
*
* reuse as desired, have fun.
*
* copyright (c) 1996, Pencom Web Works
*
*/

public class TextInteger extends TextField {
    Integer value;
    boolean numberField = true;

    public TextInteger() {
        this(10);    // always 10 columns if they don't say
    }
    public TextInteger(String s) {
        super(s);
    }
    public TextInteger(String s,int cols) {
        super(s,cols);
    }
    // no int cols constructor, since int val is required
    public TextInteger(int val) {
        super(new Integer(val).toString(),10);
    }
    public TextInteger(int val,int cols) {
        super(new Integer(val).toString(),cols);
    }

    public void setText(String s) {
        super.setText(s);
    }
    public void setValue(int n) {
        super.setText(""+n);
    }
```

```
public Integer valueOf() {
    String s = super.getText();
    if (numberField == false)
        return null;
    try {
        value = new Integer(s);
    } catch (Exception ex) {
        value = null;
    }
    return (value);
}

public int intValue() {
    if (numberField)
        return (((Integer)this.valueOf()).intValue());
       else
           return 0;
}

public boolean isNumberField() {
    return (numberField);
}

public void setNumberField(boolean state) {
    numberField = state;
}

public boolean handleEvent(Event e) {
    if (e.id == Event.KEY_PRESS) {
        String s = getText();
        int i = getSelectionStart();

        if (numberField == false)
            return(super.handleEvent(e));

        if (e.modifiers > 1 || e.key &lt ' ') {
            return false;    // let others handle special //
                             chars
```

```
        } else if (e.key == '-' || e.key == '+'  ||
            (e.key >= '0' && e.key &lt = '9')) {
            /*
            * numbers and digits
            */
            switch(e.key) {
            case '+':
            case '-':
                if (i != 0) {    // not in column one
                    e.key = 7;   // set the keystroke to a //
                                 bell
                    break;
                }
            default:        // the digits and (+- in column zero)
                if (s.length() == 0) // this key will be //
                                     only content
                    return false;    // early out
                try {     // this is so number conversion  // is
                          easy
                    value = new Integer(s);
                } catch (Exception ex) {
                    if (getSelectionStart() == 0 &&
                         getSelectionEnd() == s.length()) {
                        // next time we'll be happy :)
                    } else { // number in midst of text :(
                        e.key = 7;        // set keystroke // to
                                          a bell
                        selectAll();      // mark the whole //
                                          thing!!
                    }
                }
            }
        } else {            // all other printable chars fail
            e.key = 7;  // set the keystroke to a bell
        }
    } else if (e.id == Event.KEY_RELEASE) {
```

```
            /*
            * this code is for debug, it really
            * isn't required for normal operation
            */
            try {
                value = new Integer(getText());
//          System.out.println("Debug: TextInteger is " + value);
            } catch (Exception ex) {
//          System.out.println("Debug: TextInteger invalid " +
            getText());
                return true;    // fail this
            }
        }
        return false;  // we didn't handle it (or we're lying)
    }
}
```

ColorPanel.java

This class provides the core of a simple color picking mechanism. You may want to add event generation or colorwell drag and drop to this, but the core works fine.

```
/*
* ColorPanel is a Color selection panel that allows a user to pick
* a color by adjusting each of red, green, and blue components,
displaying
* the result color in a small canvas.  To be useful, it should be
extended
* to support better event propagation and colorwell drag and drop.
*
* ColorPanel is used to exercise custom
* objects and AWT objects for the AWT book
*/
import java.awt.*;
import java.applet.*;
```

```
import java.util.*;
import FontSelect;
import FontSample;
/*
* import any custom classes here
*/
import TextInteger;        // number field

/*
* ColorPanel is used to exercise custom
* objects and AWT objects for the AWT book
*/
public class ColorPanel extends Applet {
    Colorbar red;
    Colorbar green;
    Colorbar blue;
    ColorCanvas color;
    String ct[] = {"red","green","blue"};

    public ColorPanel() {
        this(1);
    }

    public ColorPanel(int format) {
        Panel p = new Panel();
        p.setLayout(new BorderLayout());
        p.add("North",new Label("Color"));
        p.add("Center",color = new ColorCanvas());
        p.show();
        if (format == 1)
            setLayout(new FlowLayout());
        else
            setLayout(new GridLayout(5,1));

        add(p);
        add(red = new Colorbar(Colorbar.RED,1,8));
        add(green = new Colorbar(Colorbar.GREEN,1,8));
```

```
        add(blue = new Colorbar(Colorbar.BLUE,1,8));
//        add(new Button("Reset"));
        show();
    }

    public void init() {
        Panel p = new Panel();
        p.setLayout(new BorderLayout());
        p.add("North",new Label("Color"));
        p.add("Center",color = new ColorCanvas());
        p.show();
        setLayout(new FlowLayout());
        add(p);
        add(red = new Colorbar(Colorbar.RED,1,8));
        add(green = new Colorbar(Colorbar.GREEN,1,8));
        add(blue = new Colorbar(Colorbar.BLUE,1,8));
        show();
    }

    public void paint(Graphics g) {
        Dimension d = size();
        super.paint(g);
        g.drawRect(0,0,d.width-1,d.height-1);
    }
    public Insets insets() {
        return new Insets(3,3,3,3);
    }

    public boolean handleEvent(Event evt) {
        if (evt.target == red || evt.target == green || evt.target
        == blue) {
            if (evt.id == Event.ACTION_EVENT) {
                color.setBackground(new
                Color(red.getValue(),green.getValue(),
                blue.getValue()));
                color.repaint();
            }
```

```
            return true;
        }
        return false;
    }

    public Color getColor() {
        return color.getBackground();
    }

    /*
    * main program  -- no changes here (at least usually)
    */
    public static void main(String args[]) {
        Frame x = new Frame("Scrollbar Color");
        Applet p = new ColorPanel();
//        p.init();
        x.setLayout(new BorderLayout());
        x.add("North",p);

        x.pack();
        x.show();
    }

}

/*
* ColorCanvas is a basic class that just paints the background in a
* selected color
*/
class ColorCanvas extends Canvas {
    Color color;
    ColorCanvas() {
        color = new Color(255,255,255);
    }
    ColorCanvas(Color c) {
        setBackground(c);
    }
```

```
    public Color getBackground() {
        return color;
    }
    public void setBackground(Color c) {
        color = c;
        repaint();
    }
    public void paint(Graphics g) {
        Dimension d = size();
        g.setColor(getBackground());
        g.fillRect(1,2,d.width-2,d.height-2);
        g.setColor(getForeground());
        g.drawRect(0,0,d.width-1,d.height-1);
    }
    public Dimension minimumSize() {
        return new Dimension(32,48);
    }
    public Dimension preferredSize() {
//          return new Dimension(64,64);
        return new Dimension(32,48);
    }
}

/*
* Colorbar is a basic borderlayout panel with a ColorCanvas, Label,
and
* Scrollbar.  One of these is used by ColorPanel for each color
component
* (red, green, and blue)
*/
class Colorbar extends Panel {
    int type;
    Scrollbar sb;
    ColorCanvas canvas;
    int value;
    final static int RED = 1;
```

```
final static int GREEN = 2;
final static int BLUE = 4;
final static String colorNames[] = {"Black","Red","Green",
"Yellow","Blue","Magenta","Cyan","White"};

Colorbar() {
    this(RED|GREEN|BLUE,128,1);
}
Colorbar(int colorComponent, int v, int visible) {
    int r = 0;
    int g = 0;
    int b = 0;
    value = v;
    type = colorComponent;
    setLayout(new BorderLayout());
    add("West",sb = new Scrollbar(Scrollbar.VERTICAL,v,
    visible,1,255));
    add("Center",canvas = new ColorCanvas());
    add("North",new Label(colorNames[type]));
    if ((type & RED) != 0)
        r = 255-value;
    if ((type & GREEN) != 0)
        g = 255-value;
    if ((type & BLUE) != 0)
        b = 255-value;
    canvas.setBackground(new Color(r,g,b));
    canvas.repaint();
    repaint();
}

public int getValue() {
    return 255-value;
}
public void setValue(int v) {
    value =  255-v;
    sb.setValue(v);
```

```
        repaint();
    }

    public boolean handleEvent(Event evt) {
        Event e;
        if (evt.target == sb) {
            switch (evt.id) {
            case Event.SCROLL_LINE_DOWN:
            case Event.SCROLL_LINE_UP:
            case Event.SCROLL_PAGE_DOWN:
            case Event.SCROLL_PAGE_UP:
            case Event.SCROLL_ABSOLUTE:
                break;
            default:
//                  System.out.println("idono:" + evt.id);
                break;
            }
            value = ((Integer)evt.arg).intValue();
            if (value &lt 0) {
                value = 0;
                evt.arg = (Object)new Integer(value);
            }
            if (value>255) {
                value = 255;
                evt.arg = (Object)new Integer(value);
            }
            repaint();
            e = new Event(this, evt.when, Event.ACTION_EVENT,
                    evt.x,evt.y,evt.key,evt.modifiers,
                    new Integer(255-value));
            deliverEvent(e);    // ship off ACTION_EVENT
            return true;
        }
        return false;
    }
```

```
    public void paint(Graphics graphics) {
        int r = 0;
        int g = 0;
        int b = 0;
        if ((type & RED) != 0)
            r = 255-value;
        if ((type & GREEN) != 0)
            g = 255-value;
        if ((type & BLUE) != 0)
            b = 255-value;
        canvas.setBackground(new Color(r,g,b));
        canvas.repaint();
    }

    public Insets insets() {
        return new Insets(5,5,5,5);
    }

    public String toString() {
        return "Colorbar=[sb.value=" + sb.getValue() + ", value=" +
        value;
    }
}
```

Moray.java

This is a very simple Java applet that is intended to show how to draw efficiently. Double buffering and simple display list optimization make this a fairly low overhead CPU sink. Feel free to add other patterns to this and produce your own pure Java screen waster.

```
/*
* This program is an example of moderately optimized drawing
techniques
* Double buffering, and a simple optimization of the display list
allow
```

```
* this program to quickly generate a sweeping moiré pattern in a
panel.
*
* Moray.java uses the Runnable interface to manage two threads.
*/

import java.awt.*;
import java.applet.*;

public class Moray extends Applet implements Runnable {
    Thread thread;
    static final int LINE_SKIP=4;
    private Image offScreenImage;
    private Graphics offScreenGC;
    Line lines[] = new Line[32];
    int x,y;    // the outer endpoint
    int a,b;    // the inner endpoint
    int yskip,xskip;  // which way to move the outer endpoint
    int nextLine;     // which line to draw next

    public void init() {
        x = 0;                      // start at upper left
        y = 0;
        a = size().width/2;     // inner end point at center
        b = size().height/2;
        yskip = LINE_SKIP;
        xskip = 0;
        nextLine = 0;
    }

    public void run() {
        while(thread != null) {
            repaint();
            sleep(50);     // short delay 1/20th sec
        }
    }

    public void start() {
```

```
        offScreenImage = null;
        thread = new Thread(this);
        System.out.println("Start thread = " + thread);
        thread.start();
    }

    public void stop() {
        System.out.println("Stopped thread");
        thread = null;
    }

    public void update(Graphics g) {
        if (offScreenImage == null) {
            offScreenImage = createImage(size().width,
            size().height);
            offScreenGC = offScreenImage.getGraphics();
            offScreenGC.setColor(getBackground());
            offScreenGC.fillRect(0,0,size().width, size().height);
            offScreenGC.setColor(getForeground());
        }
        paint(offScreenGC);
        g.drawImage(offScreenImage,0,0,null);
    }

    public void sleep(int millisecs) {
        try {
            Thread.sleep(millisecs);
        } catch(InterruptedException e){}
    }

    public boolean handleEvent(Event e) {
        if (e.id == Event.WINDOW_DESTROY)
            System.exit(0);
        return false;
    }

    public void paint(Graphics g) {
        int i,j;
```

```
Dimension d = size();
if (nextLine >= lines.length)
    nextLine = 0;

i = 0;
if (yskip>0) {
    if (y &lt= (d.height - LINE_SKIP)) {
        y += LINE_SKIP;
    } else {
        yskip = 0;
        y = d.height;
        xskip = LINE_SKIP;
    }
} else if (yskip == 0) {
    if (xskip>0) {
        if (x &lt= (d.width - LINE_SKIP)) {
            x += LINE_SKIP;
        } else {
            x = d.width;
            xskip = 0;
            yskip = -LINE_SKIP;
        }
    } else {
        if (x > LINE_SKIP) {
            x -= LINE_SKIP;
        } else {
            xskip = 0;
            x = 0;
            yskip = LINE_SKIP;
        }
    }

} else if (yskip &lt 0) {
    if (y > LINE_SKIP) {
        y -= LINE_SKIP;
    } else {
```

```
                yskip = 0;
                y = 0;
                xskip = -LINE_SKIP;
            }
        }

        lines[nextLine] = new Line(x,y,a,b);
        lines[nextLine].setBackground(getBackground());
        lines[nextLine].setForeground(getForeground());
        try {
            lines[nextLine].drawLine(g);
            lines[(nextLine+1)%lines.length].clearLine(g);
        } catch (nullPointerException e) {
//              System.out.println("empty line " + e);
        }
//          System.out.println("drawing " + nextLine + " from " +
            lines[nextLine]);
        nextLine++;
    }
    public Dimension minimumSize() {
        return new Dimension(128,128);
    }
    public Dimension preferredSize() {
        return new Dimension(512,512);
    }
}
/*
* Line class provides basic endpoint management and storage
*/
class Line {
    int x1,y1,x2,y2;
    Color cf,cb;

    Line() {
    }
    Line(int xp1,int yp1, int xp2,int yp2) {
```

```
        x1 = xp1;
        y1 = yp1;
        x2 = xp2;
        y2 = yp2;
    }
    public void setEndPoints(int xp1,int yp1, int xp2,
    int yp2) {
        x1 = xp1;
        y1 = yp1;
        x2 = xp2;
        y2 = yp2;
    }

    public void setForeground(Color c) {
        cf = c;
    }
    public void setBackground(Color c) {
        cb = c;
    }
    public void drawLine(Graphics g) {
        g.setColor(cf);
        g.drawLine(x1,y1,x2,y2);
    }

    public void clearLine(Graphics g) {
        g.setColor(cb);
        g.drawLine(x1,y1,x2,y2);
    }

    public int[] getEndPoints() {
        int p[] = new int[4];
        p[0] = x1;
        p[1] = y1;
        p[2] = x2;
        p[3] = y2;
        return p;
    }
```

```
    public String toString() {
        return "Line(" + x1 + "," + y1 + "," + x2 + ",
        " + y2 + ")";
    }
}
```

Other Small Examples

This section contains examples that have appeared in other places, but we felt that they were appropriate for inclusion in this book as style or methodology examples.

GUIExampleDblBuf.java

This example is from *Java Programming Basics.* It is an example of a graphics program that draws interactively, a topic we just didn't have time to cover in depth.

```
import java.applet.Applet;
import java.awt.*;          // we're using just about everything
import java.util.Vector;

// A class for drawable rectangles
class DrawableRect extends Rectangle {

    Color color = Color.black; // What color am I?
    boolean filled = false;    // Am I filled, or not?

    // constructs a drawable rectangle with the indicated
    // dimensions and attributes
    DrawableRect(int x, int y, int width, int height,
        Color color, boolean filled) {

        super(x, y, width, height);
        this.color = color;
        this.filled = filled;
    }
```

```
    // draws a rectangle taking into account the specified
    // offset
    void draw(Graphics g, int offset_x, int offset_y) {

        Color temp = g.getColor();
        g.setColor(color);
        if (filled) {
            g.fillRect(x - offset_x, y - offset_y,
            width, height);
        } else {
            g.drawRect(x - offset_x, y - offset_y,
            width, height);
        }
        g.setColor(temp);
    }
}

class CheckboxPanel extends Panel {

    // A CheckboxGroup enforces mutual exclusion
    CheckboxGroup myGroup;

    // Two checkboxes in the group
    Checkbox filledBox;
    Checkbox notFilledBox;

    CheckboxPanel() {
        // new java.awt.Panel()
        super();
        setLayout(new BorderLayout());

        myGroup = new CheckboxGroup();

        filledBox = new Checkbox("Filled", myGroup, false);
        notFilledBox = new Checkbox("Not Filled",
        myGroup, true);
        myGroup.setCurrent(notFilledBox);

        add("North", filledBox);
        add("South", notFilledBox);
```

```
    }

    // Return the state of our checkbox group
    boolean isFilled() {
        return (myGroup.getCurrent() == filledBox);
    }
}

class RectCanvas extends Canvas {
    /* for double buffering*/
    private Image offScreenImage;
    private Graphics offScreenGC;

    // mouse down point
    int orig_x;
    int orig_y;

    // where the canvas has scrolled to
    public int offset_x = 0;
    public int offset_y = 0;

    // current settings for new rectangles
    boolean filled = false;
    Color rectColor = Color.black;

    // the collection of rectangles
    int numRects = 0;
    Vector rects = new Vector(100, 10);
    DrawableRect currentRect;    // just for convenience

// create a drawable rectangle and add it to the list of rects
    DrawableRect addRect(int x, int y, int width,
    int height) {

        DrawableRect r = new DrawableRect(x, y, width, height,
                                          rectColor, filled);
        rects.addElement(r);
        numRects++;

        return r;
```

```
}

// disposes of all rectangles and starts a new list
void clearRects() {
    numRects = 0;
    rects = new Vector(100, 10);
    repaint();
}

// set the color for adding new rectangles
void setRectColor(Color c) {
    rectColor = c;
}

// set the filled attribute for adding new rectangles
void setFilled(boolean b) {
    filled = b;
}

// respond to mouseDown events
// ... called by inherited handleEvent()
public boolean mouseDown(Event evt, int x, int y) {

    // set the mouse-down point
    orig_x = x;
    orig_y = y;

    // start a new rectangle
    currentRect = addRect(orig_x + offset_x,
                          orig_y + offset_y, 0, 0);
    return true;
}

// respond to mouseDrag events
// ... called by inherited handleEvent()
public boolean mouseDrag(Event evt, int x, int y) {

    // how far have we dragged in x and y?
    int x_diff = x - orig_x;
```

```
        int y_diff = y - orig_y;

        // Rectangles can't have negative height and width.
        //     We want the Rectangle to follow the mouse.
        //         Which is the top left corner?
        int x_val = (x_diff > 0)?
                    orig_x + offset_x :
                    x + offset_x;
        int y_val = (y_diff > 0)?
                    orig_y + offset_y :
                    y + offset_y;

        //         Height and width determined by drag length.
        int width_val = Math.abs(x_diff);
        int height_val = Math.abs(y_diff);

        // Interactively reshape the rectangle
        currentRect.reshape(x_val, y_val, width_val, height_val);

        // Show the results as the user drags
        repaint();
        return true;
    }

    /* Override resize() for double buffering*/
    public void resize(int w, int h) {
        offScreenImage = null;
        super.resize(w, h);
    }

    /* Override update() for double buffering*/
    public void update(Graphics g) {
        paint(g);
    }

    // Draw all rectangles on the canvas
    public void paint(Graphics g) {
        DrawableRect r;
```

```
        /* For double buffering*/
        if (offScreenImage == null) {
            offScreenImage = createImage(size().width,
            size().height);
            offScreenGC = offScreenImage.getGraphics();
        }
        offScreenGC.setColor(getBackground());
        offScreenGC.fillRect(0, 0, size().width, size().height);

        for (int i = 0; i &lt numRects; i++) {
            r = (DrawableRect)rects.elementAt(i);

           // draw each rectangle, offset by the scroll amount
            r.draw(offScreenGC, offset_x, offset_y);
        }

        g.drawImage(offScreenImage, 0, 0, this);
    }

}

public class GUIExampleDblBuf extends Applet {

    // the top panel and its subitems
    Panel topPanel = new Panel();
    CheckboxPanel checkboxPanel = new CheckboxPanel();
    Label colorLabel = new Label("Color: ");
    Choice colorChoice = new Choice();

    // the middle panel and its subitems
    Panel middlePanel = new Panel();
    RectCanvas rCanvas = new RectCanvas();
    Scrollbar x_scroll = new Scrollbar(Scrollbar.HORIZONTAL);
    Scrollbar y_scroll = new Scrollbar(Scrollbar.VERTICAL);

    // the bottom panel and its subitem
    Panel bottomPanel = new Panel();
    Button clearButton = new Button("Clear");

    public void init() {
```

```
// create a layout manager and set our applet to use it
this.setLayout(new BorderLayout());

// SET UP THE TOP PANEL...

topPanel.setLayout(new FlowLayout());

// the color choice
colorChoice.addItem("Black");
colorChoice.addItem("Blue");
colorChoice.addItem("Red");
colorChoice.addItem("Green");
colorChoice.addItem("Cyan");
colorChoice.select("Black");

// ... add all items to the top panel
topPanel.add(checkboxPanel);
topPanel.add(colorLabel);
topPanel.add(colorChoice);

// ... add the top panel to the applet
this.add("North", topPanel);

// THE MIDDLE PANEL...
middlePanel.setLayout(new BorderLayout());

// ...set up the middle panel's RectCanvas
rCanvas.setFilled(checkboxPanel.isFilled());
rCanvas.setRectColor(getSelectedColor());
rCanvas.setBackground(Color.white);

// ...add all items to the middle panel
middlePanel.add("South", x_scroll);
middlePanel.add("East", y_scroll);
middlePanel.add("Center", rCanvas);

// ... add the middle panel to the applet
add("Center", middlePanel);

// THE BOTTOM PANEL...
```

```
        bottomPanel.add(clearButton);
        // ... add the panel to the applet
        this.add("South", bottomPanel);

        resize(350, 350);
    }

    public void paint(Graphics g) {
        // make sure the canvas gets repainted

        rCanvas.repaint();
    }

    // Read the currently selected color
    //  from the Choice item
    Color getSelectedColor() {
        if (colorChoice.getSelectedItem().equals("Black")) {
            return Color.black;
        } else if (colorChoice.getSelectedItem(). equals("Blue")) {
            return Color.blue;
        } else if (colorChoice.getSelectedItem(). equals("Red")) {
            return Color.red;
        } else if (colorChoice.getSelectedItem(). equals("Green"))
          {
            return Color.green;
        } else if (colorChoice.getSelectedItem(). equals("Cyan")) {
            return Color.cyan;
        } else {
            return Color.black;
        }
    }

    // overrides java.awt.Component.handleEvent()
    public boolean handleEvent(Event evt) {

        if (evt.target == colorChoice) {
            rCanvas.setRectColor(getSelectedColor());

        } else if (evt.target instanceof Checkbox) {
```

```
        rCanvas.setFilled(checkboxPanel.isFilled());

    } else if (evt.target == x_scroll) {
        switch (evt.id) {
            case Event.SCROLL_LINE_UP:
            case Event.SCROLL_LINE_DOWN:
            case Event.SCROLL_PAGE_UP:
            case Event.SCROLL_PAGE_DOWN:
            case Event.SCROLL_ABSOLUTE:
                // evt.arg holds the value that
                //    the scrollbar has scrolled to
                rCanvas.offset_x = ((Integer)
                evt.arg).intValue();
                break;
        }

    } else if (evt.target == y_scroll) {
        switch (evt.id) {
            case Event.SCROLL_LINE_UP:
            case Event.SCROLL_LINE_DOWN:
            case Event.SCROLL_PAGE_UP:
            case Event.SCROLL_PAGE_DOWN:
            case Event.SCROLL_ABSOLUTE:
                // evt.arg holds the value that
                //    the scrollbar has scrolled to
                rCanvas.offset_y = ((Integer)
                evt.arg).intValue();
                break;
        }
    }
    // the canvas has been scrolled, so...
    rCanvas.repaint();

    // make sure other events are handled by
    // ... the overridden event handler
    return super.handleEvent(evt);
}
```

```
    // Respond to ACTION events
    // ... called by java.awt.Component.handleEvent()
    public boolean action(Event evt, Object what) {
        if (evt.target.equals(clearButton)) {

            // clear the rectangles
            rCanvas.clearRects();

        }

        // ...just in case our parent needs the event
        return super.action(evt, what);
    }

    // Overrides java.awt.Component.reshape()
    // This method is called when the user resizes the applet
    public void reshape(int x, int y, int width, int height) {

        // allow java.awt.Component.reshape()
        //    ... to do the real work
        super.reshape(x, y, width, height);

        // Adjust the scrollbars:
        //   values, visible amounts, and ranges
        int canvasWidth = rCanvas.size().width;
        int canvasHeight = rCanvas.size().height;

        // ... use 1000 pixel "virtual" canvas
        x_scroll.setValues(rCanvas.offset_x,
                           canvasWidth,
                           0, 1000 - canvasWidth);
        y_scroll.setValues(rCanvas.offset_y,
                           canvasHeight,
                           0, 1000 - canvasHeight);

        // repaint the canvas
        rCanvas.repaint();
    }
}
```

PrintProperties.java

This example, also from *Java Programming Basics*, prints the system properties to **System.out**.

```
import java.util.StringTokenizer;

public class PrintProperties extends java.applet.Applet {
    String propString;

    public PrintProperties() {
        java.util.Properties p = System.getProperties();
        propString = p.toString();
    }

    public static void main(String args[]) {
        PrintProperties app = new PrintProperties();
        StringTokenizer st = new StringTokenizer(
            app.propString, "{,}", false);

        while (st.hasMoreTokens()) {
            System.out.println(st.nextToken());
        }
    }

    public void paint(java.awt.Graphics g) {
        StringTokenizer st = new StringTokenizer
                    (propString, "{,}", false);
        int y = 10;

        while (st.hasMoreTokens()) {
            g.drawString(st.nextToken(), 10, y+=15);
        }
    }

}
```

CalendarMonth.java

This example wasn't described in our book, but it was used to test some of the AWT platform-dependent features while writing it.

```
/*
* CalendarMonth.java -- paint a Month of buttons with labels that
match
* the month under discussion.  Month honor mouse clicks by
selecting
* that date and communicating it to CalendarMonth, who paints the
date
* in a Label at the bottom of the frame.
*/
import java.awt.*;
import java.util.*;
import DateTransport;

public class CalendarMonth extends Frame implements DateTransport{
    private boolean inAnApplet = true;
    Date startDate;    // starting date of this month
    Date selectedDate;     // current date in calendar
    Label date;          // place to show the date
    int curDate;     // index into "days" of most recently
                     // selected date
    int thisDays;    // number of days in this month
    Month window;

    public CalendarMonth() {
        this(new Date());
    }

    public CalendarMonth(Date d) {
    int i,j;
    int prevDays;     // previous months days
    startDate = d;
```

```
        curDate = startDate.getDate();  // remember his
                                        // selected start date
        if (curDate != 1) {     // make sure we talk first day // of
                                month
            startDate.setDate(1);
        }
        selectedDate = new Date(startDate.toString());
        if (selectedDate == startDate) {
            System.out.println("dates are equal... rats");

        } else if (selectedDate.equals(startDate)) {
            System.out.println("date objects are equivalent");
        }

        thisDays = new Date(startDate.getYear(),
        startDate.getMonth()+1,0).getDate();
        System.out.println(thisDays + " in this month ");

        setLayout(new BorderLayout(4,4));
        setFont(new Font("Helvetica", Font.PLAIN, 14));

         window = new Month(startDate,this);
         add("Center",window);
         setBackground(Color.lightGray);
         setForeground(Color.black);
        date = new Label((selectedDate.getMonth()+1) + "/" +
        selectedDate.getDate() + "/" + selectedDate.getYear());
        date.setBackground(Color.darkGray);
        date.setForeground(Color.white);
        add("South",date);
        pack();
    }

    public Date getSelection() {
        return startDate;
    }

    public Insets insets() {
```

```
        return new Insets(25,5,5,5);
    }

    public void setSelection(Date day) {
        selectedDate = new Date(day.toString());
        System.out.println("selected date is " +
        selectedDate.toString());
        date.setText((selectedDate.getMonth()+1) + "/" +
        selectedDate.getDate() + "/" + selectedDate.getYear());
    }
    public boolean handleEvent(Event e) {
        if (e.id == Event.WINDOW_DESTROY) {
            if (inAnApplet) {
//                  dispose();
                return true;
            } else {
                System.exit(0);
            }
        } else if (e.id == Event.ACTION_EVENT) {
        Button x = (Button)e.target;
        int i;
        System.out.println(x.toString());

        return true;
    }
        return super.handleEvent(e);
    }

    public static void main(String args[]) {
    Date d = new Date(96,9,1);
    CalendarMonth window = new CalendarMonth(d);

    window.inAnApplet = false;
    window.show();

    }
}
```

Month.java

Here's the other half of **CalendarMonth.java**, the month itself.

```
/*
* Month.java -- produces a calendar month panel (ugly, but it
works, and
* it demonstrates some of the essential ugliness of platform-
independent
* code as implemented in Java 1.0.x.  Hopefully, 1.1 will be
better:)
*/
import java.awt.*;
import java.util.*;
import DateTransport;

public class Month extends Panel implements DateTransport {
    private boolean inAnApplet = false;
    DateTransport parent = null;
    Button days[] = new Button[42];    // space for some
                                       // buttons (days)
    Date startDate;   // starting date of this month
    int startDay;     // day of week this month starts on (0-6)
    int thisDays;    // number of days in this month
    int curDate;     // index into "days" of most recently
                     // selected date

    public Month() {
        this(new Date(),null);
    }

    public Month(Date d) {
        this(d,null);
    }
    public Month(Date d,DateTransport p) {
    int i,j;
    int prevDays;     // previous months days
    Button b;
```

```
parent = p;
startDate = d;
System.out.println("New Month starts on " + d.toString());
curDate = startDate.getDate();  // remember his
                                // selected start date
if (curDate != 1) {     // make sure we talk first day // of
                        month
    startDate.setDate(1);
}
startDay = startDate.getDay();
prevDays = new Date(startDate.getYear(),
startDate.getMonth(),0).getDate();
thisDays = new Date(startDate.getYear(),
startDate. getMonth()+1,0).getDate();

setLayout(new GridLayout(0,7));
setFont(new Font("Helvetica", Font.PLAIN, 14));

// add the days of week
   b = new Button("S");
   b.disable();
   add(b);
   b = new Button("M");
   b.disable();
   add(b);
   b = new Button("T");
   b.disable();
   add(b);
   b = new Button("W");
   b.disable();
   add(b);
   b = new Button("T");
   b.disable();
   add(b);
   b = new Button("F");
   b.disable();
   add(b);
```

```
            b = new Button("S");
            b.disable();
            add(b);

          for(i=0;i&lt42;i++) {
               days[i] = new Button();
               days[i].disable();
               add(days[i]);
          }
            changeMonth(startDate);

//   System.out.println("added " + i + " days in this month ");

     }

     public void changeMonth(Date d) {
     int i,j;
     int prevDays;     // previous months days

          startDate = d;
          System.out.println("Change Month starts on " +
          d.toString());
          curDate = startDate.getDate(); // remember his
                                         // selected start date
          if (curDate != 1) {
               startDate.setDate(1);
          }
          startDay = startDate.getDay();
          System.out.println("CHGMONTH current date is " + curDate +
          "startDay is " + startDay);
          prevDays = new Date(startDate.getYear(),
          startDate.getMonth(),0).getDate();
          thisDays = new Date(startDate.getYear(),
          startDate.getMonth()+1,0).getDate();

          for(i=0;i&ltstartDay;i++) {
               days[i].setLabel(String.valueOf(prevDays+1-startDay-
               i));
               days[i].disable();
```

```
        }
        for(i=startDay;i&ltthisDays+startDay;i++) {
            days[i].setLabel(String.valueOf(i-startDay+1));
            days[i].enable();
        }
        for(j=1;i&lt42;i++,j++) {
            days[i].setLabel(String.valueOf(j));
            days[i].disable();
        }

    }

    public void repaint() {
        System.out.println("in Month repaint(), layout is " +
        getLayout().toString());
        System.out.println("Component Count is " +
        countComponents());
//        show();
//        validate();
    }

    public Insets insets() {
        return new Insets(5,5,5,5);
    }
    public void setSelection(Date sd) {

        return;
    }

    public Date getSelection() {
        return startDate;
    }

    public boolean handleEvent(Event e) {
        if (e.id == Event.WINDOW_DESTROY) {
            if (inAnApplet) {
//                dispose();
                return true;
            } else {
```

```
                System.exit(0);
            }
        } else if (e.id == Event.ACTION_EVENT) {
        Button x = (Button)e.target;
        int i;
//          System.out.println(x.toString());
            for (i=startDay;i &lt startDay+thisDays;i++) {
                if (days[i] == x ) {
                    curDate = i;
        System.out.println("current date is " + curDate + "startDay
        is " + startDay);
                    startDate.setDate(1+curDate-startDay);
                    if (parent != null)
                        parent.setSelection(startDate);
                    return true;
                }
            }
        }
        return super.handleEvent(e);
    }

}
```

DateTransport Interface

CalendarMonth.java and **Month.java** communicate via a small interface, DateTransport. Here's the source to **DateTransport.java**.

```
/*
* DateTransport.java -- two methods, set and get selection Date
objects.
* used to pass dates back and forth between containers.
*/
import java.util.Date;
```

```
interface DateTransport {
    void setSelection(Date d);
    Date getSelection();
}
```

Larger Examples

These examples are referenced briefly in the book but not really explored or described in any depth there. They include a set of Tab (tabbed `CardLayout`) objects with an example and a heavy-duty example of using layouts within layouts (the Scope example), which includes a pair of bonus objects: a `PopupDialog` and a `MsgArea` (message area).

Tabbed CardLayout Classes

This directory includes an improvement on the `CardLayout` object, donated by Vignette Corporation. I removed all Vignette proprietary code for this release. The code is not formatted quite as nicely as we would like. Still, it's in good shape, and it works beautifully.

The only two classes you should have to worry about from an API standpoint are `TabPanel` and `ExtPanel`. `TabPanel` is the mother of all tabbed objects, and all her children are instantiated through `ExtPanel` objects. You should definitely look at the source and experiment with the resources such as `TabCanvas.tabSpacing`.

TabPanel Class

`TabPanel` defines a tabbed version of a `CardLayout`. The tab information is stored in a hashed dictionary, which makes lookups fast for layouts with many tabs.

This class and its associated classes were graciously donated by Vignette Corporation.

Release: 1.0   30 Sep 1996 <*meo@pencom.com*>

Extends: ExtPanel

Imports: import java.awt.*, import java.util.*

Constructors:

```
TabPanel(String name, Container parent)
TabPanel(String name, Container parent, String layout)
```

This class assumes that its parent is managed by a `BorderLayout`. In general, use the first constructor or use the second with a layout value of `"Center"`.

For simpler applications, this is all you need from the `TabPanel` interface. The remaining work is handled by the `ExtPanel` object.

For more complete documentation, see the Pencom Web site and future editions of this book.

ExtPanel Class

`ExtPanel` manages the children (individual cards and their tabs) of a `TabPanel` object.

This class and its associated classes were graciously donated by Vignette Corporation.

Release: 1.0   30 Sep 1996 <*meo@pencom.com*>

Extends: Panel

Constructors:

```
ExtPanel(String name, Container parent)
ExtPanel(String name, Container parent, String layout)
```

In general, use the second constructor, with the information you want on the tab, in the layout argument.

This is all you need to handle basic cards and tabs.

For more complete documentation, see the Pencom Web site and future editions of this book.

Tabbed CardLayout Example

As an example of the Tab objects, we tossed together a set of tabbed cards about the various people involved with the Tab code.

Click on any of the tabs to show that card.

While the examples are all simple text widgets, each card is related to the `Panel` class and hence can be as complex as you like.

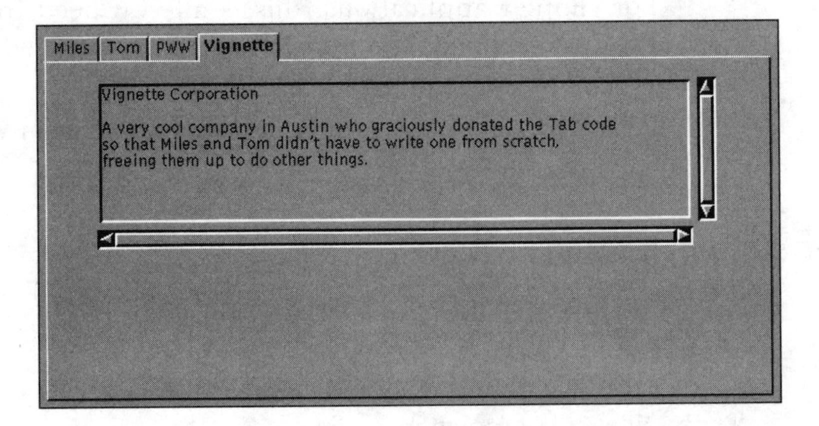

TabPanel

```
import java.awt.*;
import java.util.*;

/**
 *-----------------------------------------------------------
 * A Panel class that adds folder tabs to the CardLayout
```

```
 */
public class TabPanel extends ExtPanel {

    TabCanvas    tabCanvas;  // The tab area
    TabCardPanel cardPanel;  // The panel that holds the cards
    Hashtable    tabDict;    // Look up tab info for component
    boolean      initializing;
    int          shadowThickness = 2;    // Used around cards // and
                                         tabs
    Image        image = null;

/**
 *-----------------------------------------------------------
 * Creates a new panel
 */
    public TabPanel(Container parent) {
        this(parent, "Center");
    }

    public TabPanel(Container parent, String layout) {
        super(parent, layout);
        initializing = true;    // So that add works correctly
        setLayout(new BorderLayout());
        tabDict      = new Hashtable();
        tabCanvas    = new TabCanvas   (this, "North");
        cardPanel    = new TabCardPanel(this, "Center");
        initializing = false;   // So that add now adds to
                                // cardPanel
    }

/**
 *-----------------------------------------------------------
 * Add a component to the card panel
 */
    public synchronized Component add(String layout,
    Component comp) {

        if ( initializing ) return super.add(layout, comp);
```

```
        cardPanel.add(layout, comp);

        String  label = layout;
        TabInfo info  = new TabInfo(layout, label, image, true);

        tabDict.put(comp, info);

        return comp;
    }

/**
 *--------------------------------------------------------
 * Show or hide the tab for a component
 */
    public void showTab(Component comp, boolean show) {
        if ( show ) showTab(comp);
        else        hideTab(comp);
    }

    public void showTab(Component comp) {

        TabInfo info = (TabInfo)tabDict.get(comp);
        if ( info != null ) {
            //if ( info.visible ) return;
            info.visible = true;
        }

        show(comp);
        tabCanvas.curTab = comp;

        tabCanvas.invalidate();
        validate();
        tabCanvas.repaint(true);
    }

    public void hideTab(Component comp) {

        TabInfo info = (TabInfo)tabDict.get(comp);
        if ( info != null ) {
            if ( !info.visible ) return;
```

```
            info.visible = false;
        }

        if ( comp == tabCanvas.curTab ) {
            Enumeration tabs = cards();
            if ( tabs.hasMoreElements() ) {
                comp  = (Component)tabs.nextElement();
                show(comp);
                tabCanvas.curTab = comp;
            }
        }

        tabCanvas.invalidate();
        validate();
        tabCanvas.repaint(true);
    }

/**
 *-----------------------------------------------------------
 * Get the specified component
 */
    public Component getCard(int index) {
        return cardPanel.getComponent(index);
    }

/**
 *-----------------------------------------------------------
 * Get the card name for the specified component
 */
    public String getCardName(Component comp) {
        TabInfo info = (TabInfo)tabDict.get(comp);
        return ( info == null ? null : info.cardName );
    }

    public String getCardName(int index) {
        return getCardName(getCard(index));
    }
```

```
/**
 *----------------------------------------------------------
 * Get the label for the specified component
 */
    public String getLabel(Component comp) {
        TabInfo info = (TabInfo)tabDict.get(comp);
        return ( info == null ? null : info.label );
    }

    public String getLabel(int index) {
        return getLabel(getCard(index));
    }

/**
 *----------------------------------------------------------
 * Set the label for the specified component
 */
    public void setLabel(Component comp, String label) {
        TabInfo info = (TabInfo)tabDict.get(comp);
        if ( info != null ) info.label = label;
    }

    public void setLabel(int index, String label) {
        setLabel(getCard(index), label);
    }

/**
 *----------------------------------------------------------
 * Get the image for the specified component
 */
    public Image getImage(Component comp) {
        TabInfo info = (TabInfo)tabDict.get(comp);
        return ( info == null ? null : info.image );
    }

    public Image getImage(int index) {
        return getImage(getCard(index));
    }
```

```
/**
 *------------------------------------------------------------
 * Set the image for the specified component
 */
    public void setImage(Component comp, Image image) {
        TabInfo info = (TabInfo)tabDict.get(comp);
        if ( info != null ) info.image = image;
    }

    public void setImage(int index, Image image) {
        setImage(getCard(index), image);
    }

/**
 *------------------------------------------------------------
 * Get the visibility for the specified component
 */
    public boolean isShown(Component comp) {
        TabInfo info = (TabInfo)tabDict.get(comp);
        return ( info == null ? false : info.visible );
    }

    public boolean isShown(int index) {
        return isShown(getCard(index));
    }

/**
 *------------------------------------------------------------
 * Show the specified component.  Generate an action event.
 */
    public void show(Component comp) {
        cardPanel.show(getCardName(comp));
        postEvent(new Event(this, Event.ACTION_EVENT, comp));
    }

    public void show(int index) {
        show(getCard(index));
    }
```

```
/**
 *--------------------------------------------------------------
 * Return an enumeration of the cards
 */
    public Enumeration cards() {
        return new TabEnumeration(this);
    }

} // End TabPanel
```

ExtPanel

```
import java.awt.*;

/**
 *-----------------------------------------------------------
 * An extended Panel object
 */
public class ExtPanel extends Panel {

    static final boolean debug = false;

    int margin = 5;

// Painting variables

    protected boolean   painted;
    protected Color     bg;
    protected Color     fg;

// Used to avoid flicker

    protected boolean           doubleBuffer = true;
    protected boolean           imageValid;
    protected Image             altImage;
    protected Graphics          altG;
    protected Dimension         altSize;

/**
 *-----------------------------------------------------------
```

```
 * The base constructors are not allowed.
 */
    public ExtPanel() {
        throw new NoSuchMethodError("ExtPanel()");
    }

/**
 *--------------------------------------------------------
 * Constructs a Panel
 */
    public ExtPanel(Container parent) {
        this(parent, "Center");
    }

    public ExtPanel(Container parent, String layout) {
        super();
        parent.add(layout, this);
        painted    = false;
        imageValid = false;
    }

/**
 *------------------------------------------------------------
 * Set the margin.  Must be done before any layout to have
 * an effect.
 */
    public void setMargin(int m) {
        margin = m;
    }

/**
 *------------------------------------------------------------
 * Return the insets needed to implement the margin
 */
    public Insets insets() {
        return new Insets(margin, margin, margin, margin);
    }
```

```
/**
 *-----------------------------------------------------------
 * Users must call this to invalidate the image
 */
    public void touch() {
        imageValid = false;
    }

    public void repaint(boolean touch) {
        if ( touch ) imageValid = false;
        repaintAll();
    }

    void repaintAll() {

        repaint();

        Component[] comps = getComponents();
        int count = comps.length;
        for (int i=0; i
```

TabCanvas Class

```
import java.awt.*;
import java.util.*;
import Shadow;

/**
 * A Canvas object that draws tabs for a TabPanel
 */
public class TabCanvas extends ExtCanvas {

    static final int    arcSize = 16;

    TabPanel    tabPanel;
    int         marginWidth = 4;
    int         marginHeight = 2;
```

```
    int         expansion = 2;      // How much higher is
                                    // current tab
    int         tabSpacing = 0;
    Hashtable   bounds;             // Bounds of each tab
    Shadow      shadow;             // Around each tab
    Font        boldFont;
    FontMetrics boldMetrics;
    Component   focusTab;           // tab under mouse
    Component   curTab;             // tab whose card is shown
    Color       bright = Color.white;

/**
 * Constructs a TabCanvas
 */
    public TabCanvas(TabPanel parent) {
        this(parent, "Center");
    }

    public TabCanvas(TabPanel parent, String layout) {
        super(parent, layout);
        this.tabPanel = parent;
        bounds        = new Hashtable();
        shadow        = new Shadow(Shadow.OUT,
            tabPanel.shadowThickness);
        curTab        = null;
        focusTab      = null;
    }

/**
 *---------------------------------------------------------
 * Return the minimum width and height
 */
    public Dimension minimumSize() {
        return preferredSize();;
    }

/**
```

```
*-----------------------------------------------------------
* Return the preferred width and height
*/
   public Dimension preferredSize() {
       Dimension      dim = new Dimension(100, 100);

       if ( boldMetrics == null ) {
           Font        font = getFont();
           boldFont    = new Font(font.getFamily(),
               Font.BOLD, font.getSize());
           boldMetrics = getFontMetrics(boldFont);
       }

   // Images may affect the height of the tabs

       Image           image;
       int             imageHeight;
       int             h = boldMetrics.getHeight();
       Enumeration     tabs = tabPanel.cards();
       while ( tabs.hasMoreElements() ) {
           Component tab = (Component)tabs.nextElement();
           image = tabPanel.getImage(tab);

           if ( image != null ) {
               imageHeight = image.getHeight(null);
               if ( imageHeight > h ) h = imageHeight;
           }
       }

       int             st = shadow.getThickness();
       h += (st + marginHeight) * 2 + expansion;

// Get list of children from tabPanel

       String          name;
       int             decor = (st + marginWidth * 2);
       int             w     = 0;
       Rectangle       rect  = null;
       tabs  = tabPanel.cards();
```

```
        while ( tabs.hasMoreElements() ) {

// Add size of label

            Component   tab = (Component)tabs.nextElement();
            if ( curTab == null ) curTab = tab;

            name  = tabPanel.getLabel(tab);
            image = tabPanel.getImage(tab);
            int childW = boldMetrics.stringWidth(name) + decor;

            if ( image != null ) {
                 childW += image.getWidth(null) + marginWidth;
            }
            rect = new Rectangle(w, expansion, childW,
            h-expansion);
            bounds.put(tab, rect);

            w += childW + tabSpacing - 1;
        }

        dim.width  = w;
        dim.height = h;

        return dim;

    }  // End preferredSize

/**
 *---------------------------------------------------------
 * Draw the tabs
 */
    public void paintCanvas(Graphics g) {

        Enumeration     tabs = tabPanel.cards();

        Vector vector = new Vector(5, 5);
        Component tab;
        Component tempTab;
        Rectangle rect;
        Rectangle tempRect;
```

```
        int index = 0;
        int count = 0;
        int i = 0;

        while(tabs.hasMoreElements()) {
            tab = (Component)tabs.nextElement();
            rect = (Rectangle)bounds.get(tab);

            index = 0;
            if(count != 0) {
                for(i=0 ; i0 ; i--) {
            tab = (Component)vector.elementAt(i);

            if(tab != curTab) {
                paintTab(g, tab, true/*draw rects too*/);
            }
        }

// Draw current tab last

        paintTab(g, curTab, true/*draw rects too*/);

    } // End paintCanvas

/**
 *----------------------------------------------------------
 * Draw the specified tab
 */
    void paintTab(Graphics g, Component tab,
    boolean drawRects) {

        Rectangle rect = (Rectangle)bounds.get(tab);

//  If this is the current tab, expand it

        if ( tab == curTab )
            rect = new Rectangle(rect.x, rect.y - expansion,
                rect.width, rect.height + expansion);

        Color   bg = tab.getBackground();
        Color   fg = tab.getForeground();
```

```
        int     st = shadow.getThickness();
        if ( drawRects ) {
// Draw tab background

            g.setColor(bg);
            g.fillRect(rect.x, rect.y, rect.width, rect.height);

// Draw shadow

            bright = bg.brighter();
            shadow.reshape(rect.x, rect.y + 1, rect.width,
                rect.height);
            shadow.paint(g);

// If this is the current tab, extend the shadow along the top
// of the card

            if ( tab == curTab ) {

// Draw part to left of tab

                int     by = rect.y + rect.height;
                int     ty = by - st + 1;

                int     lx = 0;
                int     rx = rect.x + st;
                g.setColor(bright);
                g.fillRect(lx, ty, rx-lx, by-ty);

// Clear part in middle of tab

                lx = rx;
                rx = rect.x + rect.width - st;
                g.setColor(bg);
                g.fillRect(lx, ty, rx-lx, by-ty);

// Draw part to right of tab

                lx = rx + 1;
                rx = size().width - 1;
                g.setColor(bright);
```

```
                g.fillRect(lx, ty, rx-lx, by-ty);

            }  // End if this is the current card

        }  // End if we're drawing outlines

    // Center the label & image (if any)

        Image       image       = tabPanel.getImage(tab);
        int         imageHeight = 0;
        int         imageWidth  = 0;

        String      name    = tabPanel.getLabel(tab);
        Font        font    = (tab == curTab ? boldFont :
                                getFont());
        FontMetrics fm      = getFontMetrics(font);
        int         ascent  = fm.getAscent();
        int         h       = fm.getHeight();
        int         w       = fm.stringWidth(name);
        int         x       = rect.x + ((rect.width  - w)>>1);
        int         y       = rect.y + ((rect.height - h)>>1);

    // Clear the label background if we didn't already

        if ( !drawRects ) {
            g.setColor(bg);
            g.fillRect(rect.x+st, rect.y+st, rect.width -(st*2),
                                            rect.height-(st*2));
            //g.fillRect(x, y, w, h);
        }

    // Draw the image (if any)

        if(image != null) {
            imageHeight = image.getHeight(null);
            imageWidth = image.getWidth(null);

            h = imageHeight > h ? imageHeight : h;
            w += imageWidth + marginWidth;

            x = rect.x + ((rect.width - w)>>1);
```

```
            y = rect.y + ((rect.height - h)>>1);

            g.drawImage(image, x, y, null);

            x += imageWidth + marginWidth;
            y = rect.y + ((rect.height - fm.getHeight())>>1);
        }

// Draw the label

        y += ascent;
        g.setColor(fg);
        g.setFont(font);
        g.drawString(name, x, y);

    }  // End paintTab

/**
 *---------------------------------------------------------
 * Handle a mouse button release
 */
    public boolean mouseUp(Event evt, int x, int y) {

// See which rectangle contains click

        Component       tab = findTab(x, y);
        if ( tab != null ) {
            curTab = tab;
            paintNow(true);
            tabPanel.show(tab);
            return true;
        }

        return false;

    }  // End mouseUp

/**
 *---------------------------------------------------------
 * Find the tab that contains the specified position
 */
```

```
    Component findTab(int x, int y) {

// Loop through rectangles

        Enumeration     tabs = tabPanel.cards();
        while ( tabs.hasMoreElements() ) {
            Component   tab  = (Component)tabs.nextElement();
            Rectangle   rect = (Rectangle)bounds.get(tab);
            if ( rect.inside(x, y) ) return tab;
        }
        return null;
    }

} // End TabCanvas
```

ExtCanvas Class

```
import java.awt.*;
import java.awt.image.*;

/**
 *-------------------------------------------------------
 * An extended Canvas object
 */
public class ExtCanvas extends Canvas {

    static final boolean        debug = false;

    protected int   border = 0;     // Border thickness
    protected int   border2;        // Border thickness times 2
    protected Color borderColor = Color.black;  // Color of
                                                // border

// Painting variables

    protected boolean   painted;
    protected Color     bg;
    protected Color     fg;
```

```
// Used to avoid flicker

    protected boolean            doubleBuffer = true;
    protected boolean            imageValid;
    protected Image              altImage;
    protected Graphics           altG;
    protected Dimension          altSize;

/**
 *------------------------------------------------------------
 * The base constructors are not allowed.
 */
    public ExtCanvas() {
        throw new NoSuchMethodError("ExtCanvas()");
    }

/**
 *------------------------------------------------------------
 * Constructs a Canvas
 */
    public ExtCanvas(Container parent) {
        this(parent, "Center");
    }

    public ExtCanvas(Container parent, String layout) {

        super();
        parent.add(layout, this);
        border2 = border * 2;
        painted = false;
        imageValid = false;

    }  // End constructor

/**
 *--------------------------------------------------------------
 * Users must call this to invalidate the image
 */
    public synchronized void touch() {
```

```
        imageValid = false;
    }

    public synchronized void repaint(boolean touch) {
        if ( touch ) imageValid = false;
        repaint();
    }

/**
 *--------------------------------------------------------
 * Draw the canvas immediately if possible.  Don't wait for
 * a repaint
 */
    public synchronized void paintNow() {
        paintNow(true);
    }

    public synchronized void paintNow(boolean touch) {
        if ( touch ) imageValid = false;
        if ( painted ) {
            Graphics    g = getGraphics();
            paint(g);
            g.dispose();
        }
        else
            repaint();
    }

/**
 *--------------------------------------------------------
 * Draw the canvas
 */
    public void update(Graphics g) {
        paint(g);
    }

    public void paint(Graphics g) {
```

```
        Dimension       dim = size();
        if ( dim.width == 0 || dim.height == 0 ) return;

        if ( !painted ) {
            bg          = getBackground();
            fg          = getForeground();
        }

// Set up offscreen drawing

        if ( doubleBuffer ) {
            if ( altImage == null ||
              altSize.width != dim.width ||
              altSize.height != dim.height ) {
                if ( altImage != null ) altImage.flush();
                if ( altG     != null ) altG.dispose();

                altImage = createImage(dim.width, dim.height);
                altSize  = dim;
                altG     = altImage.getGraphics();
                altG.setFont(getFont());

                imageValid = false;
            }
        } else {
            altG = g;
            imageValid = false;
        }

// Build the offscreen image if necessary.  On simple
//    exposures we can re-use it.

        if ( !imageValid ) {

// Clear background

            altG.setColor(bg);
            altG.fillRect(0, 0, dim.width, dim.height);

// Draw canvas
```

```
            paintCanvas(altG);

    // Draw border

            if ( border > 0 ) {
                int w = dim.width  - 1;
                int h = dim.height - 1;

                altG.setColor(borderColor);
                for (int i=0; i
```

TabCardPanel Class

```
import java.awt.*;
import java.util.*;
import Shadow;

/**
 *---------------------------------------------------------
 * This class implements the Card portion of the tab panel
 */
public class TabCardPanel extends ExtPanel {

    CardLayout  layout;
    Shadow      shadow;        // Used around cards and tabs
    Color       bg;

/**
 *---------------------------------------------------------
 * Creates a new panel
 */
    public TabCardPanel(Container parent) {
        this(parent, "Center");
    }

    public TabCardPanel(Container parent, String layoutInfo) {
        super(parent, layoutInfo);
        int     thickness = 2;
```

```
// The shadow will be moved up so the top part does not get
// drawn. That part is drawn by the tab canvas

        shadow = new Shadow(Shadow.OUT, thickness);
        shadow.move(0, -thickness);

        layout = new CardLayout();
        setLayout(layout);
    }

/**
 *----------------------------------------------------------
 * Show a card
 */
    public void show(String cardName) {
        layout.show(this, cardName);
    }

/**
 *----------------------------------------------------------
 * Return the insets needed to avoid obscuring the shadow
 */
    public Insets insets() {

// We only use the margin on top because the shadow is not
// drawn there

        int     sm = shadow.getThickness() + margin;
        return new Insets(margin, sm, sm, sm);
    }

/**
 *----------------------------------------------------------
 * Draw the shadow on the left, right and bottom
 */
    public void paint(Graphics g) {

        if ( bg == null ) {
            bg = getBackground();
```

```
            //shadow.setBrightColor(bg.brighter());
            //shadow.setDarkColor  (bg.darker());
        }

// Add shadowThickness to the size since we moved the shadow
// up before. (See constructor)

        Dimension       dim = size();
        dim.height += shadow.getThickness();
        shadow.resize(dim);
        shadow.paint(g);

    }  // End paint

}  // End TabCardPanel
```

TabEnumeration Class

```
import java.util.*;
import java.awt.*;

/**
 *-------------------------------------------------------
 * A tabbed panel enumerator class.
 */
class TabEnumeration implements Enumeration {

    TabPanel    tabPanel;
    int         next;

/**
 *------------------------------------------------------
 * Build an enumeration of all visible tabs in a panel
 */
    TabEnumeration(TabPanel panel) {
        tabPanel = panel;
        next = -1;
        findNext();
```

```
    }

/**
 *-----------------------------------------------------
 * See if there are any more visible tabs
 */
    public boolean hasMoreElements() {
        return (next >= 0);
    }

/**
 *-----------------------------------------------------
 * Return the next visible tab
 */
    public Object nextElement() {

        int     tab = next;
        findNext();
        return tabPanel.cardPanel.getComponent(tab);
    }

/**
 *-----------------------------------------------------
 * Find the next visible tab
 */
    void findNext() {

        int     count = tabPanel.cardPanel.countComponents();
        while ( ++next
```

TabInfo Class

```
import java.awt.*;

/**
 *---------------------------------------------------------
 * This class holds information about each tab
```

```
 */
public class TabInfo {

    String      cardName;           // Used for card layout;
    String      label;
    Image       image;
    boolean     visible;

    public TabInfo(String name, String lab, Image img,
      boolean vis) {
        cardName = name;
        label    = lab;
        image    = img;
        visible  = vis;
    }
}
```

Shadow Class

```
import java.awt.*;

public class Shadow {

    static final boolean        debug = false;

    public static final int     FLAT            = 0;
    public static final int     IN              = 1;
    public static final int     OUT             = 2;
    public static final int     ETCHED_IN       = 3;
    public static final int     ETCHED_OUT      = 4;
    public static final int     DASHED          = 5;
    public static final int     maxThickness    = 16;

    int         thickness;
    int         type;
    Color       darkColor;
    Color       brightColor;
```

```
    Color       darkMidColor;
    Color       brightMidColor;
    Rectangle   bounds;

    public Shadow() {
        this(OUT, 2);
    }

    public Shadow(int type) {
        this(type, 2);
    }

    public Shadow(String type) {
        this(type, 2);
    }

    public Shadow(int type, int thickness) {
        bounds = new Rectangle(0, 0, 10, 10);
        setType(type);
        setThickness(thickness);
    }

    public Shadow(String type, int thickness) {
        bounds = new Rectangle(0, 0, 10, 10);
        setType(type);
        setThickness(thickness);
    }

/**
 * Return the current shadow type
 */
    public int getType() {
        return type;
    }

/**
 * Return the current shadow size
 */
    public int getThickness() {
```

```
        return thickness;
    }

/**
 * Return the current bright shadow color
 */
    public Color getBrightColor() {
        return brightColor;
    }

/**
 * Return the current dark shadow color
 */
    public Color getDarkColor() {
        return darkColor;
    }

/**
 * Return the current bright shadow color
 */
    public Color getBrightMidColor() {
        return brightMidColor;
    }

/**
 * Return the current dark shadow color
 */
    public Color getDarkMidColor() {
        return darkMidColor;
    }

/**
 * Set the shadow type
 * @param type The type of shadow to be drawn
 */
    public void setType(int type) {
        switch (type) {
            case FLAT:
```

```
                case IN:
                case OUT:
                case ETCHED_IN:
                case ETCHED_OUT:
                case DASHED:
                    this.type = type;
                    return;
            }
            throw new IllegalArgumentException(
                "invalid shadow type: " + type);
        }

    /**
     * Set the shadow type
     * @param type The type of shadow to be drawn
     */
        public void setType(String type) {
            if ( type == null || type.equalsIgnoreCase("out") )
                setType(OUT);
            else if ( type.equalsIgnoreCase("flat"      ) )
                setType(FLAT);
            else if ( type.equalsIgnoreCase("in"        ) )
                setType(IN);
            else if ( type.equalsIgnoreCase("etched_in" ) )
                setType(ETCHED_IN);
            else if ( type.equalsIgnoreCase("etched_out") )
                setType(ETCHED_OUT);
            else if ( type.equalsIgnoreCase("dashed") )
                setType(DASHED);
            else
                throw new IllegalArgumentException(
                    "invalid shadow type: " + type);
        }

    /**
     * Set the shadow thickness
```

```
 * @param size The thickness of the shadow
 */
   public void setThickness(int size) {
       if ( size >= 0 && size
```

Tab Sample Usage

```
//
// Tab - test driver for TabPanel (Tabbed CardLayout) object.
//

// Release 1.0 30 Sep 1996 meo@pencom.com

import java.applet.*;
import java.awt.*;
import ExtPanel;
import TabPanel;
import TabCardPanel;

public class Tab extends Applet {

// The Tab stuff requires a borderLayout for the parent.

    BorderLayout borderLayout = new BorderLayout();

// The top object must be a TabPanel; its children should be
// ExtPanels.  ExtPanels act pretty much like Panels from an
// API standpoint.

    TabPanel tabPanel;
    ExtPanel author1, author2, author3, author4;
    TextArea meo, tom, pww, vig;

    String meoText = "Miles O'Neal" +
        "One of the primary authors of the book, and the guy who" +
        "removed all the extraneous Vignette code from the Tab" +
        "objects.";

    String tomText = "Tom Stewart" +
```

```
        "One of the authors of the book, who was too busy doing
        other"
        "cool stuff like the table object to hack on the Tab
        objects.";

    String pwwText = "Pencom Web Works" +
        "A brilliant, fun bunch of people who do cool IntraNet
        work," +
        "many of whom helped Tom and Miles with this book but were"
        +
        "busy helping customers and so didn't hack the Tab
        objects.";

    String vigText = "Vignette Corporation" +
        "A very cool company in Austin who graciously donated the
        Tab" +
        "code so that Miles and Tom didn't have to write one from"
        +
        "scratch, freeing them up to do other things.  In
        particular," +
        "Neil worked through the issues so we could include" +
        "the code, and Greg Hilton (the author of this truly" +
        "elegant piece of code) proofed it after we removed the" +
        "proprietary Vignette bits.";

    public void init() {
        this.setLayout(borderLayout);
        tabPanel = new TabPanel(this, "Center");

        author1 = new ExtPanel(tabPanel, "Miles");
        meo = new TextArea(meoText, 8, 60);
        meo.setEditable(false);
        author1.add("thing1", meo);

        author2 = new ExtPanel(tabPanel, "Tom");
        tom = new TextArea(tomText, 8, 60);
        tom.setEditable(false);
        author2.add("thing2", tom);

        author3 = new ExtPanel(tabPanel, "PWW");
```

```
            pww = new TextArea(pwwText, 8, 60);
            pww.setEditable(false);
            author3.add("author3", pww);

            author4 = new ExtPanel(tabPanel, "Vignette");
            vig = new TextArea(vigText, 8, 60);
            vig.setEditable(false);
            author4.add("author4", vig);
        }
    }
```

Scope and PWT Classes

This section includes a sample GUI for a wave generator scope (`Scope` class) with displays and the PWT classes. The `Scope` class is strictly an example of GUI design and implementation with the AWT. The scope uses the `Scope` class and a `Display` class, which emulates a simple LCD or CRT.

The PWT set of classes is very minimal at this point. It contains a `MsgArea` class for simplified message handling and a `PopupDialog` class for use with applets, because the stock AWT Dialog classes only work with Java apps, not applets.

Introduction

This section began as a project to learn the AWT. It contains examples of moderately sophisticated AWT features such as `GridLayout`, ways to handle common problems (such as a message box), and an applet `HelpDialog`, so we decided to include it on the CD accompanying the book.

I (Miles) have been working with electronics since I was a child, so an oscilloscope was a natural project—there was no input, so it devolved into a waveform generator with scope displays. Obviously, this isn't a real scope, but the GUI developed can be used for one.

The waveform generation was a quick hack. It's not solid or very elegant in this early version. In the future, it will be fleshed out; watch the Pencom World Wide Web server for details. If anyone feels like playing with the wave shape generator, feel free to send me better versions.

Layout and Design Notes

The scope is composed of six horizontal sections:

- The logo
- Two wave generation modules (class `baseModule`)
- Two wave mixer modules (class `opsModule`)
- A message box

The logo panel is, of course, nothing more than Hello World as applied to products.

Wave Generation Modules

These modules are based on `GridBag`-controlled panels. Each module contains checkboxes with a common `CheckboxGroup` (wave shape and Off), labels, a `TextField` (frequency control), an ungrouped checkbox (Invert), and a display (described elsewhere). Half the problem with any GUI is determining the proper controls and layout; these modules took a little work to fit properly on an average monitor without sacrificing usability. The only concession to the virtual world made here was the text field for frequency selection.

Mixer Modules

These are basically simpler versions of the wave generation modules, from a GUI layout standpoint. They could have been laid out several ways, but good GUI design calls for consistency.

Message Box

Most GUIs have a variety of message mechanisms, with About boxes, popups, splash screens, and so forth. Because this was an applet, I decided that things like About and splash screen information should be built into the Web page. These could have been done in fancier ways, but the main thing here is the scope, so I kept the rest simple. Instead of having a variety of popups for information, warnings, errors, and so on, I went with a simple message box at the bottom of the screen. A bench-top wave generator or scope doesn't usually have too many popups, anyway.

The message box initially contains copyright information. Messages are numbered and added to the end of the message text, which scrolls automatically, to make it easy to determine when a new message has been displayed.

While the scope itself doesn't use the box very much, the message box is a good general-purpose tool to have around.

Help

A good GUI should be as intuitive as possible, but it's still a good idea to have some help available. Because there is no `PopupDialog` for applets, I developed one for this project. Eventually, it will have some real help text in it.

Display

The `Display` class is an extension of the `Canvas` class; it emulates an LCD or vacuum tube display. It plots a set of Y coordinates against a standard X-axis. The number of points must currently equal the display width in pixels less 2. The Y-axis auto-scales to fill the display.

PopupDialog Class

`PopupDialog` consists of a popup dialog box with text and a **Done** button. Events/actions are provided to pop the dialog down when the **Done** button is pressed and to destroy the object and clean up when a Window Destroy event occurs.

Release: 1.0   28 Sep 1996 <*meo@pencom.com*>

Extends: Frame

Constructors:

```
PopupDialog(String name, String text, int rows, int cols)

PopupDialog(String name)
```

Public Interfaces:

```
void setPopupText(String text)
Set the popup text.

void popupPopup()
Pop up the popup dialog.
```

Example code:

```
        :
import PopupDialog;
```

```
public class Newbie extends CaveNewt {
        :
    PopupDialog helpDialog = null;
        :
    Button help = new Button("Help");
        :
    public boolean action(Event e, Object arg) {
        Panel p = (Panel) ((Component) e.target).getParent();

//      If the popup doesn't exist, create it.
//      Otherwise, just pop it up again.

        if (e.target instanceof Button) {
            if (helpDialog == null)
                helpDialog = new PopupDialog("Help",
                    "Sorry, I'm clueless!", 4, 40);
            else
                helpDialog.popupPopup();
        }
        :
}
```

MsgArea Class

`MsgArea` implements a simple message box. There is an initial message capability, separated from further messages with a line of dashes. Subsequent messages are numbered and appended to the end of the message list. The box always scrolls to the end to display new messages.

Release: 1.0   28 Sep 1996 <*meo@pencom.com*>

Extends: TextArea

Constructors:

```
MsgArea(int rows, int cols)
```

Public Interfaces:

```
public void setMsgAreaInitial(String text)
```

Set initial text (no line numbers).

```
public void addMsgAreaMessage(String text)
```

Add a message with a line number. Add a separator line first if there was initial text.

Example code:

```
public class Volcano extends Crevice {
        :
    MsgArea messages;
        :
    messages = new MsgArea(3, 60);
        :
    messages.setMsgAreaInitial(
        "Copyright 1900, the talk.bizarre public trust");
        :
    messages.addMsgAreaMessage("User marked for deletion.");
        :
}
```

Functionality

From the (somewhat tongue-in-cheek) help page that accompanies the Scope: "Welcome to the PWW AWT-990 Wave Generator & Display Scope. This totally useless product lets you generate sine, square and triangle waves at almost any frequency between 0 and infinity, although it can only reliably display sine waves, and those only to around 30 Hz or so. Higher frequencies generate interference patterns (some quite cool).

"Please to read the instructions arriving with your PWW AWT-990. Instructions will arriving by commuter aircraft, and possessing ID badges to better you scrutinize. This end up.

Unscrewing the screws is not permitted, as no screw class has been derived. Use no hooks. Clean screen daily only with approved screen cleaner. Not aciding based products to apply, the better to serve you with.

"Sine waves generally work, but clean waves are available only to around 30 Hz or so. Higher frequencies generate interference patterns (some quite cool).

"Triangle waves are so crudely generated that the frequency is usually off by a noticeable fraction of a wavelength. Square waves are not even generated yet.

"All waves scale to completely consume the available display space."

Parts Is Parts

The first two modules are raw wave generators. Select a wave type, and it will be displayed. Wavelengths beyond 30 Hz may look absurd. Try **3333333333333333** (that's 16 3s), or the numbers from 100 to 110, for example. The **Invert** button does as you would expect (or as you should expect, anyway).

Square waves are currently unimplemented. There's a reason for this, but national security is involved, and if we told you, well, you'd be stuck using a 3270 in a cell somewhere near Thule for the rest of your life.

Modules 3 and 4 display waveforms based on munging the waves from Modules 1 and 2 together in various ways. Currently, only sum and difference are supported, but we might add more eventually. These modules only display data if both Modules 1 and 2 are active.

At the bottom of the scope is a message area.

In Progress

More accurate wave generation functions, and adding square waves.

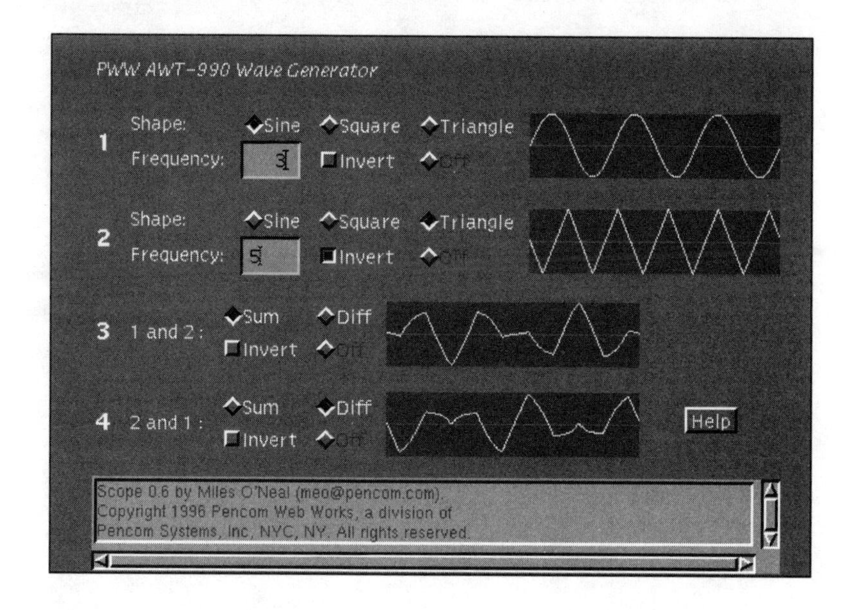

Display Class

```
import java.applet.*;
import java.awt.*;

public class Display extends Canvas {
    int[] data;
    int numPoints;
    boolean pointsSet = false;

    private int midy = 0;                // middle y coords
    private int maxx = 0, maxy = 0;      // maximum x & y coords
    private int maxpx = 0, maxpy = 0; // max plottable coords

    public Display(int width, int height) {
        Dimension d = new Dimension(width, height);

        resize(d);

        // set the drawing area parameters

        maxx = width - 1;
```

```
        maxy = height - 1;
        midy = height / 2;
        maxpx = maxx - 1;
        maxpy = maxy - 1;

        // create the data holders

        numPoints = maxpx;
        data = new int[numPoints];
        pointsSet = false;
    }

    public void paint(Graphics g) {
        Color bg;
        Rectangle rect;

        // clear the display

        g.setColor(this.getBackground());
        rect = this.bounds();
        g.fillRect(rect.x, rect.y, rect.width, rect.height);

        // draw the display's edges & center line

        g.setColor(Color.green);
        g.drawLine(0, midy, maxx, midy);
        g.drawRect(0, 0, maxx, maxy);

        // display data if present

        if (this.pointsSet) {
            g.setColor(Color.white);
            for (int i = 0; i
```

MsgArea Class

```
//  Constructors:
//      MsgArea(int rows, int cols)
//
```

```
//  Public Interfaces:
//      setMsgAreaInitial(String text) - set initial text
//          (no line numbers)
//      addMsgAreaMessage(String text) - add message with
//          line number

import java.awt.*;

public class MsgArea extends TextArea {

    private int msgNum = 1;
    private boolean sepNeeded = false;

//  CONSTRUCTORS

    public MsgArea(int rows, int cols) {
        super(rows,cols);
        setFont(new Font("Helvetica", Font.PLAIN, 12));
        setBackground(Color.lightGray);
        setForeground(Color.red);
        setEditable(false);
    }

//  PUBLIC INTERFACE METHODS

//
// setMsgAreaInitial(String text) - set initial text
//      (no line numbers)
//
    public void setMsgAreaInitial(String text) {
        this.appendText(text);
        sepNeeded = true;
    }

//
//  addMsgAreaMessage(String text) - add message with
//      line number. Add a separator line first if there
//      was initial text.
//
```

```
    public void addMsgAreaMessage(String text) {
        if (msgNum == 1 && sepNeeded)
            this.appendText(
                "--------------------------------------");
        this.appendText("");
        this.appendText((new Integer(msgNum++)).toString());
        this.appendText(": " + text);
    }
}
```

PopupDialog Class

```
//  CONSTRUCTORS
//   PopupDialog(String name, String text, int rows, int cols)
//   PopupDialog(String name)
//
//  PUBLIC INTERFACE METHODS
//      void setPopupText() - set popup text
//      void popupPopup()   - pop up the popup dialog

import java.awt.*;

public class PopupDialog extends Frame {
    private protected String pText;
    private protected TextArea popupText;
    private protected Button done;
    private protected static String notext =
        "Sorry - this PopupDialog was invoked with no text.";
    private protected int rows = 1, cols = 40;

//  CONSTRUCTORS

    public PopupDialog(String name, String text, int rows,
      int cols) {
        super(name);
        create(text, rows, cols);
```

```
    }

    public PopupDialog(String name) {
        super(name);
        create(notext, 1, 40);
    }

//
//  create() - common code for both constructors.
//      The super() method can only be called from
//      a constructor, which is why it's not called
//      here, also.
//
    public void create(String text, int rows, int cols) {
        this.rows = rows;
        this.cols = cols;
        this.pText = text;
        this.init();
    }

// PRIVATE INSTANCE METHODS

//
//  init() - general initialization code
//
    private protected void init() {
        GridBagConstraints gbc;
        GridBagLayout layout;
        Panel p;

//      general appearance-related stuff

        this.setBackground(Color.lightGray);
        this.setForeground(Color.black);
        this.setResizable(true);
        this.setCursor(HAND_CURSOR);

//      Use a GridBag, with (mostly common) constraints
```

```
        layout = new GridBagLayout();
        this.setLayout(layout);
        gbc = new GridBagConstraints();
        gbc.fill = GridBagConstraints.VERTICAL;
        gbc.gridwidth = 1; gbc.gridheight = 1;
        gbc.anchor = GridBagConstraints.CENTER;
        gbc.gridx = 0;

//      create & set up the popup text area (on top)

        popupText = new TextArea(this.pText,
            this.rows, this.cols);
        popupText.setEditable(false);
        gbc.gridy = 0;
        layout.setConstraints(popupText, gbc);
        this.add(popupText);

//      create & setup the Done button (on bottom)
//      NOTE: button colors may not work under Windows

        done = new Button("Done");
        done.setBackground(Color.red);
        done.setForeground(Color.white);
        gbc.gridy = GridBagConstraints.RELATIVE;
        layout.setConstraints(done, gbc);
        this.add(done);

        this.pack();
        this.show();
    }

//  PUBLIC INSTANCE METHODS

//
//  setPopupText() - set popup text (for external access)
//
    public void setPopupText(String h) {
        this.pText = h;
        this.popupText.setText(this.pText);
```

```
    }

//
// popupPopup() - pop up the dialog
//
    public void popupPopup() {
        this.show();
    }

// EVENTS

//
// action() - handle the Done button event
//
    public boolean action(Event e, Object arg) {
        if (e.target instanceof Button) {
            this.hide();
            return true;
        }
        return false;
    }

//
// handleEvent() - when window manager sends a
//     destroy window event, get rid of this object.
//
    public boolean handleEvent(Event e) {
        if ( e.id == Event.WINDOW_DESTROY) {
            this.dispose();
        }
        return super.handleEvent(e);
    }
}
```

Scope Class

```
// Scope implements a basic wave generator/oscilloscope. The //
base modules
```

```
//  (at the top of the scope) handle basic wave generation.  // The
ops modules
//  (underneath the base modules) mix the waves from the base //
modules and
//  display the results.

//  Some constrain methods were obtained from the examples
// distributed
//  with the book _Java in a Nutshell_, as were some constrain //
method
//  invocations.  That code came with the following copyright:
//      This example is from the book _Java in a Nutshell_ by //
David Flanagan.
//      Written by David Flanagan.  Copyright (c) 1996
// O'Reilly & Associates.
//      You may study, use, modify, and distribute this
// example for any purpose.
//      This example is provided WITHOUT WARRANTY either
// expressed or implied.

//  CONSTRUCTORS
//      no new constructors
//  PUBLIC INTERFACE METHODS
//      there really isn't anything to be accessed externally // at
this point

import java.applet.*;
import java.awt.*;
import java.net.*;
import Display;
import MsgArea;
import PopupDialog;

public class Scope extends Applet {
    Label logo;
    Panel module1, module2, module3, module4;
    PopupDialog helpDialog = null;

    MsgArea messages;
```

```
    static private Font mainFont, logoFont, moduleFont;

//  The layout manager for each of the containers.

    GridBagLayout gridbag = new GridBagLayout();

//  Main is included for standalone usage.

    public static void main(String args[]) {
        Frame frame = new Frame("Scope");
        Scope scope = new Scope();
        scope.init();
        scope.start();
        frame.add("Center", scope);
        frame.show();
    }

    public String getAppletInfo() {
        return ("Scope 0.6 by Miles O'Neal (meo@pencom.com)." +
            "Copyright 1996 Pencom Web Works, a division of" +
            "Pencom Systems, Inc, NYC, NY. All rights reserved.");
    }

    public void init() {
        Button help = new Button("Help");
        logoFont = new Font("Dialog", Font.ITALIC, 14);
        mainFont = new Font("Dialog", Font.PLAIN, 14);
        moduleFont = new Font("Dialog", Font.BOLD, 18);

        this.setBackground(Color.gray);
        this.setForeground(Color.white);
        this.setFont(mainFont);

        logo = new Label();
        logo.setFont(logoFont);
        logo.setText("PWW AWT-990 Wave Generator");

        module1 = baseModule("1");
        module2 = baseModule("2");
        module3 = opsModule("3", "1 and 2 :");
```

```
        module4 = opsModule("4", "2 and 1 :");

        messages = new MsgArea(3, 60);

        this.setLayout(gridbag);
        constrain(this, logo, 0, 0, 2, 1,
            GridBagConstraints.VERTICAL,
            GridBagConstraints.NORTHWEST,
            0.0, 1.0, 10, 10, 1, 1);
        constrain(this, module1, 0, 1, 2,
            1, GridBagConstraints.VERTICAL,
            GridBagConstraints.NORTHWEST,
            0.0, 1.0, 10, 10, 1, 1);
        constrain(this, module2, 0, 2, 2,
            1, GridBagConstraints.VERTICAL,
            GridBagConstraints.NORTHWEST,
            0.0, 1.0, 10, 10, 1, 1);
        constrain(this, module3, 0, 3, 1,
            1, GridBagConstraints.VERTICAL,
            GridBagConstraints.NORTHWEST,
            0.0, 1.0, 10, 10, 1, 1);
        constrain(this, module4, 0, 4, 1,
            1, GridBagConstraints.VERTICAL,
            GridBagConstraints.NORTHWEST,
            0.0, 1.0, 10, 10, 1, 1);
        constrain(this, help, 1, 4, 1, 1,
            GridBagConstraints.NONE,
            GridBagConstraints.CENTER,
            0.0, 0.0, 0, 0, 0, 0);
        constrain(this, messages, 0, 5, 2, 1,
            GridBagConstraints.BOTH,
            GridBagConstraints.CENTER,
            0.0, 1.0, 10, 10, 1, 1);
    }

    public void start() {
```

```
    messages.setMsgAreaInitial(getAppletInfo());
}

public Panel baseModule(String num) {
    Display display;
    Checkbox[] ops;
    CheckboxGroup ops_group;
    Panel modulePanel;
    TextField freq;
    Label moduleNum = new Label(num);

    moduleNum.setFont(moduleFont);
    display = new Display(201, 51);
    display.setBackground(Color.darkGray);

    ops_group = new CheckboxGroup();
    ops = new Checkbox[4];
    ops[0] = new Checkbox("Sine", ops_group, false);
    ops[1] = new Checkbox("Square", ops_group, false);
    ops[2] = new Checkbox("Triangle", ops_group, false);
    ops[3] = new Checkbox("Off", ops_group, true);
    ops[3].setForeground(Color.red);
    freq = new TextField("     1");
    freq.setForeground(Color.black);

    modulePanel = new Panel();
    modulePanel.setLayout(gridbag);

    constrain(modulePanel, moduleNum, 0, 0, 1, 2);

    constrain(modulePanel, new Label("Shape:"),
        1, 0, 1, 1);
    constrain(modulePanel, ops[0], 2, 0, 1, 1);
    constrain(modulePanel, ops[1], 3, 0, 1, 1);
    constrain(modulePanel, ops[2], 4, 0, 1, 1);

    constrain(modulePanel, new Label("Frequency:"),
        1, 1, 1, 1);
    constrain(modulePanel, freq, 2, 1, 1, 1);
```

```
        constrain(modulePanel, new Checkbox("Invert"),
            3, 1, 1, 1);
        constrain(modulePanel, ops[3], 4, 1, 1, 1);

        constrain(modulePanel, display, 5, 0, 1, 2,
            GridBagConstraints.EAST);

        return modulePanel;
    }

    public Panel opsModule(String num, String s) {
        Display display;
        Checkbox[] ops;
        CheckboxGroup ops_group;
        Panel modulePanel;
        Label moduleNum = new Label(num);

        modulePanel = new Panel();
        modulePanel.setLayout(gridbag);
        moduleNum.setFont(moduleFont);

        ops_group = new CheckboxGroup();
        ops = new Checkbox[3];
        ops[0] = new Checkbox("Sum", ops_group, false);
        ops[1] = new Checkbox("Diff", ops_group, false);
        ops[2] = new Checkbox("Off", ops_group, true);
        ops[2].setForeground(Color.red);

        display = new Display(201, 51);
        display.setBackground(Color.darkGray);

        constrain(modulePanel, moduleNum, 0, 0, 1, 2);
        constrain(modulePanel, new Label(s), 1, 0, 1, 2);

        constrain(modulePanel, ops[0], 2, 0, 1, 1);
        constrain(modulePanel, ops[1], 3, 0, 1, 1);

        constrain(modulePanel, new Checkbox("Invert"),
            2, 1, 1, 1);
        constrain(modulePanel, ops[2], 3, 1, 1, 1);
```

```
    constrain(modulePanel, display, 4, 0, 1, 2,
        GridBagConstraints.EAST);

    return modulePanel;
}

//  Based on the ORA constrain methods, this one was added
//  by PWW.

public void constrain(Container container,
    Component component, int grid_x, int grid_y,
    int grid_width, int grid_height, int grid_loc)
{
    if (grid_loc == GridBagConstraints.EAST)
        constrain(container, component, grid_x, grid_y,
            grid_width, grid_height,
            GridBagConstraints.HORIZONTAL, grid_loc,
            0.0, 0.0, 0, 0, 0, 0);
    else if (grid_loc == GridBagConstraints.CENTER)
        constrain(container, component, grid_x, grid_y,
            grid_width, grid_height,
            GridBagConstraints.HORIZONTAL, grid_loc,
            0.0, 0.0, 0, 0, 0, 0);
    else if (grid_loc == GridBagConstraints.RELATIVE)
        constrain(container, component, grid_x, grid_y,
            GridBagConstraints.RELATIVE, grid_height,
            GridBagConstraints.HORIZONTAL,
            GridBagConstraints.EAST,
            0.0, 0.0, 0, 0, 0, 0);
    else if (grid_loc == GridBagConstraints.NONE)
        constrain(container, component, grid_x, grid_y,
            grid_width, grid_height,
            GridBagConstraints.HORIZONTAL,
            GridBagConstraints.WEST,
            0.0, 1.0, 0, 0, 0, 0);
    else
        constrain(container, component, grid_x, grid_y,
```

```
                grid_width, grid_height,
                GridBagConstraints.NONE, grid_loc,
                0.0, 0.0, 0, 0, 0, 0);
    }

//  BEGIN ORA CONSTRAIN METHODS

    public void constrain(Container container, Component component,
        int grid_x, int grid_y, int grid_width,
        int grid_height,
        int fill, int anchor, double weight_x,
        double weight_y,
        int top, int left, int bottom, int right)
    {
        GridBagConstraints c = new GridBagConstraints();
        c.gridx = grid_x; c.gridy = grid_y;
        c.gridwidth = grid_width; c.gridheight = grid_height;
        c.fill = fill; c.anchor = anchor;
        c.weightx = weight_x; c.weighty = weight_y;
        if (top+bottom+left+right > 0)
            c.insets = new Insets(top, left, bottom, right);

        ((GridBagLayout)container.getLayout()).
        setConstraints(component, c);
        container.add(component);
    }

    public void constrain(Container container,
    Component component,
        int grid_x, int grid_y, int grid_width,
        int grid_height)
    {
        constrain(container, component, grid_x, grid_y,
            grid_width, grid_height,
            GridBagConstraints.NONE, GridBagConstraints.WEST,
            0.0, 0.0, 0, 0, 0, 0);
    }
```

```
    public void constrain(Container container,
    Component component,
        int grid_x, int grid_y, int grid_width,
int grid_height,
        int top, int left, int bottom, int right)
    {
        constrain(container, component, grid_x, grid_y,
            grid_width, grid_height, GridBagConstraints.NONE,
            GridBagConstraints.CENTER,
            0.0, 0.0, top, left, bottom, right);
    }

    // END ORA CONSTRAIN METHODS

    // EVENT HANDLING

    public boolean action(Event e, Object arg) {
        Panel p = (Panel) ((Component) e.target).getParent();

        if (e.target instanceof Button) {
            if (helpDialog == null)
                helpDialog = new PopupDialog("Help",
                    "Sorry, I'm helpless!", 4, 40);
            else
                helpDialog.popupPopup();
        } else if (e.target instanceof TextField) {
//          in module1 or module2
            TextField t = (TextField) e.target;

            CheckboxGroup cbg =
                ((Checkbox) p.getComponent(2)). getCheckboxGroup();
            Display d = (Display) p.getComponent(9);
            makeWave((cbg.getCurrent()).getLabel(), t, d);
            return true;
        } else if (e.target instanceof Checkbox) {
            Checkbox cb = (Checkbox) e.target;
```

```
if (p == module1 || p == module2) {
    Display d = (Display) p.getComponent(9);
    String pressed = cb.getLabel();
    if (pressed == "Invert") {
        d.invert();
        d.repaint();
        updateOps(d);
        return true;
    } else {
        if (pressed == "Off") {
            d.pointsSet = false;
            d.repaint();
            updateOps(d);
            return true;
        } else {
            TextField t = (TextField) p.
            getComponent(6);
            makeWave(pressed, t, d);
            return true;
        }
    }
} else if (p == module3 || p == module4) {
    Display d = (Display) p.getComponent(6);
    String op = cb.getLabel();
    if (op == "Invert") {
        d.invert();
        d.repaint();
        return true;
    } else if (op == "Off") {
        d.pointsSet = false;
        updateOps(d);
        return true;
    } else {            // "Sum" or "Diff"
        return opWaves(p, d, op);
    }
```

```
            }
        }
    return false;
    }

// PRIVATE METHODS

// makeWave creates a wave's y-coordinate data for the
// specified
// wave type & frequency.  It then invokes the display's
// repaint()
// method to display the data.

    private void makeWave(String type, TextField freqT,
      Display display) {
        Double freqD = new Double(freqT.getText());
        double freq = freqD.doubleValue();
        boolean inv =
            ((Checkbox)((display.getParent()).
            getComponent(7))).getState();

        if (type == "") {
            display.pointsSet = false;
        } else {
            display.pointsSet = true;
            if (type == "Sine") {
                double x = 0.0;
                double dx;    // delta X to map frequency to
                              // display size
                double datum;

                dx = (freq * 2.0 * Math.PI) / (double)
                display.numPoints;
                for (int i = 0; i  display.getMaxPY()) {
                        // datum -= (2.0 * slope);
                        slope = -slope;
                    }
                    // now invert it for proper display
                    if (inv == false)
```

```
                    display.data[i] = (int)
                        (((float) display.getMaxY()) - datum);
                else
                    display.data[i] = (int) datum;
            }
        }  if (type == "Square") {       // NOT IMPLEMENTED
            messages.addMsgAreaMessage(
                "Functionality not implemented yet");
            display.pointsSet = false;
        }
        display.repaint();
        updateOps(display);
    }
}

// if the ops modules (3 & 4) are active, update them as //
well

private void updateOps(Display display) {
    Display d;

    d = (Display) module3.getComponent(6);
    if (display.pointsSet == false)
        d.pointsSet = false;
    opWaves(module3, d, null);
    d.repaint();

    d = (Display) module4.getComponent(6);
    if (display.pointsSet == false)
        d.pointsSet = false;
    opWaves(module4, d, null);
    d.repaint();
}

private boolean opWaves(Panel p, Display d, String opp) {
    String op;
    boolean inv =
        ((Checkbox)(d.getParent().getComponent(4))).getState();
```

```
int minpy = 1;
int maxpy = d.getMaxPY();
int midy = (maxpy - minpy) / 2;
int tmp_maxy = maxpy, tmp_miny = minpy;
Display d1, d2;

op = opp;
if (op == null) {
    Checkbox cb1 = ((Checkbox)p.getComponent(2));
    Checkbox cb2 = ((Checkbox)p.getComponent(3));
    if (cb1.getState() == true)
        op = cb1.getLabel();
    if (cb2.getState() == true)
        op = cb2.getLabel();
}
if (op == null)
    return false;

if (p == module3) {
    // wave 1 op wave 2
    d1 = (Display) module1.getComponent(9);
    d2 = (Display) module2.getComponent(9);
}  else {
    // wave 2 op wave 1
    d1 = (Display) module2.getComponent(9);
    d2 = (Display) module1.getComponent(9);
}
if (d1.pointsSet == false || d2.pointsSet == false) {
    d.pointsSet = false;
    d.repaint();
    return false;
}
if (op == "Sum") {
    for (int i = 0; i  tmp_maxy)
        tmp_maxy = d.data[i];
    else if (d.data[i]  maxpy || tmp_miny
```

APPENDIX B

Java Links

Even though this book provides a great deal of information, there is not enough space available to describe every trick, feature, or bug associated with Java and the AWT. This appendix lists some of the WWW links that we've found useful over the past few months. We checked each of these just before publication, but we obviously can't guarantee that they will still be active when you try them.

Don't forget, almost all of these sites have their own list of Java links. You should be able to work your way to almost any information you need by starting at any of these sites.

If we had to choose one site, we'd pick *The Java Developer* at

`http://www.digitalfocus.com/faq/.`

But, since we can't pick just one, we think you also ought to look at *The Java Store* at

`http://www.javastore.com/`

Java—Programming for the Internet

`http://java.sun.com/`

This is the JavaSoft home page. From here, you can find out about everything going on at JavaSoft. Press releases, documentation, software downloads, FAQ lists, and other useful things are all linked off this page.

Some quick shortcuts to stuff of immediate interest follow.

`http://java.sun.com/java.sun.com/aboutJava/`

This page is called "All About Java" and provides links to many of the other pages at JavaSoft. You can look at this for an overview of what JavaSoft's web server contains.

`http://java.sun.com/java.sun.com/products/`

This page contains links to the various supported products that JavaSoft is producing. Some products are officially released, others are in alpha or beta releases.

`http://java.sun.com/java.sun.com/devcorner/`

This page shows release dates for the various things that you as a developer can download over the network.

`http://java.sun.com/applets/applets.html`

This page contains Sun's Beta Java applets. They should run under Netscape Navigator 2.x/3.x and the JDK appletviewer.

The Java Store

http://www.javastore.com/

The Java Store is designed to help you quickly find and obtain Java applets, applications, and related development products. There are two major "departments" in The Java Store.

The AppSearch Database

The AppSearch Database is a worldwide database of Java applets, applications and related products. If you need an applet for a specific project or if you just want to see what's been done in a particular area of Java, you won't find a better place to start than right here!

Java Products

Java Products is a listing of Java development products, utilities and toolkits that may be obtained directly from the vendors listed later in this appendix.

Java Programming Basics

http://www.pencom.com/javabasics/

This is the home page for Pencom Web Works previous MIS:Press book, *Java Programming Basics* by Edith Au, Dave Makower, and Pencom Web Works. If you don't have this book, we suggest you buy it; it will make our boss happy.

NetScape

```
http://www.netscape.com/
```

If you haven't been to NetScape's home page, you aren't getting the whole picture on Java. This page has a lot of graphics and a lot of information, but you can navigate through it fairly easily. The DevEdge pages are definitely worth looking through, as is their information on Server-side Java.

You can check out their applets page at

```
http://www.netscape.com/comprod/products/navigator/version_2.0/java
_applets/
```

Also, try

```
http://developer.netscape.com/library/ifc/
```

for information about their Java foundation classes. According to NetScape, the IFC includes classes for

- Windowing and application framework, overlapping windows
- Advanced user interface controls, including color picker and font chooser
- Animation
- Drag and drop
- Timers
- Multifont text support
- Persistent Store/Object Archive System

Developers can expect:

- Compatibility with all standard Java SDKs and popular IDEs

- An open API for adding custom objects or subclassing existing objects
- Bundling with future versions of the Navigator
- Documentation, examples, and newsgroup development support from Netscape

The Java Developer

http://www.digitalfocus.com/faq/

This site provides an online forum/FAQ list that gives huge numbers of links to Java Sites. Try their Resources page for web sites, and lists of books and newsletters. We think this site is great. Their online forum/FAQ list at

http://www.digitalfocus.com/faq/howdoi.html

is an easy way to check out solutions to problems that other folk have already solved.

ObjectSpace, Inc. Java Generic Library

http://www.objectspace.com/jgl/

This is a freely available library of Java classes that provide support generic data structures including sorting, multiple forms of lists and containers, and a whole lot more. If your application needs sophisticated data structures, check this library out—besides, it's free.

Microline Component Toolkit

`http://www.mlsoft.com/mct/mct.html`

The Microline Component Toolkit 3.0 provides a powerful set of user-interface objects for Java. The toolkit is written entirely in Java and extends classes contained in Sun's Abstract Windows Toolkit, a part of the standard Java distribution.

Borland Online

`http://www.borland.com/internet/`

Borland has spent a lot of time with Java. Their Latte product promises to be one of the better commercial developer tools.

Symantec Java Central

`http://www.symantec.com/javacentral/`

Symantec's Cafe was the first commercial Java developer product released.

Natural Intelligence, Inc.'s Roaster

`http://www.natural.com/pages/products/roaster/`

Roaster is the first and most popular Java developer tool for Macintosh.

SunSoft Java Workshop

`http://www.sun.com/sunsoft/Developer-products/java`

This is SunSoft's attempt to produce a pure Java development environment. It provides a fairly large run time library, visual GUI builder, and reasonable source code control.

Gamelan: Earthweb's Java Directory

`http://www.gamelan.com/`

This is one of the premiere applet repositories. If you want to check out what other people are doing or just find an applet that solves your problem, then Gamelan is worth checking out.

APPENDIX C

CD-ROM Contents

The CD-ROM included with this book contains the source code and/or binaries for many of the program examples in the book, as well as several additional products and packages. The CD-ROM is provided as a multiplatform disk, with partitions accessible from Macintosh, Windows, and UNIX systems. For the most part, each CD-ROM partition is identical, except:

- Text files are in the appropriate format for each platform.
- The Mac partition contains the distribution archive of Alpha, a shareware text editor with a syntax-colored Java mode and other neat features.
- On the Mac partition, the Microline Component Toolkit is provided in expanded form, and the sources for the examples have been compiled. The way it is set up, the demos can be run directly from Netscape or from the Mac JDK, without setting the `CLASSPATH` variable.

- The **Microline Component Toolkit** folder on the Mac partition contains an additional **README** file. On the Mac partition, all files have their type and creator set appropriately.

Naturally, each partition contains only the version of the JDK for that platform. Any files that are only on one platform or another are noted as such in the following list.

RealWorldAWT/

This directory contains the many small examples found in this book. Also included are two useful custom classes: `ButtonCanvas.java` and `LabelCanvas.java`. In addition, you'll find two large examples that are referenced briefly in the book but not really explored or described there. They include a set of product quality Tab (tabbed `CardLayout`) objects with an example and a heavy-duty example of using layouts within layouts (the Scope example), which includes a pair of bonus objects: a `PopupDialog` and a `MsgArea` (message area).

The tabbed `CardLayout` classes are an improvement on the `CardLayout` objects provided by Vignette Corporation. I removed all Vignette proprietary code for this release, but the code is not formatted quite as nicely as we would like. It's in good shape, however, and it works beautifully.

All of the `RealWorldAWT` examples are free for your use. Any restrictions are included in the copyright information in each file.

ccc/

Corey Trager's Choo-Choo-CAD is a little diversion meant to demonstrate the specialty of the Premisys Corporation: creating specialized CAD software.

The tracks in Choo-Choo-CAD are not merely blocks of lines and arcs. Rather, they are "intelligent" graphical counterparts to real-world tracks. They "know" they are tracks, and they behave like tracks. For example, they won't allow themselves to be attached to the end of a track that has already received another track, they know when they form a closed loop, and so on.

The Premisys Corporation has created somewhat more serious customized CAD systems for GE Medical Systems, Honeywell, IBM, Marvin Windows and Doors, Trane Corporation, Comsat, and others. For the online documentation, try *http://www.mcs.net/~ctrager/html/class/rrtrain.htm.*

JavaBasics/

This directory contains two useful drawing examples from *Java Programming Basics.* The `GUIDrawingExample` provides examples of double buffering, mouse dragging, image resizing, and interactive drawing examples. Also provided in this directory is a small Java application called `PrintProperties` that prints the system properties of the environment that invokes the application. System properties are similar to the UNIX environment variables, Xdefaults properties, or Windows Registry items.

mct/

This folder contains a demonstration version of Microline Software's Microline Component Toolkit (© 1996 by Microline Software).

The file **mct3csdk.zip** is the unmodified zip file as available from Microline's WWW site. The folder **mct.3c** is essentially what you get if you unzip the archive, but we've made a few largely inconsequential changes to smooth out the process of running it on a Mac (the file types and creators are set to appropriate values). An unzipped copy of the class files in the archive **:mct.3c:lib:mct3_0.zip** were placed inside the **Examples** directory so that they will be found by a Web browser when browsing the HTML pages in that directory. Also, the **.java** files in the **Examples** directory were compiled with Sun's JDK 1.0.2 for the Macintosh, so that the demos could be run without first compiling the source files.

The Microline Component Toolkit itself and the demo programs that come in the archive are unmodified. As a result, any platform-specific issues (including, but not limited to those mentioned in the file **:mct.3c:README.txt**) remain.

Alpha.6.5.sit

This is a freely available Mac editor program with Java syntax coloring. Alpha is included only on the Mac partition.

JDK

The JavaSoft JDK (Java Developer's Kit) is included, within the appropriate platform partitions. The 1.0.2 JDK on the CD is the same as the version available on **ftp.javasoft.com** as of mid-October 1996.

APPENDIX D

AWT 1.1 Overview

This appendix addresses the new AWT features that will be available in Sun's JDK 1.1 release. While the 1.1 version of the JDK has no announced release date, many of the other packages have been released individually in alpha format. The AWT 1.1 release is not available to the public in any form yet, but JavaSoft recently provided some informal design point documentation. We will summarize the features JavaSoft described and try to indicate how this will impact existing development projects.

According to JavaSoft, the AWT enhancements in release 1.1 are tasked with improving the quality and performance of Java applications. A stronger component set and additional APIs for GUI development will include:

- a simple printing API (an interface where the paint functionality renders print images)

- more sophisticated scrolling (a new scrolling container and better event handling)
- pop-up menus (in addition to the existing drop-down menus)
- a copy/paste clipboard API (no drag and drop yet)
- better cursor management
- delegation-based event handling (in addition to the existing methods)
- general performance and quality enhancements
- a completely rewritten Win32 version of the AWT

We'll try to comment on each of these briefly, but you should understand that the AWT 1.1 design and implementation is not yet set in stone, so you probably don't want to use this appendix to "predevelop" code for the 1.1 release. After going over our commentary, you can keep up-to-date by periodically checking the JavaSoft Web site at:

```
http://www.javasoft.com/products/JDK/1.1/designspecs/awt/
```

You can also use the `designspec` pages to check out other feature of the JDK 1.1 release, like remote method invocation, internationalization, and JAR files (a big performance enhancement).

Printing

Did you wonder why we didn't talk about printing in this book? It's because there is no support for printing in Java 1.0.x. AWT 1.1 will provide a simple but useful model for printing components. Basically, the new API uses a separate graphics context for print imaging. The normal paint/repaint mechanisms are used to render an image suitable for shipping to the printer.

The toolkit provides a new method:

```
public abstract PrintJob getPrintJob(Frame frame,
                                     String jobtitle,
                                     Properties props)
```

Along with getPrintJob, a new class called java.awt.printJob allows your code to obtain specific information about the printer being used, the page size, and the imaging model, and it finalizes the print job and dispatches it to the print queue manager.

After establishing a print job, the printer graphics context is provided by a new interface, java.awt.PrintGraphics. The printer graphics context is obtained from the PrintJob object via the method Graphics getGraphics(). This object is passed into the existing paint() method, which merely renders the image as it does now. Of course, you may want to extend or modify your imaging code to recognize that a print image rather than an onscreen image is being generated. Most often, you will want to recognize that the printer is typically a monochrome device with much greater resolution. Your code might attempt to render halftones (like a newspaper) instead of color and might draw images that have much more detail. To detect that the graphics context is a print context, you can add the following excerpt to your code:

```
public void paint(Graphics g) {
      if (g instanceof PrintGraphics)
            // render print image
      else
            // render screen image
```

You should realize that the image rendered in the paint() method is just a simple bitmap. Each platform-specific AWT implementation would normally have specific hidden optimizations to generate an image that is suitable for the printing subsystems common for those platforms. Typically, Mac and PC systems will print the bitmap as is, while UNIX systems and network printers will generate PostScript for the text and other objects. For example, the `Graphics.drawText()` method could just generate PostScript directly, rather than rendering a bitmap into the image. What will be implemented for these optimizations remains to be seen, but you can expect further optimizations to be made in each release of the AWT.

One interesting point to consider in printing is pagination. If you've printed a Web page from Netscape Navigator, you probably noticed that it may break the page in the middle of a character line. This is because Navigator thinks of a Web page as a single long piece of paper, rather than a print document with multiple pages of paper. In AWT 1.1, each call to `getGraphics()` obtains a new piece of paper. The dimensions of the paper can be obtained from a call to `PrintJob.getPageDimension()`; the resolution comes from `PrintJob.getPageResolution()`. Each of these methods can be used in your `paint()` method to decide how to image the component.

The process of invoking all these methods is basically up to you. The API provides a new method called `Component.printAll(Graphics g)`. This method would normally be called from an event handler in response to some user action. Typically, this would be a Print menu item or a button on a container. The `printAll()` method will traverse the entire container hierarchy, calling the `print()` method in each component. The default `print()` method inherited from `Component` will just call `paint()`, which would presumably use the excerpt given earlier to realize that we are printing rather than imaging to the screen. Native components (buttons, scroll bars, etc.) will all emulate this behavior, even though they don't directly implement the `paint()` method.

Here's a simple excerpt that shows how this will all work:

```
public boolean action(Event evt, Object arg) {
```

```
        if ("Print".equals(arg)) {
            PrintJob job = Toolkit.getPrintJob(container,
                                  "Printout", (Properties)null);
            if (job != null) {
                Graphics g = job.getGraphics();
                if (g != null) {
                    printAll(g); // render container hierarchy
                    g.dispose(); // flush page
                }
                job.end();
            }
            return true;
        }
        return false;
    }
```

Note that you could put the calls to `getGraphics`, `printAll`, and `Dispose` into a loop and print a multipage report. Also, there is no reason that the components must be display components. A traditional report might never be displayed onscreen, but it would still use the same class structure.

Print Limitations

Printing in AWT 1.1 is not all roses. There are serious restrictions on printing within applets. For example, untrusted applets cannot create a PrintJob object. They can, however, print to an existing PrintGraphics object if you create one for them. This might allow an applet to generate a print image and send it back to the Web server to be printed. Basically, normal applet security applies to printing.

Many applications add special features to the native platform Print dialog box. The AWT 1.1 print implementation does not provide this capability. JavaSoft's stated intention is to add this capability later.

Desktop Colors

One of the problems associated with the 1.0.x release of AWT was the lack of "desktop" colors. Most windowing systems implement some set of user-configurable colors that apply to the basic components of the desktop. For example, the background, borders, text, text background, error text, component shadows, and many other features may be part of the desktop color set.

AWT 1.1 will provide a set of predefined `Color` objects that correspond to the commonly available desktop features. Some platforms may have desktop features that are not in this set, and some platforms may not use all these features. However, the addition of these objects will greatly simplify the layout of visually pleasing (or at least coordinated) color models for Java containers.

Here is the list of supported desktop colors in AWT 1.1:

```
Color desktop; // Background color of desktop
Color activeCaption; // Background color for captions
Color activeCaptionText; // Text color for captions
Color activeCaptionBorder; // Border color for caption text
Color inactiveCaption; // Background color for inactive captions
Color inactiveCaptionText; // Text color for inactive captions
Color inactiveCaptionBorder; // Border color for inactive captions
Color window; // Background for windows
Color windowBorder; // Color of window border frame
Color windowText; // Text color inside windows
Color menu; // Background for menus
Color menuText; // Text color for menus
Color highlight; // color for highlight
Color highlightText; // color for highlighted text
Color control; // Background color for controls
Color controlText; // Text color for controls
Color controlLtHighlight; // Light highlight color for controls
Color controlHighlight; // Highlight color for controls
```

```
Color controlShadow; // Shadow color for controls
Color controlDkShadow; // Dark shadow color for controls
Color inactiveControlText; // Text color for inactive controls
Color scrollbar; // Background color for scroll bars
Color info; // Background color for spot-help text
Color infoText; // Text color for spot-help text
```

Note that all these objects are declared `public final static`. This means that you cannot set them in your code. They represent the color of the corresponding desktop objects at the time of use. If the desktop color set is modified during an application's lifetime, these colors may not reflect the new color set.

Pop-up Menu

The menu style implemented in AWT 1.0.x is named *drop-down* because the menu items are attached to a menubar at the top of the associated frame. When a menu on that menubar is selected, the menu drops down to show all the menu items.

The concept of pop-up menus is an attempt to avoid having a menubar. Typically, the user initiates a pop-up menu by using a different mouse button to activate the pop-up. For example, the right mouse button on Win32 systems pops up a menu for the underlying application.

Essentially, AWT 1.1 implements pop-up menus by providing a new subclass of `Menu` called `PopupMenu`. This subclass is essentially identical to `Menu`, except that it implements a single `show(Component origin, int x, int y)` method. This method, when invoked, will cause the pop-up menu to appear at the *x,y* coordinates of the origin object. The coordinates relate to the origin object rather than the triggering event coordinates.

`PopupMenu` must be attached to a component. Unlike `Menu`, it can be added to any `Component` via the `add(PopupMenu` popup) method and removed with remove(MenuComponent). Note that the PopupMenu can be owned (added) only by a single component at a time.

To implement sensible behavior, the triggering mechanism for pop-up menus is implemented as a new Event.POPUP_TRIGGER event type. This allows the event handling code to detect the event as "probably" a pop-up event (the handler could neglect to call show, essentially ignoring the pop-up).

Pop-up menu handling (and most event handling) will be made much easier with the new event model in AWT 1.1.

ScrollPane

The concept of a scrolling container is central to every windowing system. While AWT 1.0.x required developers to implement their own scrolling containers, with the ScrollBar primitive, AWT 1.1 provides a new ScrollPane object. The AWT 1.0.x model caused serious performance issues, because each scroll event caused several round trips between the native and Java environments.

The new ScrollPane container provides integrated operation for scrolling container operation, entirely within Java. ScrollPane supports three modes for scroll operation:

- Automatic (SCROLLBARS_AS_NEEDED)—show scroll bars (horizontal and vertical) as needed; perhaps only one direction would display scroll bars in a particular display size environment
- Always (SCROLLBARS_ALWAYS)—always show scroll bars, even when the container is completely visible
- Never (SCROLLBARS_NEVER)—never show scroll bars, the program must perform all scrolling actions

A new interface called `java.awt.Adjustable` allows the program to manipulate the various increments, sizes, and position attributes of the `ScrollPane`. This interface also provides the new event handler methods to add and remove listeners, who expect to be notified about scroll events:

```
ScrollPane mypane;
public void init() {
	mypane = new ScrollPane(ScrollPane.SCROLLBARS_AS_NEEDED);
	mypane.add(new CustomCanvas());
	Adjustable vadjust = mypane.getVAdjustable();
	Adjustable hadjust = mypane.getHAdjustable();
	hadjust.setUnitIncrement(10);
	vadjust.setUnitIncrement(10);
	mypane.resize(100, 100);
	add(mypane);
}
```

Mouseless Operation

AWT 1.0 provides no support for mouseless operation. AWT 1.1 will provide the very basic capabilities of focus traversal and menu shortcuts.

Focus traversal will be implemented only in the simplest of forms. The **Tab** and **Shift-Tab** keys will cause focus to move forward and backward through components in a container. The order of movement will be the order of containment (the order in which the components were added to the container). If the components were added with the optional position operand, then the traversal will follow that imposed ordering. Note that components that are not editable or otherwise wish to not receive the focus should override `public boolean isFocusTraversable()` to return `false`. The default returned by `Component` is `true` for those components that can take advantage of the focus.

The basic steps to add support for your custom components is as follows:

- Override `isTabbable()` to return `true` (`Canvas` returns false by default)
- Catch the mouse-down event on the component and invoke `requestFocus()` (to implement click to type for your component)
- When your component gets focus, provide visual feedback indicating that it has the focus

Menu shortcuts are implemented in AWT 1.1 via a new class called `java.awt.MenuShortcut`, which is a subclass of `java.awt.event.KeyEvent`. This new class should hide some of the complexities of dealing with menu shortcut events.

Essentially, the `MenuItem` and `MenuBar` classes receive new methods that tie a Shortcut object to the menu component. When the shortcut keypress occurs, the corresponding `MenuItem` is activated. Note that the application shortcuts all have a common key modifier, depending on the platform:

- **Command** on Macintosh
- **Ctrl** on Windows and Motif (UNIX)

A new Toolkit method has been added, called `public int getMenuShortcutKeyMask()`. It provides the modifier for the current platform.

The AWT 1.1.design spec contains the following comment about the **Alt** key: **Alt** isn't supposed to be used for application shortcuts, other than **Quit,** which is already mapped by the AWT.

Data Transfer

The AWT 1.1 release supports fundamental cut, copy, and paste capabilities via the `java.awt.datatransfer` package. This package contains interfaces and classes to provide the basic data transfer framework. For the primitive and common cases, the AWT implements convenience classes to perform most of the work. For example, `StringSelection` performs the required action to cut, copy, and paste a string selection.

The underlying implementation depends on what JavaSoft engineers call "data flavors." Each transfer requires negotiation of the flavor of data to be transferred (text, rich text, binary, etc.), as well as the actual transmission and reception of the data.

Information encapsulated by the flavor includes a well-chosen nameset (both internal and human-readable) and the representation class that is used to carry the data within the transmission.

JavaSoft engineers have chosen to use MIME type/subtype nomenclature for the logical name. This allows most of the registration aspects to be handled in an internationally recognized standard and it provides support for most of the common data types. MIME is also extensible for custom unregistered data types via the `x-` prefix to the type name.

If you examine the JavaSoft design spec carefully, it appears that most of the data transfer protocol is still in the design stage. While the framework is documented and the design rationale is there, most of the language indicates that there will be changes to the implementation. Because of the tentative tone of the current document (as of October 15, 1996), we've chosen not to discuss the data transfer implementation in depth. Suffice it to say that there will be a representation class to carry data from transmitter to receiver and a flavor class to encapsulate the transfer negotiation.

Delegation Event Model

If you look at most of the event handler examples in this book and at the more complex example code on the CD-ROM, you'll quickly come to the conclusion that event handling can be complicated. In AWT 1.0, efficient event handling is almost impossible to impose, and it is very easy to induce "feature" bugs. AWT 1.1 will continue to provide the 1.0 event handling model to support pre-existing code. However, a new and improved model will also be provided.

Delegation event handling, as implemented in AWT 1.1, has the following stated design goals:

- Simple to use and easy to learn
- Support a clean separation between application and GUI code
- Facilitate the creation of robust event handling code that is less error-prone (strong compile-time checking)
- Flexible enough to enable varied application models for event flow and propagation
- For visual tool builders, enable run-time discovery of both events generated by a component as well as the events it may observe
- Support backward binary compatibility with the old model

Delegation

AWT 1.1 event types have been encapsulated in a new class hierarchy rooted at java.util.EventObject. This class hierarchy provides for the delegation of events from source to listener objects.

Listeners implement a specific EventListener interface that maps to the subclass of event desired. Sources originate or fire events. Listeners register for events from a source by calling the set<EventType>Listener or add<EventType>Listener methods that each event source object provides. Source objects can either single-cast (by providing only set-methods) or multicast (by providing add-methods).

In AWT 1.1, the source objects are typically GUI components, and the listener objects are application objects (commonly called *adapter* objects) that respond to the events by modifying application logic.

Event Hierarchy

The AWT 1.1 events are represented by a hierarchy of event classes rather than the single event class of AWT 1.0.x. However, each subclass may still represent more than one event type. For example, mouse up, down, drag, and move events are all handled by the `MouseEvent` subclass. Similarly, keyboard events are handled by a single event subclass.

Each event subclass now completely hides the internals of the event. No longer can you directly manipulate the instance variables of the event from your handler. All access to the event attributes is encapsulated with `get` and `set` methods; each event subclass defines only the attribute methods that make sense for that event.

Additional event subclasses may be defined by subclassing any of the AWT classes in the event hierarchy.

The AWT-provided event hierarchy consists of the following classes. These are properly divided into low-level and semantic events by the AWT documentation. However, the programmatic aspects of all event classes are equivalent. The provided event classes that event sources can generate are:

```
java.util.EventObject
      java.awt.event.AwtEvent
            java.awt.event.ComponentEvent       (component resized,
moved, etc.)
                  java.awt.event.FocusEvent       (component got focus,
lost focus)
                  java.awt.event.InputEvent
```

```
                         java.awt.event.KeyEvent     (component got key-
press, key-release, etc.)
                         java.awt.event.MouseEvent    (component got
mouse-down, mouse-move, etc.)
            java.awt.event.ActionEvent       ("do a command")
                   java.awt.event.AdjustmentEvent       ("value was
adjusted")
                   java.awt.event.ItemEvent       ("item state has
changed")
Listeners implement support for the event classes via the following
interfaces:
java.util.EventListener
            java.awt.event.ComponentListener
            java.awt.event.FocusListener
            java.awt.event.KeyListener
            java.awt.event.MouseListener
            java.awt.event.MouseMotionListener
            java.awt.event.WindowListener
            java.awt.event.ActionListener
            java.awt.event.AdjustmentListener
            java.awt.event.ItemListener
```

While all AWT events will operate in a multicast environment, the AWT 1.1 implementation makes no guarantees about order of delivery to multicast listeners. Also, each listener receives a copy of the original event attributes, not the adjusted contents from a previous listener.

Registering for Events

Listeners register to receive events via the `add<EventType> Listener` methods. The low-level AWT GUI components provide methods of this type for the events that they source. Here is the list of methods (and event listener types) for AWT 1.1–provided classes:

```
java.awt.Component
      addComponentListener(ComponentListener l)
      addFocusListener(FocusListener l)
      addKeyListener(KeyListener l)
      addMouseListener(MouseListener l)
      addMouseMotionListener(MouseMotionListener l)
java.awt.Dialog
      addWindowListener(WindowListener l)
java.awt.Frame
      addWindowListener(WindowListener l)
java.awt.Button
      addActionListener(ActionListener l)
java.awt.Choice (implements java.awt.ItemSelectable)
      addItemListener(ItemListener l)
java.awt.Checkbox (implements java.awt.ItemSelectable)
      addItemListener(ItemListener l)
java.awt.CheckboxMenuItem (implements java.awt.ItemSelectable)
      addItemListener(ItemListener l)
java.awt.List (implements java.awt.ItemSelectable)
      addActionListener(ActionListener l)
      addItemListener(ItemListener l)
java.awt.MenuItem
      addActionListener(ActionListener l)
java.awt.Scrollbar (implements java.awt.Adjustable)
      addAdjustmentListener(AdjustmentListener l)
java.awt.TextField
     addActionListener(ActionListener l)
```

Extended Component Event Handlers

The model just described is used to implement delegate model event handling where the listener is implemented as an application adapter object. When you develop extended objects (typically custom subclasses of AWT-provided components, like `Canvas`) you would be required to implement separate listener objects to receive the events generated by your component. To avoid this problem, each component class implements a set of protected handler methods that are responsible for dispatching the events from the component. Your custom components can override these methods to handle some events internally without ever implementing the listener object. Of course, the inherited dispatch code is still available via `super`. For example, you could implement the following methods to provide custom behavior, while still dispatching the event properly:

```
public class CustomCanvas extends Canvas {
boolean haveFocus = false;
protected void handleFocusGained(FocusEvent e) {
      if (!haveFocus) {
            haveFocus = true;
            // custom behavior here
      }
      super.handleFocusGained(e); //let superclass dispatch to
listeners
}
protected void handleFocusLost(FocusEvent e) {
      if (haveFocus == true) {
            haveFocus = false;
            // undo custom behavior here
      }
      super.handleFocusLost(e); //let superclass dispatch to
listeners
}
```

Provided Adapter Classes

The AWT 1.1 release provides basic adapter classes for the defined event types. These classes provide core functions for handling events and greatly simplify development of your custom adapters. By inheriting from the appropriate base adapter, you are required to implement only the handlers for the particular event types and handling you need:

```
java.awt.event.ComponentAdapter
java.awt.event.FocusAdapter
java.awt.event.KeyAdapter
java.awt.event.MouseAdapter
java.awt.event.MouseMotionAdapter
java.awt.event.WindowAdapter
java.awt.event.ActionAdapter
java.awt.event.AdjustmentAdapter
java.awt.event.ItemAdapter
```

Performance Benefits

By moving to the delegation-based event model, AWT 1.1 will be able to make improvements in performance as well as reliability. The division of labor between source and listener allows AWT 1.1 to impose order on the dispatching of events. Each class of event goes only to the registered handlers (listeners), rather than to the entire hierarchy of event handlers. The subsequent improvements in dispatch time allow the AWT to be more responsive and to simplify your code by prequalifying each event you receive.

However, the overall requirement for your event handler to run synchronously is still necessary, and the corresponding requirement to efficiently execute the event response also remains.

Other AWT 1.1 Enhancements

In other areas, the 1.1 release of the AWT provides bug fixes, better component implementations, and, in the case of Win32 releases, a complete rewrite of the AWT. This rewrite will do more than anything else to elevate the status of Java to a production-quality programming environment.

Also, the changes in the event model and the data transfer protocols provide the underpinnings for support of the upcoming Java Beans architecture.

Index

A

B

C

D

E

F

G

H

I

J

K

L

M

N

O

P

R

S

T

U

V

W

Y